# THE FOUNDING FATHERS OF
## SOCIAL SCIENCE

# THE FOUNDING FATHERS
# OF SOCIAL SCIENCE

*Edited by Timothy Raison*
*Revised Edition by Paul Barker*

A series from *New Society*

SCOLAR PRESS
LONDON

First published in *New Society*

Copyright © *New Society* 1963, 1964, 1965,
1966, 1967, 1977, 1978, 1979

First published in volume form 1969 by Penguin Books Ltd
Harmondsworth, Middlesex, England

This revised and reset edition published 1979
by Scolar Press
39 Great Russell Street, London WC1B 3PH

ISBN 0 85967 458 4 (cloth)
0 85967 459 2 (paper)

Printed in England by
Whitstable Litho Ltd
Whitstable, Kent

# CONTENTS

# Contents

# PREFACE

SINCE its first publication in 1969, *The Founding Fathers of Social Science* seems to have established itself as a useful book for both students and teachers. With some revision and addition, the Scolar Press thought that its usefulness could be prolonged. Hence this new edition.

I explain later in this note exactly what changes have been made. But the important thing to say first is that, though he decided not to become involved in the revision in any way, this remains essentially Timothy Raison's book. The articles which went into the original edition were entirely commissioned by him as founder-editor of *New Society*. The new ones which appear in this edition are intended to follow very much the same lines.

In his introduction to the first edition, he explained how the idea arose:

One of the more intriguing problems which faced us when, in October 1962, we launched *New Society* as a weekly devoted to the social sciences and society was how best to tackle theoretical sociology. Obviously, a social science journal which ignored social theory would not be doing what it claimed to do. On the other hand, theoretical sociology and social anthropology are not easily put over to an audience which, however intelligent, must include a substantial number of laymen.

It was not long before we decided that the most effective approach, by and large, would be through the lives and works of the leading social scientists, whom we dubbed – perhaps a little portentously – the Founding Fathers of Social Science. We began the first series on 28 March 1963 with a study of Émile Durkheim by John Rex.

The contributors – apart from the American, Everett C. Hughes – were all British: and this remains true of the revision. I also, after some reflexion, decided to retain the all-but-veto on living social scientists, however major (Talcott Parsons had been the only exception). This meant leaving out, for example, Professors Habermas and Lévi-Strauss. But it is much harder to assess the living in this kind of context. And, after all, the living ought to be able to speak to us direct.

Six articles have been added for this edition. They range in time from Montesquieu, an important precursor, to Gramsci, who is a much more controversial and (in the literal sense) 'contemporary' figure. The other four are Freud, G. H. Mead, Mauss and Adorno. They emphasize the European, rather than the American, tradition in social science. (Two other names which were almost included, Lukács and Walter Benjamin, would have emphasized this further.)

All the existing articles and booklists were (where possible) sent by the publisher to their authors for revision. In the remaining cases, Stephen Struthers took the task on.

My own involvement, therefore, has been confined to the commissioning of the new articles. I am grateful to Stephen Struthers for his help with the booklists, and to Anthony Giddens, Geoffrey Hawthorn, Professor Donald MacRae, Alan Ryan and Professor Laurie Taylor for their help in deciding what should be added – though the final choice of subjects and authors was, of course, mine.

Tim Raison ended his own preface by saying: 'I would like to record . . . my indebtedness to my father, Maxwell Raison, and Collin Shepherd for all they have done for *New Society*.'

Let me just add that I see this book as one of the reminders of what Tim Raison, also, did for *New Society*. He was an excellent editor. No one could have launched the magazine better.

PAUL BARKER

# INTRODUCTION

*A science which hesitates to forget its founders is lost.*
Alfred North Whitehead

*But to forget something, one must have known it in the first place. A science ignorant of its founders does not know how far it has travelled nor in what direction; it, too, is lost.*
Alvin Gouldner

AT the present time, sociologists display a certain ambivalence towards the history of their discipline. In order to sustain the claim that sociology is a science, it seems necessary to show how sociological knowledge can be made progressively more exact and systematic. And this means emphasizing the importance of increasingly powerful techniques of investigation and analysis and of more integrated and rigorous theory. The end in view is a highly professional, 'value-free' and well-organized field of study. From this standpoint, the history of sociology must in several ways be an embarrassment. For it is evident that the work of the men generally recognized as the 'founding fathers' was rarely cumulative, was often characterized more by passion than by precision, by imagination rather than by order, and indeed was sometimes *not* scientific on any definition – nor, perhaps, even intended to be.

This is, therefore, a dangerous heritage for the modern sociologist to claim. Some would, in fact, deny it; and others would gladly leave its use and enjoyment to the historians of ideas. Yet, for the large majority, to forget the founders is still something they cannot do, whatever the consequences may be. Reluctantly perhaps, but repeatedly, they find themselves drawn back to the great sociological literature of the nineteenth and earlier twentieth centuries. Indeed, some names from the past – Marx, Durkheim, Weber – are still as often invoked in sociology today as are those of the most important contemporary writers. And many lesser figures in the sociological Pantheon are still, generation by generation, 'rediscovered' and reinterpreted.

How, then, is this intellectual piety to be accounted for? Why does the history of sociology retain so strong an influence over its present-day practitioners? And why, too, is it capable of exciting interest among a much wider public?

In seeking to answer such questions, the first and perhaps most important point to be made is a rather paradoxical one: that in one sense much of the work of the founding fathers is not in fact part of the *history* of sociology at all. Rather, it is still *current* sociology in that the substantive topics which are discussed and the issues of theory and method which are raised are still live ones, and remain focal points of contemporary inquiry and debate. The sociology of the past, in other words, often retains an immediate significance for both the society and the sociology of the present.

For example, one set of problems of major interest to many of the founding fathers – from Ferguson onwards – relates to the wider implications of the increasing division of labour in society; that is, to the largely unintended, and often unwanted, consequences of man's attempts to gain greater technical and economic efficiency through greater 'specialization'. The Marxian theme of the alienation of the industrial worker, the quest of Comte and of Durkheim to discover new bases of social consensus amid economic conflict and moral diversity, Weber's preoccupation with the necessary evil of bureaucracy – all these are aspects of a deeply felt concern with the human and social costs of material progress. And the undeniable point is that the discussion of these issues in the sociological classics *remains* of quite unrivalled importance today. Certainly, some of the problems of an extreme division of labour are now being investigated more systematically and in greater detail than ever previously – through studies of work satisfaction, occupational mobility, organizational change, the social effects of technological innovation, etc. But nevertheless, the ways in which such problems are defined and approached are still essentially the same as in the works of the 'founders'; and in these respects, as in not a few others that could be cited, we are still largely engaged in pursuing, if sometimes critically, the lines of analysis which they pioneered.

Furthermore, illustrations of the way in which the 'history' of sociology lives on into the present are yet more readily encountered at the level of basic methodological issues. There is, for instance, the crucial question of how sociology should respond to the fact that it is ultimately concerned with human beings, whose behaviour may be of a purposive or otherwise subjectively meaningful kind; that is to say, may be oriented towards the achievement of goals, the realization of values, the expression of sentiment, and so on.

On the one side, it has been claimed that if sociology is to gain the status of a science, it must avoid any involvement with questions of will and intention: subjective categories must be eliminated from sociological explanation. Sociology should take as its subject-matter those demonstrable regularities in social life which can be considered independently of individual motivation, and should attempt to account for these on, as it were, their own terms. Societies can, for example, be thought of as constituting some kind of 'system'; and explanations of observed patterns of social relationships can then be sought in terms of the principles by which the structure and functioning of such systems are governed. On the other side, however, the counter-claim has been advanced that it is both unnecessary and undesirable for sociologists to deny themselves the possibility of investigating social behaviour and social structure 'from the actors' point of view': unnecessary because this *can* be done in quite scientific ways, and undesirable because without this human society cannot in fact be made intelligible. Any attempt to understand the collective existence of human beings in the same way as one would that of ants or of chickens – i.e. without reference to the subjective meaning of behaviour – will clearly be inadequate. For this must mean disregarding the distinctively human phenomenon of *culture*: that is, the set of learnt beliefs, values and symbols in which groups of individuals have to some extent to share as a condition of social life being carried on at all.

The arguments outlined here have been many times rehearsed in the literature of sociology. But it could scarcely be questioned that the most cogent, yet sophisticated, statements are still to be found in some of the original presentations – as, for example, in the discussions of sociological method in the work of Durkheim on the one hand or of Weber on the other. It is true, and important, as Talcott Parsons and others have shown, that the methodological positions these writers explicitly adopt are not ones they are always able to uphold as they grapple with substantive sociological problems: implicitly, at least, they are often forced to concede a good deal to the opposing point of view. And this in itself is then a strong indication that the two contrasting approaches should be seen as complementary rather than contradictory. Yet at the same time the question of how they should actually be *integrated* is one that still awaits a satisfactory answer – the efforts of Parsons and his associates notwithstanding. And for so long as this is the case, the classical expositions of the issues that are involved must clearly remain a necessary starting point and foundation for any serious study of sociological theory.

It is not difficult, then, to point to instances, and of an important kind, where the sociology of the past continues to form an essential part of the sociology of today: often, the founding fathers cannot be forgotten because they are still figures of great contemporary relevance. However, this is in no way to suggest that sociology has no 'real' past at all – an argument which would, of course, imply that it has no achievements, no progress to show. This is not in fact the case. On the contrary, the history of sociological thought is of further considerable value – and not only in this respect to sociologists themselves – precisely as a means of assessing the advances which *have* been made, both within the context of specifically sociological enquiry and also more generally in, as it were, society's consciousness of itself.

From the point of view of sociology as a field of study, countless particular illustrations of progress in knowledge and understanding could be offered. Many will be indicated in the essays which follow. But perhaps the most significant line of development which might be noted here is that whereby sociology *as a discipline* has established its right to exist and its intellectual independence.

The case for sociology in this sense was first made out by the great polymaths of the nineteenth century: Saint-Simon and Comte in France and Spencer in England. But while their arguments were enthusiastically pressed, and characterized by a fine *esprit de système*, they did not spell out in any detailed way the precise nature either of sociological problems or of sociological analysis. Rather, their conceptions of the new science which they called into existence tended to be of an over-arching, all-embracing kind. It was, therefore, the task – and the achievement – of a later generation on the one hand to disentangle sociology from unfortunate embroilments with the philosophy of history, political theory and evolutionary biology, and on the other to show how it was related to, yet distinct from, such sister disciplines as psychology and economics. In this way, through the efforts of Durkheim, Weber, Simmel, Pareto and others, the field of sociology became subject to more thoughtful, if less ambitious, definition. It was recognized that it could not be the aim of sociology to offer any *total* interpretation of man, history and society but that its proper objective was to develop its own analytical perspectives and, on this basis, its own distinctive theories and research procedures.

Such a programme has, then, in general been accepted by sociologists in the modern period. And while it has not, even now, been fully realized, it has none the less made possible the two major achievements of recent decades: the more refined conceptualization of the analytical elements with which sociology is concerned (as in the work of Parsons); and the fashioning of techniques through which these elements may be quantified and their interrelationships assessed. In this manner, sociology has been brought to a level of development at which its status as an autonomous discipline is difficult to challenge, and to a point where it can at least begin to speak the language of science without appearing merely pretentious.

Concomitantly with this emergence of sociology as a discipline, and equally illuminated by the history of sociological thought, a progressive movement can also be traced in the understanding of social life implicit in (to use a Durkheimian notion) the 'collective consciousness'. In part, such a development may be seen as a prerequisite of continuing achievement of a specifically sociological kind; but in part too it can be regarded as a consequence of this achievement – the reshaping of generally accepted ideas and values. In this latter perspective, two advances would appear to be of particular significance.

The first of these consists in our growing awareness of the manifold relationships which link the different aspects of the culture of a people to the structure of the society in which they live. From its earliest origins, an essential feature of sociological thought has been its refusal to regard the 'realms' of knowledge, belief, morality or aesthetic style as separate from, and independent of, specific types of economic organization, political régime, status hierarchy and so on. The existence of some socio-cultural 'whole' has always been insisted upon. It is true that for some time the positions from which this claim was made tended to diverge widely: at one pole, the Comtean assertion '*les idées gouvernent le monde*'; at the other, the contention of Marx and Engels that social being determines social consciousness. Nevertheless, both from these extreme points of view and from the later, more sophisticated approaches of such writers as Weber, Hobhouse, Sorel and Mannheim new insights were gained which have come to exert a profound and distinctive influence on all our contemporary thinking about the interconnexions of 'mind' and 'society'.

For example, in any informed analysis of, let us say, the problems of new nations, it would now be fairly commonplace for observations to be made on the effects on economic development of prevailing religious beliefs, or on the way in which traditional moral ideas prevent the efficient working of bureaucratic administration; on the importance of 'social myths' in inspiring radical political movements, or on the relationship between the content of dominant ideologies and the social character of the elites which uphold them. And all such observations would reflect the extent to which advances in sociological understanding have been assimilated into our discussion of public issues; advances which the history of sociology records.

The second progression that should be noted is, to put the matter briefly, in our widening appreciation of exactly *how* man is a social animal. When in the later eighteenth century Ferguson and other Scots philosophers decisively rejected the idea of the 'social contract', they rejected also the possibility that any adequate theory of society could be logically derived from some initial conception of 'human nature'. For the nature of man, it was argued, is rather *created in* society; and the fact that man is always to be found existing in social relationships with others must not then be simply remarked upon but must, as Ferguson put it, 'be admitted as the foundation of all our reasoning relative to man'. From this point on, the investigation of the ways in which individual experience, conduct and even personality are shaped by social forces has been central to sociological endeavour. On the one hand, writers as diverse in outlook as Marx, Le Play and Booth have emphasized the extent to which the individual's life-chances – whether for mere survival, material well-being, cultural attainment or personal fulfilment – are determined by the social, and particularly by the economic conditions in which he is born and has to exist. On the other hand, a tradition of inquiry inspired primarily by Durkheim has made us increasingly aware of the processes through which social values and norms are 'internalized' by individuals and thus become part of their own selves; and furthermore, of how in this way strains and tensions within the social order may be manifested in the individual in the form of 'deviant' behaviour or personal disequilibrium.

As the implications of these advances have become generally realized, our outlook on a wide range of social questions has been inevitably transformed. We no longer believe, for example, that poverty exists simply because the poor are either undeserving or, as individuals, unfortunate. We see poverty, rather, as an outcome of the way in which given economic and social systems operate. Similarly, the problems of crime and other kinds of social deviance can no longer be discussed merely in terms of 'original nature', individual responsibility, and the failure of moral restraints. We now recognize not only that, as Durkheim remarked, 'crime is normal' but moreover that some forms of society – like ours today – are far more 'crimogenic' than others. Through the development of our greater sociological understanding into a new mode of social consciousness, we have been made to recognize, on issue after issue, the full sense in which we are indeed 'members of one another'.

In the end, then, it proves far less surprising than it might at first appear that the founding fathers of sociology continue to be so widely read and revered. They have still much to tell us, about sociology and about ourselves. And if, eventually, sociologists *are* in fact able to heed Whitehead's dictum and put the past decisively behind them, one hopes that even then they will, with other civilized men, retain at least an acquaintance with the work of their predecessors. For the significance of the latter will still extend beyond the fact that they have begotten a science.

JOHN H. GOLDTHORPE

# MONTESQUIEU

## (*1689–1755*)

### Salvador Giner

WE are all followers of Montesquieu now, and yet no one calls himself by that name. This 18th century French lawyer's influence on the history of social theory, political sociology, constitutional thought and, more generally, on modern men's ways of reasoning about their society and finding civilized solutions to its problems is, quite simply, second to none. In contrast to the legacy of men like Rousseau, Marx or Freud, Montesquieu's work shows a greater diffuseness of impact. But that does not diminish its importance.

His influence shows itself in the very way in which his witting or unwitting disciples express themselves. His writings were an inspiration for critical and rational thought, a ground for a secular morality, and a plea for a re-definition of freedom. They were *not* a closed and specific doctrine about the world, let alone a pretext for ideological degradations.

During his lifetime, Montesquieu's work was received as a revelation by a small but growing number of people who were aware of the need for a new science of society. He also reached wider, enlightened audiences (the audience of the Enlightenment, in fact) who were already, though perhaps unconsciously, favourably predisposed towards any systematic presentation of their social world in secular terms. They sought an explanation of human affairs which went further than the satire of Swift or Voltaire (Montesquieu's almost exact contemporaries). They sought an explanation which went further, even, than Montesquieu's own early subtle account of the weaknesses of European civilization, as given in the earliest of his three masterpieces, the *Lettres Persanes* of 1721.

Later on, when the time was ripe for the great revolutions with which many believe that the modern world began, Montesquieu was invoked by the new men of action everywhere. In

America and in France his opinions on constitutional law, and his celebrated doctrine on the necessary separation of powers in a government fit for free men, became an essential part of the emerging political world which hoped to bury the harsh spirit of Machiavelli and Hobbes with the help of gentler minds like his own, Locke's, and the men of the Scottish Enlightenment.

At least two leading members of the latter group, John Millar and Adam Ferguson, were explicit in their unqualified recognition of Montesquieu's importance in developing a new science of history and society. No Frenchman since has so consistently won the praise and respect of social scientists and theorists in the English-speaking world. Did not John Maynard Keynes consider him the greatest French economist, who stood 'head and shoulders above the Physiocrats'? Much earlier, Auguste Comte had said that he was the father of political science. So did Émile Durkheim, who wrote a dissertation to demonstrate that Montesquieu had founded political sociology. Others, from marxists to conservatives of different shades, have at different times added to this unbroken chain of recognition and admiration. But, again, hardly anyone has felt able or willing to fit into a possible 'Montesquieu school'.

Nothing would please the Baron de Montesquieu more than this state of affairs, were he to look down on us from his heavenly (though not entirely Catholic) abode. He was born in 1689 not far from Bordeaux, at the family castle of La Brède. This was a place to which he remained attached all his life, looking after its fields and improving its vineyards with loving care and remarkable expertise. He belonged to a noble family who had served the kings of Navarre before Henry of Navarre merged that realm with France. The Montesquieu family had been, at different times, in both the Protestant and the Catholic camps in the seventeenth century wars of religion. But by the time Charles de Secondat, the future Baron de La Brède et de Montesquieu, was born, the family had definitely cast its allegiance with the Catholics.

That did not prevent Montesquieu marrying a rich and devout Huguenot lady on whom he seems to have put no pressure to change her religion. (This may have been only one aspect of his neglect of her, in the tradition of a class openly committed to marriages of convenience.) He was then made president of the Bordeaux parlement, a judicial post he inherited as part of his uncle's will, rather than as a consequence of the legal training he had received earlier on.

He was bored by procedural law, though the issues themselves interested him. He became a keen defender of regional autonomy, and the independence (and privileges) of his noble caste, against the levelling tendencies of central government and, as he saw it, the growing despotism of the king. Vulgar interpreters of Montesquieu have not failed to point out that his defence of decentralization and local government was merely a poor disguise for his feudal loyalties. But this misses the essential paradox that it was precisely Montesquieu's *esprit de corps*, and his desire to preserve the traditional rights of the nobility (in open conflict with his equally strong rationalism and acute sense of social justice), that led him to develop a broad system of political principles specifically intended to preserve pluralism and institutionalize tolerance. (Such a system was partly embodied in the American Constitution of 1787.) He was painfully conscious of the contradictions into which he had been led by his defence of 'feudalism'. But unlike his more important theories, that defence was without enduring effect.

In his early years as an author, Montesquieu's interests were extremely wide – a point that worried him. Later he realized that the strong unity and coherence which marks his mature work could not have been achieved without the bewildering variety of his earlier efforts. Thus, before the *Lettres Persanes* appeared, he wrote several essays on such scientific subjects as weight, acoustics and glands; and shortly after that book's publication, a *Peinture poétique de la volupté*, a short and frivolous erotic divertimento. This was followed by a considerable number of moral, economic and political essays, travel notes, political projects, and general reflections on the most diverse subjects.

Some of these brief works were considered by his friends and peers to be of sufficient substance: they opened for him the doors, first, to the Bordeaux Academy, then to the select Paris salon, the Club de l'Entresol and, finally, earned him membership of the Royal Society during his momentous stay in London from 1729 to 1731.

He saw England as the embodiment of freedom, and her constitution as reconciling liberty with equality: 'A Londres, liberté et égalité.' Critics have seen Montesquieu's interpretation of the English polity as a complete misunderstanding of its real nature. But nowhere did he propose that other nations should ape Albion's institutions – rather that they should consider the advantages of grasping the spirit that made the best of them possible.

If it was a misunderstanding, it was a fortunate one for the future of the political theory of liberalism. Montesquieu took his interpretation beyond the limitations of Locke's individualistic conception; he put much greater emphasis on the rights of, and guarantees for, organized groups and associations. Locke and his disciples are to this day ontological (and hence methodological) individualists – i.e. they believe that only individuals are ultimately real in society. Montesquieu and his modern followers are what is usually called 'holists' (ontological and methodological 'collectivists'): they believe that groups, institutions, classes, castes, and indeed in some cases, societies themselves, are part of the proper study of social life; and that they are real entities – i.e. they are not merely convenient metaphors.

The *Lettres Persanes* only foreshadowed all this. This, the most popular and amusing of Montesquieu's works, was written in epistolary form. In it, two Persians gave their opinions, reactions and reflections on the western societies they visited, and especially France. With a stroke of genius, Montesquieu reversed the traditional ethnocentric European perspective which had inspired countless books about distant and foreign lands since Marco Polo. And the land he depicted was not an imaginary one (unlike the one which Gulliver was to explore only five years later) but, to his readers, the most familiar of all.

He had invented a genre, and there were notable imitators like the Irishman Oliver Goldsmith in his *Citizen of the World*, or the Spaniard José Cadalso in his *Moroccan Letters*. But these later writers did not give their books the constant changes of perspective and multiple layers of criticism that imbue Montesquieu's. He was not only looking at Europe as if it were an exotic and strange world, full of weird laws, customs and beliefs (which made religious authorities ban the book in horror). He was also studying the nature of despotic rule ('Asiatic despotism', as he would later call a phenomenon on which rivers of ink have since flowed from the pens of social scientists), and reflecting on the sources of a social order not based on terror and naked domination.

Through a series of letters written to the travelling Persians by the guardian eunuchs of the seraglio, and by wives and concubines, Montesquieu showed how Europeans, despite their still barbarous customs (witch-hunting here, *autos de fé* there), had come upon some solutions for a more decent life.

These were based, first and foremost, on what he called *vertu* and *patriotisme*. By these words he mainly meant what is now often called a political culture based on constitutional consensus, and the acceptance of peaceful competition in trade, industry and politics. A story inserted in the Persians' correspondence, the famous Myth of the Troglodytes, took civic virtue as the only permanent bulwark against despotism and corruption at all levels of social life. He kept his interpretations of public *vertu* from being too optimistic about human nature by adapting Mandeville's claim, put forward in the *Fable of the Bees* (1705), that private vices produce 'publick benefits' and underpin the 'wholesome mixture of a well-ordered society'. But under what conditions could Mandeville's noted paradox produce its beneficial effects? And under what conditions would a well-ordered society – both based on and strengthening public virtue – grow or, for that matter, decline?

These questions are rooted in ancient themes in the history of western social thought. He tried to answer them in his *Considerations on the Causes of the Romans' Greatness and Decline*, which appeared in 1734. It was overshadowed by Gibbon's later masterpiece on the same subject, though the English historian freely recognized the root of his inspiration in the French one.

In contrast to the *Decline and Fall of the Roman Empire*, Montesquieu's work was essentially an essay. It was uncritical of evidence and often took statements by the most diverse Latin authors at their face value. As a source on the history of Rome, it should not be read. As an investigation of the unintended consequences of human action through time, and an effort to comprehend the historical process of a given period as possessing an internal logic of its own (without recourse to metaphysical notions about Progress or Providence), it is unsurpassed.

Some of the ideas and theories that he put forward in his *Considerations* are now platitudes, but were then revolutionary. Witness his assertion that there are: 'general causes, whether moral or physical, which act upon every monarchy, which advance, maintain, or ruin it. All accidents are subject to these causes. If the chance loss of a battle – that is, a particular cause – ruins a state, there is a general cause that created the situation whereby this state could perish by the loss of a single battle.'

It was now obvious that Montesquieu had found the main theme of his lifework, the search for the general cause of concrete social events. The task demanded no less than a general theory of human society. To this end he now devoted most of his energies. He ceased to travel abroad (he knew several countries well), dividing his time between La Brède and Paris. He became active in the work of the French Academy, to which he had been elected; here he continued to converse with the men of his time.

He was fully a man of his century (he was, for instance, a freemason). But he remained impervious to several of the overriding beliefs of the age, notably the belief in progress; and this despite his friendship with its very champion, Fontenelle. By now, Montesquieu knew exactly what he was after – an explanation of human society which would satisfy the scientific modern mind. That is, an explanation in terms not of fortune (or mythical will), but of regularities; not of essences (or metaphysical will), but of relationships; not of congeries of events, but structures. This he achieved in his *L'Esprit des Lois*, on which he worked till he went blind from reading and writing, and which he finally published in 1748, only eight years before his death.

In its author's words, *L'Esprit des Lois* is a study of the 'necessary relations that derive from the nature of things' as they occur in human society. These relations Montesquieu calls *laws*, anchoring his thoughts in the doctrines of philosophers of Natural Law who preceded him. But he went beyond their conclusions in his much more secular interpretation. Montesquieu's laws are the rules which preside over the activity of any conceivable phenomenon – including the Supreme Being and human intelligence, as well as all the creatures and bodies in the universe.

Human intelligence, however, is 'far from being as well governed as the physical world'. Man, as a physical being, is ruled by the invariable laws that govern all other bodies; but, as a thinking being, 'never ceases violating those laws established by God, and changing others he has himself made'. This tension between the two dimensions of human reality – necessary relations which are immutable, and change brought about by the human mind always bent on innovation – is ultimately the subject of Montesquieu's work.

The origin of social change is to be traced back to man's passions, his needs and beliefs, though these are in turn largely determined by the physical conditions of existence and the social structure in which he lives. These two last components he sees as the sources of what is permanent in each society. They go a long way, he thinks, towards explaining the variations in ethics, belief, political regime, wealth and welfare in each society. (Hence the usual misinterpretation of Montesquieu that he was a commonplace determinist. Everyone seems to know that he claimed the climate determined people's love of, or aversion from, work!) Montesquieu was the first social theorist to establish the all-important analytical distinction between social structure and social change. He was perhaps the first to speak distinctly of social structure at all.

Nearly all of the many chapters of *L'Esprit des Lois* bear the word 'relationship' in their titles. He wanted to impress on his readers that every single phenomenon occurring in a society had to be seen as a bundle of interactions, resulting from a specific set of combinations of the factors present in it. To illustrate his point with empirical data, he painstakingly analysed an enormous mass of material and documents about the most diverse societies, past and present; classified it; and marshalled it under his rigorous central criteria of inquiry. This path was to be trodden again by Victorian social scientists like Herbert Spencer and Sir James Frazer, as well as by certain of the modern sociologists like Pitirim Sorokin.

Montesquieu wanted to show how every institution (slavery, polygamy, aristocracy, science, free trade, tyranny) could be largely explained by given combinations of factors (cultural, demographic, economic, climatic). But he carefully avoided the pitfalls and poverty of the mere 'factorial analysis' into which many of his successors have fallen. Montesquieu was, above all, a 'structuralist'. He showed that 'the general properties of society' – the social whole, or structure – in its unity, imposed a specific character upon the entire range of phenomena occurring within it. What he called the *esprit général d'une nation* – i.e. its social structure and culture – he saw as the chief cause entering into the lives of its members. This was, after all, a nation's central mode of organizing itself economically, politically and culturally. Its true meaning or spirit could not be grasped if we saw it only as the sole sum of its parts. Once constituted, it had a life and an internal logic of its own.

Montesquieu left us a system and a method. I have emphasized some of the strengths, and have pointed to the extent of his sociological contribution. What are the weaknesses?

One of the most serious is that he could not ultimately solve the moral dilemmas into which his own approach inevitably led him. On the one hand, he abhorred despotic rule, warfare and slavery. On the other he showed, with the 'fatalism' and detachment of the scientist, how in certain circumstances they were inevitable and therefore in a sense necessary.

But he did not have any patience for the logically 'impeccable' argument that we live in the best of all possible worlds (the Leibnitzian argument that Voltaire gave, in irony, to Pangloss in his *Candide* of 1759). Some of Montesquieu's readers, however, have not realized this. They mistakenly believe that his serene style and remarkable moderation in judgment betray some sort of moral indifference. There is open, if always restrained, anguish in the whole of Montesquieu's work at the realization that he could not overcome the contradiction between freedom and necessity. Have his successors been more capable than he was?

### FURTHER READING

WORKS IN ENGLISH TRANSLATION

*The Persian Letters*, tr. J. Robert Loy (Meridian, 1961).

*The Spirit of the Laws*, tr. Thomas Nugent, revised ed., two vols. (Hafner, 1962).

CRITICAL STUDIES

Louis Althusser: *Politics and History: Montesquieu, Rousseau, Hegel and Marx* (New Left Books, 1972).

Raymond Aron: *Main Currents of Sociological Thought*, vol. 1 (Weidenfeld and Nicolson, 1965; Penguin, 1968).

Émile Durkheim: *Montesquieu and Rousseau: forerunners of sociology* (Paris, 1953; English translation, University of Michigan Press, 1960).

Paul Hazard: *European Thought in the Eighteenth Century* (Paris, 1946; English translation, Hollis and Carter, 1954; Penguin, 1965).

S. M. Mason: *Montesquieu's Idea of Justice* (Nijhoff, 1975).

Melvin Richter: *The Political Theory of Montesquieu* (Cambridge University Press, 1977).

Robert Shackleton: *Montesquieu: a critical biography* (Clarendon Press, 1961).

# ADAM FERGUSON
## (*1723–1816*)

### Donald G. MacRae

IT is very easy, given ignorance and ill-will, to dismiss the history of the social sciences as a subject deserving no serious consideration. There are still people stupid enough to ask what are the social sciences, what have they achieved, that they should have a history? This sort of thing need hardly be taken seriously: the social sciences may be regrettable, but even if they are mistaken and delusory, they are yet facts of our life, our government and our administration, and more important still, they are crucial forms of human self-awareness in the twentieth century. The real attack on the history of the social sciences comes rather from social scientists themselves, most of whom I suspect can see little case for time being spent on the observations and speculations about social structure and social change of a nearly forgotten eighteenth-century Chaplain to the Black Watch – a man who had the temerity to practise sociology before the term had even been invented by Comte.

The anti-historical charge against us is one of triviality and sterility. What have we to do with the errors and conjectures of more ignorant, methodologically unsophisticated, times? Is the historiography of sociology not the mere making of chronicles, in no way superior to the reconstruction of the time-tables of dead railways? Surely the being and vitality of a living science is in the urgency of the present and the anticipation of the future? And so on; even the excuse sometimes put forward for studying the past of the natural sciences – and a shabby, needless excuse it is – may hardly be urged, for the history of, say, sociology cannot be suggested as an educational bridge subject, civilizing scientists, scientizing humanists.

Against this I claim that the history of social science is an intrinsic part of the various disciplines, and that the work of Adam Ferguson can show us why this is so. His claim to attention is not merely that he was the first real sociologist – and I do not forget Vico, Montesquieu or Herder. Far less is it that he influenced Marx or Sombart (or, for that matter, Schiller!). Such points are perhaps antiquarian or pious. The issue is more general: the relationship of the social sciences to their past differs in strength, though not I think in kind, from that of the natural sciences to their specific histories.

Firstly, every contribution to social science is at once a document of and a clue to the structural and cultural situation of its time and place. So much the sociology of knowledge leads us to expect. Secondly, every piece of social science has a potential, a charge, because it is itself a social fact, capable of altering and affecting the subsequent acts of men. We are all familiar with this notion if only because of Keynes's epigram about the sway of dead economists over live politicians. If we pause for a moment, the present is a good time to see sociology itself influence, corrupt if you like, contemporary social structure and culture at a dozen points from education to marketing to the conduct of elections. Thirdly, discoveries, original work in social science, assume new values in new situations. It is never safe to assume that we have exhausted or even fully incorporated the endeavour and insight of the past by our own work. In an age of tyrannies, for example, the work of Montesquieu and Ferguson on despotism becomes relevant and illuminating again, and analytically most helpful. What Adam Smith had to say about the division of labour is always important but in advanced industrial society Ferguson's account of the fragmentation of personality by the division of labour seems more relevant today than Smith's more directly economic analysis.

Now all these points, *mutatis mutandis*, also apply to natural science, but the second and third apply to a lesser degree or in a different form. Through technology natural science operates powerfully on society, of course. And past work can become relevant in a new and startling context – as, for example, Hamilton's mathematics reached out of the nineteenth century into the quantum physics of the 1920s and today. Nevertheless, the difference of degree is real; it is important for sociologists today to study Ferguson and it is important for the subject that we understand why the achievement of eighteenth-century Scottish social thought was not cumulative and for so long contributed so little to knowledge and understanding. It is improbable that any branch of natural science is in a similar condition *vis-à-vis* its founding fathers. One heretical suggestion to explain the difference may be permitted: natural scientists have done their history consistently better than the sociologists. . . .

Ferguson's life cannot much concern us here. Three facts however must be stressed. The Scotland of the eighteenth century was, for reasons not fully explained, intellectually vigorous and culturally creative as never before or since. Edinburgh vied with Paris and surpassed London or Philadelphia as a capital of the Enlightenment. The Scots knew this – as any reader of Hume's correspondence will realize – but they could scarcely credit their own knowledge. In this milieu, extraordinary in its cordiality considering its intense intelligence, Ferguson was a considerable figure, surpassed in contemporary reputation perhaps only by Hume, Smith and Robertson. The modern world would, rightly I believe, place him above the last of these three.

Yet in one way Ferguson was an alien in this informed and brilliant society. He was a Highlander whose origins were in Perthshire, on the marches of two cultures, one animated by honour, martial virtue and tribal bonds, the other by commerce, speculation and orthodox learning. Marginality is no disadvantage to a sociologist. Being an alien, familiar with, yet estranged from, two cultures is an undoubted gain. In addition, if Gibbon profited from service in the militia, how much more did Ferguson learn from his years of service with the Black Watch? (Alas, one must probably dismiss Sir Walter Scott's anecdote that Ferguson abandoned the Bible for the claymore at Fontenoy.)

And, like Adam Smith, Ferguson was a moralist. I mean by this more than that he was Professor of Moral Philosophy at Edinburgh. His sociology is rooted in his ethical theory precisely as is true of Durkheim, of Hobhouse and of Weber. (Of the classical sociologists perhaps Pareto alone has no specific system of ethics.) Unfortunately his theory of morals is eclectic and unconvincing, rhetorical precisely where it should be closely logical. There is much good sociology in his widely-translated

*Institutes of Moral Philosophy* (1772) and more in his *Principles of Moral and Political Science* (1792). There is acute criticism of Smith and of Hume. But the total effect is small, and his success as an ethical thinker far less than his contemporary influence as a moralist. But the moral impulsion underlies the great *History of Civil Society*, and his moral concern drives him into sociology. He wishes to understand the moral conduct of man, and for this it is his conviction that a science of society is required. So also is a science of the laws of the human mind, a psychology, but while he recognizes this necessity he does no more than to make a few very general observations, and one realizes with a shock how recent is the strict separation of mental from moral science. Yet this proves an advantage, for Ferguson is not tempted, as so often and so unsuccessfully has happened, to try to deduce his sociology from a system of psychology.

What *An Essay on the History of Civil Society* (1767) does is to elaborate, without the name, a systematic, widely informed, developmental sociology. The book constantly acknowledges the influence of Montesquieu, but it is in fact different in kind from *L'Esprit des Lois* precisely because it does not merely contain flashes of sociological insight in the midst of an ill-organized and polemical disquisition on politics, but is an attempt to outline the necessary structural elements of any society, to examine the principal actual varieties of such structures, and to explain change within them. Ferguson, of course, lacks the genius and felicity of Montesquieu, but he is a sociologist, the first.

Nor should one underestimate Ferguson's prose. Leslie Stephen called him, 'a facile and dexterous declaimer'. This seems to me nowhere just about the *Civil Society*, and though I understand Stephen's point and his irritation with some of the moral writings, yet here too there is a misunderstanding. Ferguson was largely and openly engaged in publishing lectures in the rhetoric of his century. His fine writing when he is in difficulties seems sad rather than dexterous, laborious rather than facile. In *Civil Society* the language is customarily terse and the formal periods dense with meaning, abrupt in their sequence. 'The maxims of conquest are not always to be distinguished from those of self-defence.' 'The most equitable laws on paper are consistent with the utmost despotism in administration.' Remarks such as these are not epigrams, but they remain in the mind. There are few pages without them.

Ferguson uses a wide range of comparative material, but as his editor, Dr Duncan Forbes, points out, he never mentions his own central experience as a Highlander, Gaelic speaking, and knowing by acquaintance, not description, the reality of 'barbarian' life, and puzzled justly to assess what is gained, what lost, in social change. Yet this Highlandness is one of the clues to the understanding of the book. He repeats a truism of his age when he says that in contemporary primitives we see 'as in a mirror, the features of our own progenitors'. But in his pages the truism comes alive – just as today it comes alive in the novels of African writers like Achebe or Beti. The comparative references he employs most openly for his account of barbaric society are to North American Indians, the Mongols, the early Germans, and the most ancient Greeks known to him. (He was indeed a pioneer in the interpretation of the literary records of early Greece and Rome, not as veridical history but as documents, sociological clues, and political assertions.)

The result is excellent. He is concerned with the politics of savage and barbarous society. From conversation with those who knew the Indians of the eastern forests and from Lafitau and Charlevoix, he elaborates an accurate and operative sociological model. It is true that he has little to say which analyses the structure of kin, but kin as a principle of organization cannot escape the eye of a man who knew the Clans. He is also – through prudence, prejudice or indifference – inclined to neglect the religious factor in social life. (We know how, but imperfectly why, he left the Ministry of the Church of Scotland.) Indeed Ferguson's handling of the American Indians almost causes one to despair of anthropology, and to reflect on how much its attention has been an affair of fashion, imperial history and accident. Certainly there has been progress in the last two generations, but to what a remarkable degree it has been in extent and rigour rather than depth.

Ferguson perhaps does not allow enough for culture contact in his analysis of social change. He allows much in social solidarity and invention to arise from the wars, feuds, and rivalries of groups. But, 'any singular practice of one country . . . is seldom transferred to another, till the way be prepared by the introduction of similar circumstances. Hence our frequent complaints of the dulness of obstinacy of mankind, and of the dilatory communication of arts, from one place to another.' This belief may explain his failure in later versions ever to refer to those developments of Indian polity of which he must have been aware and which we associate with such men (Indians despite their European names) as Joseph Brant with the Mohawk and Alexander McGillivray of the Creek. But it saves him from the romantic diffusionism of his French contemporaries.

Social change that is theoretically interesting is thus what we have learned to call endogenous change, change generated within a society. The progress of societies involves public dangers; it does not necessarily improve the lot or the individual integrity of the individual. Indeed the savage can neither comprehend nor tolerate a society where the social division of labour produces men 'ignorant of all human affairs, and who may contribute to the preservation and enlargement of their commonwealth, without making its interests the object of their regard or attention'. The division of labour serves 'to break the bonds of society': its advance injures civic commitment and may end in 'an attempt to dismember the human character, and to destroy those very arts we mean to improve'. Here we come to two cardinal elements in Ferguson's thought: his theories of 'alienation' as we have been taught to call it, and of property.

Now two great names intrude, those of Adam Smith and Marx. *The Wealth of Nations* was published in 1776: Marx, who praised Ferguson, believed that Smith's analysis of the division of labour leans on Ferguson. But Smith thought otherwise, and we now know the content of Smith's Glasgow lectures first published in 1896 (*Justice, Police, Revenue and Arms*) with its famous phrase that 'man is an anxious animal.' The two Scots seem to me, as I said above, to be concerned with different aspects of the same thing, and it matters little if Ferguson already knew Smith's views. *Civil Society* is about the solidarity, differentiation and evolution of societies, not about markets and productivity.

Ferguson's economics are the *ad hoc* necessities of the sociologist.

The point about the sociological implications of the increasing division of labour in society is that acts and devices intended for purposes of immediate advantage, social or economic, have consequences additional and far other from those intended by the actors. This was an idea beloved of the Enlightenment – central, for example, to Mandeville's *Fable of the Bees*. It is none the less important: without it no sociology is possible. Ferguson sees a functional relationship between social stratification and the division of labour. Classes are the product in part of variations in inherent ability, in part of the unequal distribution of property, and most originally of the effects of the division of labour whereby, in our language, different sub-cultures and different personality types are formed. These sub-cultures and personalities are defective because partial: hence flows Ferguson's contribution, the theory of alienation.

I must confess that most of what is written about alienation seems to me void. What Ferguson says goes, as Dr Forbes says, beyond Rousseau, and is I believe realistic and suggestive. But it seems to me less exciting than his study of the institution of property as a social phenomenon. This after all remains the great and one of the least studied questions in sociology, probably our biggest reproach. Behind him are Harrington and Locke, but when he speculates that it is the distribution of property which gives a society its character he goes further than them, for he understands by society a structure of more than power and wealth, and he has no specific theory of class struggle though one may find in him something richer, the beginning of a theory of social conflict. Property is 'a matter of progress', i.e. of social development, and is therefore a matter of secondary rather than primary causation in society. He traces its growth and influence in an abstract argument illustrated by his usual command of comparative data. His merits largely result from his avoiding three theories which pervaded the thought of his time.

He was not haunted by a 'state of nature' either of idyllic virtue and peace or of the war of all against all. He believed, quite simply, that he knew better. Secondly, he does not adopt a 'means of subsistence' scheme of stages of social development such as is employed from Smith to Hobhouse, Wheeler and Ginsberg – and for his purposes he is right. His categories are savage, barbarous and 'polished'. (The anthropologist will think of L. H. Morgan a century later.) These are the names of types of social structure. Thirdly he uses the word 'progress' to mean something like developmental change of social structure. This progress is not inevitable. Nor is it simply beneficent. Its accompaniment is a measure of alienation. It is in constant danger of despotism. Social regression becomes in Ferguson a sociological category, not just a sort of moral threat or convenient denunciation of the present by the disillusioned, disappointed or old.

And while Ferguson may seem to follow Montesquieu very closely in the most striking part of his political sociology, here too his unique quality is evident, so that criticizing Wittfogel's *Oriental Despotism* some ten years ago I found the classical formulation of the sociological theory of despotism in Ferguson. Here Ferguson's emotional commitments, his moral concern, are always evident. They do not corrupt his judgement. He does not hold out easy hopes for freedom. He shows how when under despotism, 'human nature appears in the utmost state of corruption, it has actually begun to re-form'. But this is a process of generations, it involves a return (though not a repetition; one is reminded of Vico) to an earlier style of social organization. Human life is not easy, every society buys its structure at a price. The attainment and maintenance of a civilization is a dangerous achievement, under constant threat from within. *Civil Society* is a social evolution if you like, but it is a realistic one in that it is a theory of developmental sequences, not of a triumphal march from the 'infancy of society' to our present perfections.

I have been looking at Ferguson, correctly I believe, as the first sociologist. He is other, connected, things as well. I hope some day to examine his place in the historiography of the Roman republic and revalue his three-volume study of its progress and death. I would like to understand how at least three years before Malthus he could write 'that the numbers of mankind in every situation do multiply up to the means of their subsistence'. I would like to have contrasted him with Smith, John Millar and Kames. I should have compared his proto-sociology of literature with those of Vico and Herder. Professor David Kettler in a recent book has examined Ferguson as an early example of the specialized intellectual and some very contemporary aspects of his theory of politics – not, I think, the most vital points, but I confess that not all the concerns of political theorists make sense to me. But on most of these matters (and there are many others I have not mentioned) Ferguson seems to me essentially and genuinely 'an interesting historical figure'. In sociology he is more than that, and after two centuries he is relevant to the concerns and the difficulties of the subject. He could not employ, of course, the vocabulary of special words and usages which sociology and anthropology have now developed, but read with attention he is not merely instructive and helpful, he can surprise with novel suggestions, insights and ideas that deserve consideration and research. We should not permit a change of terms to veil him from us.

A fascinating question remains: why did sociology not develop directly out of the theories and analyses of Ferguson and Millar, the eighteenth-century use of comparative sources – historical and ethnographic – which were far more extensive and exact than most people today believe, and the empirical techniques of Sir John Sinclair and Sir Frederick Eden? The ingredients of a developing and worth-while discipline, even though without a specific name (and it is easy to forget how recent are the specific names of some of the major divisions of natural science: names are only sometimes magical) were in existence by the time of Ferguson's death. Practically nothing happened. Men as intelligent as J. S. Mill knew their Ferguson, but could not see the point of *Civil Society*. Comte named the discipline but distorted its growth. The question seems to me particularly interesting and pressing two centuries after the writing of *Civil Society* when, for all its vogue and activity, sociology is faltering intellectually. The specific answer lies in the movement of European culture we call romanticism, in the novel political experience of 1789–1815, in the economic and social transformations of the industrial 'take-off', and above all in changes in Scottish social and cultural arrangements and in her self-image in relation to England and the world. But this specific answer might yield general conclusions for us in the 1960s.

What is certain is that sociology began with Ferguson. He realized its essential nature and from this realization developed propositions new in kind and novel above all in their systematic inter-relationships. Sociology is not firstly about people, but about society: as Albert von Salomon said, Ferguson first discovered 'the specific character of sociological generalizations as presenting a rational construction in abstractions, not reality'. Many who call themselves sociologists have not yet learned that lesson.

### FURTHER READING

WORKS

Duncan Forbes (ed): *An Essay on the History of Civil Society, 1767* (Edinburgh University Press, 1966).

CRITICAL STUDIES

Gladys Bryson: *Man and Society: the Scottish Inquiry of the eighteenth century* (Princeton, 1945).

Herta H. Jogland: *Ursprünge und Grundlagen der Soziologie bei Adam Ferguson* (Duncher and Humblot, Berlin, 1959).

David Kettler: *The Social and Political Thought of Adam Ferguson* (Ohio State University Press, 1965).

William C. Lehmann: *Adam Ferguson and the Beginnings of Modern Sociology* (Columbia University Press, New York, 1930).

Donald G. MacRae: *Ideology and Society* (ch. xii, Heinemann, 1961).

# SAINT-SIMON
## (1760–1825)

### Steven Lukes

SAINT-SIMON has been variously and correctly described as 'the most eloquent prophet of the rising bourgeoisie in its most generous and idealistic mood', 'the prophet of a planned industrial society', the philosopher of 'the age of organization', the precursor of totalitarian authoritarianism, and a utopian socialist.

Engels said of him that he was, 'with Hegel, the most encyclopedic mind of his age' and that almost all the ideas of later socialism were 'contained in his works in embryo'. François Perroux, the distinguished French economist and technocrat, has remarked that in the modern age, 'we have all become more or less saint-simonians' – observing that Saint-Simon's thought will remain relevant 'as long as it is necessary to seek an organization which renews elites, while preventing industry from destroying society and society from destroying industry and either from destroying man', and that with Saint-Simon and his followers 'the religious aspiration and industrialism are linked in a harmonious fashion'. Émile Durkheim saw Saint-Simon, rather than Comte, as the founder of positivism and sociology: there were 'few doctrines richer in fertile observations than his and it led simultaneously in three directions – to 'the idea of extending to the social sciences the method of the positive sciences, out of which sociology has come, and the historical method ...; the idea of a religious regeneration; and finally, the socialist idea'.

Claude-Henri, Comte de Saint-Simon, was more than half mad and led a life that was almost as bizarre as the legend cultivated by his disciples after his death. The legend, to which he himself contributed, has it that he was a direct descendant of Charlemagne, who appeared before him, while he was in prison during the French revolutionary Terror, with the words, 'Since the world began no family has had the honour to produce both a hero and philosopher of the front rank ... My son, your success as a philosopher will equal mine as a soldier and a statesman.' The legend tells that the mathematician d'Alembert supervised his education, that his valet would wake him every morning with the words, 'Get up, Monsieur le Comte, you have great things to do!' and that he proposed to Madame de Staël by exclaiming, 'Madame, you are the most extraordinary woman in the world, and I am the most extraordinary man. Between us, we would, without doubt, have an even more extraordinary child,' adding (according to one version) that they should consummate their union in a balloon.

In fact, the story of his adult life can be divided, in his disciples' words, as follows: 'Seven years he consecrated to the acquisition of pecuniary resources and seven years to the acquisition of scientific materials; ten years to the renovation of philosophy and ten years to the renovation of politics.' In his last year of life he turned to the founding of a new religion, the 'New Christianity', but without genuine religious enthusiasm: it was left to his followers to create from his thought a romantic and mystical cult with its own esoteric jargon and rituals. He always remained a rationalist and a child of the Enlightenment, a philosopher whose aim was the total reconstruction of society and of thought.

Born into an old noble family in 1760 (his great-uncle was the famous Duc de Saint-Simon, the chronicler of Louis XIV's court), he fought in the American revolution, whence he wrote to his father that, when his ideas were anchored, he would 'achieve a scientific work useful to humanity – which is the principal aim I am setting for my life.' On the conclusion of peace, he tried to persuade the viceroy of Mexico to build a canal linking the Atlantic and Pacific Oceans in Nicaragua and then spent some time in Spain, drawing up plans to link Madrid with the sea. With the outbreak of the French revolution, he renounced his noble titles (his relatives fled) and loudly proclaimed revolutionary sentiments. He was none the less imprisoned (by mistake) for nine months.

His chief activity during the revolutionary period was to engage in financial dealings in national lands. He was, indeed, one of the revolution's great speculators, and during the Directory he lived lavishly, with twenty servants and a famous chef. Then, after a major quarrel with his business partner over his extravagance and reckless commercial ventures, he turned to scientific self-education and surrounded himself with scientists and artists. He took a house opposite the École Polytechnique and invited the outstanding physicists and mathematicians to dinner. Then he took a house opposite the École de Médicine, where he studied physiology in similar fashion. Journeys to England and Germany completed his education.

The rest of his life was spent in writing, amid increasing poverty. From 1803 to 1813 he was concerned primarily with the reconstruction of the intellectual realm, as a precondition for reorganizing society. The first need was to develop what he variously called philosophy, religion and 'a general theory of the sciences' – by which he meant a unified system of scientific knowledge, including the sciences of man and society. Saint-Simon believed that institutions are only ideas in action and that 'Every social regime is an application of a philosophical system and consequently it is impossible to institute a new regime without having previously established the new philosophical system to which it must correspond.' Thus, 'the crisis in which the European peoples are involved is due to the incoherence of general ideas: as soon as there is a theory corresponding to the present state of enlightenment, order will be restored, an institution common to the peoples of Europe will be reestablished, and a priesthood adequately educated according to the present state of knowledge will bring peace to Europe by restraining the ambition of peoples and kings.'

During these years Saint-Simon's words fell on deaf ears. The scientists treated him as a buffoon and took no notice when he advised them to 'choose an idea to which others can be related and from which you would deduce all principles as consequences. Then you will have a philosophy. This philosophy will certainly be based upon the law of Universal Gravity, and all your works will from that moment on assume a systematic character.' Neither the scientists nor Napoleon I, to whom Saint-Simon repeatedly addressed himself, showed any interest in the 'religion of

Newton', or in any of Saint-Simon's successive schemes for instituting an intellectual elite – an elite of 'scientists, artists and men of liberal ideas', in conjunction with the propertied, the bankers and industrialists.

In 1805 his money ran out. For a time he was a copyist in a pawnshop and was then taken in to the house of a former servant. For several years he lived in great poverty and fell dangerously ill, but his fortunes improved with the fall of Napoleon. He acquired a secretary in Augustin Thierry, the future historian, who was succeeded in 1817 by Auguste Comte: these brilliant young men enabled the wild and fertile ideas of Saint-Simon to acquire some coherence. With the restoration of the French monarchy, he turned his attention to the industrial and commercial bourgeoisie, to whom he henceforth addressed himself in a series of periodicals and pamphlets in the interests of the practical reorganization of society. His attention moved from science to economics and politics.

At first the capitalists and liberals, and especially the financial aristocracy, supported him, for he argued for the primacy of industry and government non-interference. But with the publication of the third volume of the periodical *L'Industrie*, in which the constitutional monarchy and the sanctity of property were mildly criticized, there was a sudden flight of the subscribers and a subsequent trial for subversion, which brought him acquittal and welcome publicity. Saint-Simon and Comte continued to publish further periodicals, exploring in detail the features of the emerging industrial society of the future and exhorting the 'industrial class', and in particular the leaders of the bourgeoisie, to bring it into being and demolish the theological-feudal order of the past.

In a sudden crisis of demoralization due to the lack of support for his ideas, Saint-Simon attempted suicide in 1823, but survived for another two years. In his last years, he turned to the consideration of the role of religion in the industrial society and became much more concerned about the condition of the working class. He also quarrelled with Comte, who derived most of his main ideas from Saint-Simon but thenceforth denied this, calling Saint-Simon 'a depraved juggler'. He died in 1825 and became apotheosized soon thereafter.

It was during the restoration period that Saint-Simon's most important ideas achieved expression. Although, in an important sense, his life's work constitutes a unity, it is his ideas about the significant features of industrial society that constitute his genius and mark him as a founder not only of sociology and socialism, but also of philanthropic capitalism, planning and technocracy. The unity of his thought hinges on his belief, already mentioned, in the causal priority of ideas, both for maintaining social order and for engineering social change. His philosophical-cum-scientific constructions bear all the marks of the autodidact systematizer, and the scientists were, on the whole, justifiably unmoved, although his belief in incorporating the social sciences (what he called 'social physiology') in the system of the positive sciences does have considerable historical importance, exercising, through Comte, a profound influence on the future development of sociology. As Durkheim put it, it was with Saint-Simon that 'a new conception of [the laws of social life] appeared . . . he was the first to offer the formula for it, to declare that human societies are realities, original . . . and different from those which are to be found elsewhere in nature, but subject to the same determinism.'

Saint-Simon's starting point was his perception of the condition of France, indeed of Europe, in the aftermath of the French revolution. 'The general upheaval experienced by the people of France,' he wrote, had led to a situation in which 'all the existing relations between the members of a nation become precarious, and anarchy, the greatest of all scourges, rages unchecked, until the misery in which it plunges the nation . . . stimulates a desire for the restoration of order even in the most ignorant of its members.' Society was 'in a state of extreme moral disorder; egoism is making terrible progress . . .' and the problem was to put an end to the 'profound agony which society has had to endure in the period from the decadence of the old political system' to the final constitution of the new.

This diagnosis had much in common with that of the counterrevolutionary thinkers of the time, theocratic and romantic reactionaries of all kinds. But, unlike them, Saint-Simon discerned new forces at work in society and a new principle of social cohesion: since the revolution the 'theological and feudal powers ... have not sufficient force or credit to hold society together. Where shall we find ideas which can provide this necessary and organic social bond? In the idea of industry; only there shall we find our safety and the end of revolution ... the sole aim of our thoughts and our exertions must be the kind of organization most favourable to industry.'

By industry Saint-Simon meant 'every kind of useful activity, theoretical as well as practical, intellectual as well as manual.' Man, he thought, was essentially a productive animal; indeed, properly considered, politics was the science of production. Thus all societies hitherto had been in contradiction with human nature and it was only the society of the future that would render human fulfilment for the first time possible. (On his deathbed, his last words were, 'The essence of my life's work is to afford all members of society the greatest possible opportunity for the development of their faculties.') The history of the world (or rather the history of Europe, for, like Hegel, Saint-Simon was ethnocentric) was the history of the development of the preconditions for modern industry, and the motor of change was the conflict between the productive and the unproductive classes.

Organic periods (in which the social and political institutions were 'in harmony with the state of civilization') were succeeded by critical periods, which were transitional and marked by conflict and destructive criticism. The last organic period had been the 'feudal-theological system', which reached maturity around the eleventh and twelfth centuries, but the germ of its destruction was born at the very time of its fullest flowering: 'from the philosophical aspect it is since the Arabs introduced into Europe the practice of the experimental sciences, and from the political aspect it is since the emancipation of the towns, that the human mind has obviously advanced towards a general revolution.' The present transitional period had reached a point of crisis. With the decline of the medieval system, the leadership had been taken by the lawyers and the metaphysicians, both equally unproductive and parasitic, who had carried through the French revolution proclaiming the deceptive and irrelevant ideas of 'liberty' and 'the rights of man'. The immediate task was to form a cohesive industrial class, made up of merchants, bankers, engineers, the productive professions and the workers, and put an end to the rule of the 'unproductive' classes.

Saint-Simon illustrated his thesis concerning the functional necessity to modern society of the *industriels*, or productive classes, and the functional irrelevance of the unproductive, the idlers or drones, in a famous parable. Imagine, he wrote, that France should suddenly lose three thousand of her leading scientists, artists, engineers, bankers, businessmen, farmers, professional men and artisans of all kinds. The nation would become 'a lifeless corpse'. Suppose, however, that France should lose instead thirty thousand of her nobility, bureaucrats, ecclesiastics and rich landowners. There would ensue 'no political evil for the state'. Their places could easily be filled, but in any case they only maintained their positions by propagating superstitious falsehoods hostile to positive science, and 'in every sphere men of greater ability are subject to the control of men who are incapable.'

What was the organization that Saint-Simon considered 'most favourable to industry'? It consists, he wrote, in 'a government in which the political power has no more force or activity than is necessary to see that useful work is not hindered; a government so arranged that the workers, who together form the real community, can exchange directly and with complete freedom the products of their labours; a government under which the community, which alone knows what is good for it, what it wishes and prefers, will also be the sole judge of the worth and utility of its labours. Consequently the producer will depend solely on the consumer for the salary for his work.' Thus a wholly new principle of authority and type of social integration, a quite new social structure, based upon the functional requirements of industrial production, would supersede the old system of hierarchy and subordination. 'The government of men would give way to the administration of things,' and political action would be 'reduced to what is necessary for establishing a hierarchy of functions in the general action of men on nature.' The class struggle would come to an end and 'the desire to dominate, which is innate in all men, has ceased to be pernicious, or at least we can foresee an epoch when it will not be harmful any longer, but will become useful.'

The influence of Saint-Simon's ideas was immense, though posthumous. There were his immediate disciples, a band of young Jewish intellectuals, mostly from banking families, who had lost their civil rights under the restoration, and who were later, after their religious phase, to become a major force behind French economic expansion during the Second Empire (especially in the development of banks, railways and the Suez Canal). Saint-Simon also had a distinctive influence upon English liberalism (especially through Mill), on Russian liberalism and socialism (especially through Herzen), on Italian nationalism (through Mazzini), on Marx and on Engels, and, of course, on French socialism. As to his influence on European positivism and sociology, it is impossible to separate it from that of Comte, a less original though more systematic thinker.

If his theory of progress was somewhat shallow, if his theory of class is inferior to that of Marx (which some are now inclined to doubt), if his doctrine of the increasing irrelevance of politics and the essentially peaceful and internationalist character of industrial society now has a utopian ring, if the unity of his total system breaks down before the contradiction between the demands of rationalism and the secular religion he thought industrial society required, it none the less remains true that no thinker has had a more pervasive influence on modern European thought and a greater claim to being considered the founder of sociology.

FURTHER READING

WORKS IN ENGLISH TRANSLATION

Ghita Ionescu (ed): *The Political Thought of Saint-Simon* (Oxford University Press, 1976).

F. M. H. Markham (ed): *Henri Comte de Saint-Simon: Selected Writings* (Basil Blackwell, 1952).

Keith Taylor (ed): *Henri Saint-Simon (1769–1825): Selected Writings on Science, Industry and Social Organisation* (Croom Helm, 1975).

CRITICAL STUDIES

Émile Durkheim: *Socialism and Saint-Simon* (1928; tr. Routledge and Kegan Paul, 1959).

Friedrich A. Hayek: *The Counter-Revolution of Science* (Free Press of Glencoe, 1952), Part 2.

George G. Iggers: *The Cult of Authority* (Martinus Nijhoff, 1958).

Frank E. Manuel: *The New World of Henri Saint-Simon* (Harvard University Press, 1956; paper, University of Notre Dame Press, 1963).

Frank E. Manuel: *The Prophets of Paris* (Harvard University Press, 1962).

# AUGUSTE COMTE
## (*1798–1857*)

### Julius Gould

AUGUSTE COMTE (1798–1857) was a tormented, dogmatic genius: and, as his 'image' emerges from his copious writings, a somewhat rebarbative one as well. Showing, from an early age, both literary and mathematical prowess he won a place at sixteen at the École Polytechnique in Paris. Before long he was involved in a student protest: the École was closed by the authorities and Comte was expelled. After a short sojourn in his native Montpellier he returned to Paris and resumed his studies – this time on a wider scale and with an eye to political action.

Paris, then as now, was the centre of many currents – messianic, technocratic and socialist: and Comte was quickly drawn into the circle of Henri de Saint-Simon – becoming for a while his secretary. During this period Comte produced his 'Plan of the Scientific Operations Necessary for Reorganizing Society' – an early work that combined his constant themes – a profound intellectualism (a belief that the human mind passed through certain stages and that these stages determined the course of history) and an equally profound activism – as shown in his desire to reorganize society to suit the latest scientific, or 'positive', stage. Comte was well set to be one of the 'Prophets of Paris' – elaborating his theories, quarrelling with his contemporaries, recovering from mental breakdown, and enjoying some quite disastrous love affairs.

Students of the history of sociology readily accept a few cant facts about him. We all know that it was he who, quite literally, gave 'sociology' its name: that he was a 'positivist' and placed sociology at the apex of a hierarchy of the sciences: that he propounded the Law of the Three Stages. We know too that he was a 'morality intoxicated' man – who gave to the familiar eighteenth- and nineteenth-century ideas of progress some new and puzzling twists: that he was out to eliminate 'moral anarchy' and spent his zeal in the service of 'social regeneration'. We see him betrayed into ludicrous authoritarian notions, establishing, with himself as Pontiff, a novel Religion of Humanity.

It is tempting, I confess, to dismiss so bizarre a figure – one who speaks to us, at enormous length, from a distant age. Even where his contribution is a real one, there is a risk that we may exaggerate its novelty. He may well have given sociology its name – but in no real sense can he be said to have discovered the subject. Many of the ideas which, quite properly, he set out as sociological concepts had been in the air in eighteenth-century France and Scotland. Nor did he 'discover' positivism: as we shall see, this key term in his work is none too rigorously defined by Comte and it certainly cannot be equated with scientific empiricism.

Indeed, for all his scientific claims, he was in the main a social prophet – insisting, from the very beginning but with growing frenzy, that his own 'synthesis' of human knowledge could be used to create a new social order. His claim was a bold one. Such a synthesis had awaited the tremendous growth of 'positive' scientific knowledge: and in the chaos of post-Napoleonic Europe the time was ripe for its application to the study of man. It was a unique conjuncture of science, the *zeitgeist* – and Auguste Comte...

'Positive' methods are so central to Comte's theme that it is surprising that he gave so little time to making clear what 'positivism' meant. In his famous *Cours de philosophie positive* (based on lectures that he gave in the 1820s) he observes that 'the fundamental character of all positive philosophy is to regard all phenomena as subject to invariable natural *laws*, whose precise discovery and reduction to the smallest number possible is the aim of all our effort'. But this assertion does not tell us how we are to distinguish phenomena from each other or how we are to know which natural (or social) events can be classified as identical, similar or comparable phenomena. The process of sifting and classification is a constructive 'mental' process – and with the philosophical difficulties presented thereby Comte was blithely unconcerned. Indeed he helped to codify a rather *naif* gambit – the position that 'facts' are directly given to the investigator and that the relationship between them can be directly apprehended.

Comte then proceeded to advance some special advice for the pursuit of 'social physics' – or, as he came to call it, sociology. In studying social phenomena we should use the established scientific methods of observation, experiment and comparison: but to them he added a fourth method of especial relevance to sociology – the historical method. In principle this was a signal for a healthy advance from the arid and often ahistorical deductions that had previously been dominant in social thinking. But, as was often the case with Comte, he gave the good advice a special and limiting nuance. What *he* meant by the historical method was not what practising historians would understand by historiography. Indeed for practising historians (mere chroniclers) he had a grave contempt. Historical method for Comte meant the search, often in disregard of historical data, for abstract 'developmental social series' – collections of events and trends which fit in to an often conjectural scheme of historical change. Just as his notion of positivism begged many tough philosophical questions, so did his idea of 'history in the abstract' evade the challenges of concrete, if limited, historiography.

In mapping this 'abstract history' a key place was held by his Law of the Three Stages. He distinguished between three stages (not necessarily in all contexts consecutive) in the development of the human mind – the theological, the metaphysical and the positive. Simplifying his analysis rather drastically, we may say that he meant something like this. In interpreting natural phenomena mankind has come to rely less and less upon explanations in terms of supernatural causes: nor do we now find it useful to talk of nature, as for example medieval philosophers had done, in terms of abstract Essences or Ideas or Forces. We now seek to account for natural events by reference to 'laws of coexistence and succession' – hence the advances made in the late eighteenth century in physics and chemistry. These sciences had reached the 'positive' stage. Would not the study of human actions, if based on the same methods (plus some additions), now take an equally impressive turn?

Comte's answer was an enthusiastic 'yes'. In his enthusiasm to unite all knowledge under the banner of sociology and abstract history Comte once more was indifferent to major issues of method. Indeed, both in his early *Cours* and in his later *System of Positive Polity*, these issues were brushed briskly aside. He ignored, as many critics have complained, the way in which human beings have a kind of inside knowledge of themselves which they do not have with regard to external objects or events. Furthermore, in his quest to establish sociology in its own right, Comte had no time for the achievement or the promise of psychology. These are among the traditional 'loose ends' of social analysis – and I do not claim that subsequent writers have tied them all up. But – admittedly with hindsight – both Durkheim and Weber grappled energetically with such issues. For Comte to have done so would have revealed that his system was scientifically insecure.

Comte's stress on the Law of the Three Stages symbolizes his concern with 'social dynamics' – with the processes of change. What he has to say on social statics is relatively brief and bald. He was not concerned primarily with the empirical study of social structures – his job was to expound the 'laws' by which such structures are transformed. These laws are those of the development of the human mind (its growing rationality). And knowledge of these laws must be applied to human affairs if our happiness is to grow in step with our technological skills. It followed for Comte that those who like himself possess such insights should form a spiritual elite: this elite would evolve a 'subjective synthesis' of all useful knowledge geared to the interests and wants of mankind.

We may smile at this view: and smile again when we recall firstly that this spiritual elite (led by Comte) would be, in the ideal society, the sole countervailing power to the temporal rulers, and secondly, that the temporal rulers, in each state, would consist of the three most important bankers. Freedom of speech would, of course, be allowed: but Comte did not expect that the teachings of persons outside the spiritual elite would enjoy much prestige or influence. In the minute details of the new social order, and of the supporting Religion of Humanity, Comte became pathologically absurd: and upon the absurdities, and their sources in his stormy private life, it is best to draw a veil. But the enterprise of which Comte wrote is worth some attention.

His confidence arose from his basic view that there are invariable laws that govern human relationships. This positivist view is, at best, a heuristic assumption. With astonishing self-confidence Comte used it as assumption *and* as conclusion of his arguments. For the Law of the Three Stages is not a law about a given, 'unconstructed' reality. It is rather an interpretation which arises from thinking about *some* relevant evidence on human history. But obviously it is an interpretation that owes much to the perspective of the interpreter, the time at which he lived, and the motives that moved him. This does not mean that the interpretation is 'false' – only that other verdicts, prior, contemporary or subsequent, may be just as 'true'.

I do not want to be misunderstood. Such interpretations have their uses – and their place in sociology. Comte's case was of interpretation gone astray: but his wildness does not mean that interpretation (even of a utopian kind) is itself absurd. Comte's hubris lay in his belief that he knew what the 'laws of social development' looked like and how to apply them. Like so many enthusiasts for the happiness of mankind he became indifferent to the happiness – and freedom – of individual human beings. Even his elite were to think with freedom only within hallowed Comtean lines. This is more than an intellectual error: it is a moral enormity. No elite, whatever its scientific pretensions, can either know or coordinate the wants and interests of all mankind – or even of the citizens of one nation state. Happiness, after all, is a many-sided objective. The state can certainly create the prerequisites of human happiness: but it cannot create it uniformly according to a blueprint. This kind of 'scientific' planning is an enemy of 'real' planning – planning, with faith and vision, for what is possible in a non-plastic world.

Positivism involves more than an assertion that there are 'invariable laws'. It stresses the links between knowledge, prediction and action. Indeed Comte's maxim – *savoir pour prévoir* – might serve as a copy-book rule for social science. Today – though not in Comte's own day – many short-run, actuarial-type predictions are, of course, quite possible – in criminology, for example, or in applied economics. And in the computer age the raw data needed for such predictions can be analysed with a speed and rigour unimaginable in Comte's day. Yet, as is notorious, this kind of statistical projection was viewed by Comte with undisguised distaste. There is irony here – for Comte, in so far as he earned his own living, did so as a skilful mathematician.

As will by now be clear, Comte's interest in prediction lay in a very different direction. He believed that the coming of sociology itself was part of a determinate pattern of historical change. Once the sociologist has discovered the laws of such change it was his task to use the discovery in order to mastermind the political course of 'social regeneration'. What is more, this insight possessed by the sociologist was an insight into ethically valuable policies and purposes – that is, those policies which will advance 'progress'. Comte slips, in other words, very gently from the indicative into the imperative mood.

Comte made things far too easy for the sociologists. In the first place, sociology – in Comte's day and in ours – does not have a special technique for solving ethical questions or for laying down the course of social policy. If presented with a plan that is politically ordained and clearly set out, the sociologist can assist in its execution. But his special skill lies not in legitimizing the policy or in conferring upon it a seal of approval. Of course the plan, as politically ordained, may be inadequate to meet some moral or social emergency: or, quite conceivably, it may be a wicked or immoral plan. Then the sociologist, like any other citizen, has the right or duty to protest: but he cannot rest his protest upon any special status as a *sociologist*.

Secondly, Comte has a rather significant technique for setting out the context within which planning is to be conducted. It has often been noted that he is ambiguous about whether the field in which his 'laws' operate (or in which they should be applied) is Humanity taken as a whole, or Western Europe or merely his own country, France. He does refer to each of these possibilities. But he is not careful or exact on this score. Where he *is* consistent is in his view that he is discussing the fate of a 'total' self-contained reality. He postulates a field for prediction and planning which is, in a special sense, a 'system' – something within which there are no significant breaks or discontinuities. This assumption is linked with the analogy between the subject matter of the biological and the social sciences – an analogy upon which Comte, like other founders of sociology, drew very heavily.

Something of what this implies has been set out by John Plamenatz in the second volume of his *Man and Society* (Longmans, 1963). Comte, he observes, was not the first writer to insist on the social importance of knowledge as a factor in social development. '... Turgot and Condorcet, though they take it for granted that the increase of knowledge affects other sides of man's life in society, do not assume that all activities are so closely connected that they all change in a fixed order: they do not assume that there is a fixed course of *integral*, social change.' Comte, argues Plamenatz, did make such an assumption.

Like Plamenatz I do not regard this assumption as one for which there is real evidence. Unfortunately it produces a kind of picture thinking that has a deep hold over sociologists and those concerned with social reform. Comte, in my view, helped materially to legitimize as, par excellence, *sociological* what is, after all, but one possible view of the nature of society – the view that society is an interlocked system of interacting activities – but without significant breaks that might arouse theoretical concern. It is of interest too that Marx operated with rather similar intellectual machinery: we should not be misled by the neat classification of Comte as a prophet of social order and of Marx as a prophet of social conflict. So far as their effect on sociological imagery is concerned there are remarkable similarities.

Imagery, too, has its place in sociology – but there are times when it becomes a straitjacket for the selection, manipulation and, in the last resort, the suppression of data. The image of a society which follows a 'fixed course of *integral* social change' is especially attractive and dangerous. It is convenient for those who wish to 'plan' without the hard labour of assessing evidence. Once one has postulated a continuous 'fabric' – that, metaphysically, is that. One does not then need to worry about the discontinuities that may be seen in actual social arrangements. Whether they result from human inertia, historical legacies or unanticipated consequences, they can be dismissed at once: for they do not *really* exist.

Nor on such assumptions would we concern ourselves, any more than did Comte, with the priorities, moral or social, that have to be assigned to conflicting goals or with seeing how scarce means (human and material) can be employed in the service of competing ends. In real life we have to ask how the statistical and other projections that emerge from one study may be married with those that come out of another: or how to effect a divorce when the marriage has no further value. For a true Comtean positivist these problems have no meaning.

This review of Comte, in short, is a cautionary tale. For all his eccentricities Comte developed certain styles that his more 'normal' successors have unwittingly absorbed. For all his theoretical roots he became an anti-intellectual. His contemporary John Stuart Mill concluded: 'It is no exaggeration to say that M. Comte gradually acquired a real hatred for scientific and all purely intellectual pursuits, and was bent on retaining no more of them than was strictly indispensible.' And a more recent critic has noted Comte's practicality and his 'disdain for truth' – citing Comte's idea that 'the intellect's proper function is as servant for the social sympathies'. Comte's passion for social regeneration warped him and unfitted him for the *intellectual* study of society and its institutions. And, as Mill acutely argued, this *theoretical* backsliding meant a distinct loss, too, at the level of *practical* results.

Is it *naif* to believe that there is a warning here for us all – a century or more after Comte's death? Is not the vocabulary of modern sociology shot through with motifs drawn from this nineteenth-century founder of the subject – the language of 'integral', organic social systems? And do we pause to reflect whether this language is really relevant to the study of what happens within *actual* societies?

## FURTHER READING

WORKS IN ENGLISH TRANSLATION

*The Catechism of Positive Religion*, tr. Richard Congreve (London, 1858).

*A Discourse on the Positive Spirit*, tr. E. S. Beesly (Wm. Reeves, 1903).

*A General View of Positivism*, tr. J. H. Bridges (Routledge and Kegan Paul, 1908).

*The Positive Philosophy*, tr. and abridged by Harriet Martineau, two vols. (Trübner, London, 1853; George Bell, 1896).

*System of Positive Polity*, tr. Bridges, Beesly, Congreve, Harrison (Longmans Green, 1875–77).

CRITICAL STUDIES

Pierre Arnaud: *Sociologie de Comte* (Presses Universitaires de France, Paris, 1969).

Donald G. Charlton: *Positivist Thought in France during the Second Empire 1852–1870* (Clarendon Press, 1959).

Ronald Fletcher: *The Making of Sociology*, vol. 1 (Nelson, 1971), esp. ch. 2.

Morris Ginsberg: 'Comte' in *Essays in Sociology and Social Philosophy*, vol. 1. *On The Diversity of Morals* (Heinemann, 1956).

Leonard T. Hobhouse: 'The Law of the Three Stages' (*Sociological Review*, 1904).

Walter M. Simon: *European Positivism in the Nineteenth Century. An essay in intellectual history* (Cornell University Press, Ithaca, 1963).

Kenneth A. Thompson: *Auguste Comte: the foundation of sociology* (Nelson, 1976).

# JOHN STUART MILL
## (*1806–73*)

### Alan Ryan

In the course of a not particularly long life Mill gained a quite remarkable ascendancy over the intellectual life of England, as a philosopher, as an economist, and as a critic of literature, of politics and of society. He had in a sense been born to this position, for his father and Bentham had decided upon him as the prophet of the Utilitarian reformation, and had resolved to educate him into this role. The details of this extraordinary education are well known, and are recounted both vividly and movingly in his *Autobiography*. The results of it are rather more difficult to assess. On the one hand there is Mill's complaint that he 'never was a boy', that he never played games, never met children of his own age; on the other, his admission that by the age of sixteen he had a quarter of a century's start on his contemporaries.

That this education fitted him for the role of preceptor to a rapidly changing society is certain; and to this extent his teachers' hopes were to be fulfilled in good measure. The direction of his advice would have pleased them less, for once his critical faculties were aroused, Mill focused them most fiercely on the social and political views of his father and Bentham. His education and his reaction to it created the most notable of Mill's intellectual characteristics, his readiness to accept new ideas, new sights of the truth, at whatever cost to his present opinions.

The eminence Mill achieved was the more remarkable in being the work of the scanty leisure left him by his duties at the India House. One of the qualities that make his work more readable than that of most of his contemporaries is precisely the vigour which lights up his terse, economical style. He was for three years Liberal Member of Parliament for Westminster (1865–8). Opinions vary about his parliamentary effectiveness – Disraeli greeted his arrival with 'here comes the finishing governess', and Mill aroused opposition by defending Fenian terrorists, advocating dramatic measures of land reform in Ireland, and, above all perhaps, by insisting that atheists such as Charles Bradlaugh should be seated in the House of Commons. But he was always listened to with attention, even by the landowners whose holdings he patiently demonstrated to be a sort of theft from their employees. He came closer to securing the vote for women than did anyone before it was conceded in 1918 – he himself got 73 votes for an amendment to the 1867 Reform Bill which everyone expected to be ridiculed out of the House, and his allies got a majority on first reading in 1870.

The catholicity of Mill's interests and the scope of his influence was almost bound to provoke a reaction. The last quarter of the nineteenth century was in no political mood for Mill's brand of liberalism; the rise of Hegelianism discredited his philosophical opinions, and for the first thirty years or so of this century, he was merely another target for sophisticated sneers at nineteenth-century naivety. Today, Mill has very largely been rehabilitated. There have been many recent books and essays dedicated to doing justice to the extraordinary intellectual range of his work. His 'pure' philosophical work continues to look dated and unsophisticated in some respects – though recent work on problems of identity and reference have made him seem oddly up to date – but his social and political theory turns out to have much more life in it than anyone would have expected forty years ago.

As a young man, Mill was in closer contact with the French thinkers who coined the term 'sociology' and set the subject on its way than any other man of comparable ability in England. There were strong practical grounds for his enthusiasm for the nascent science. The Saint-Simonians were Utopians of the wildest kind, and Mill was under no illusions about that; but he shared their belief that effective reform must be solidly based upon a knowledge of the laws governing the concomitance and succession of social facts – in other words upon *Social Statics* and *Social Dynamics*. Unlike Saint-Simon and the later Comte, Mill saw his task as primarily an intellectual one, that of clearing the ground of outmoded doctrine and inherited prejudice that cluttered the path of progress. The direction in which Mill hoped progress would be made diverged increasingly from the aims of Comte or the Saint-Simonians, but his belief that the social sciences were the indispensable foundation of controlled progress remained unshaken.

At the time when Mill wrote it was widely held that to study society as a part of the natural world was either impossible or else ethically inadmissible. Some writers, of whom Macaulay was one, held that the complexity of society was such that there could be no hope of finding laws of social behaviour; only very limited foresight and control was possible. This is a position of political quietism, which tends to be contented with nothing more than maintaining the status quo or at most making limited small-scale reforms. The other common attitude was that of Burke, that society was governed by the will of God, which it was presumptuous to inquire into, and both foolish and blasphemous to oppose.

Both positions Mill thought little of; they seemed to him despicable shifts to cover intellectual poverty and selfish conservatism. It is scarcely an exaggeration to say that the chief object of the *System of Logic* was to silence such opponents and secure the foundations of the *scienza nuova*. The sixth, and final, book of the *Logic* was the first to be written. It is entitled *Of the Moral Sciences*, and deals with all the sciences of human behaviour, which for Mill included history, psychology, economics and sociology. The first five books lay the foundation for Mill's defence of the scientific status of these inquiries, a status which many writers still wish to deny them.

Mill did nothing that we should recognize as empirical sociological research. For all that, he had a number of perennially important views about the probable future development of mass society. There are, perhaps, three main areas in which Mill's views remain completely fresh. The first is the whole area of relations between society, and particularly the state, and individuals; the second is that of the relations of capital and labour, where Mill tried to steer a careful line between the tidy oppression of state socialism and the unjust chaos of capitalism in defending his own theory of cooperation; and the third is that of religion and the role it, or its surrogates, might play in a secular society. All of these are, of course, related; like other nineteenth-century thinkers, Mill was obsessed with the problem of preserving the individual's newly won independence of traditional ties without subjecting him either to new forms of tyranny or mere anomie. He gained, from De Tocqueville's *Democracy in America* and from his own voluminous reading, the impression that society was yearly becoming more conformist, more egalitarian, and less able to tolerate and admire distinction and superiority.

The question that dominates Mill's political writings is how to secure the free and spontaneous growth of individuality in the face of the pressures exerted by an industrial democracy. All the conditions of life were tending to stifle individuality. In industrial society the work of most men was mechanical, repetitive and dull; their reading was limited and trivial; their interests were few and mostly selfish and narrow. What could they do but exert a stifling pressure on society when they once had political power? It was not that Mill had any hostility to working people; he did not think them stupid or ineducable or wicked. He simply recognized that, given the conditions under which they lived, they were likely to be oppressive political masters. Nor did he think this oppression would be due to their despotic inclinations, for he saw they had none; it would be the despotism of unimaginative, uneducated mass society.

In many ways Mill set greater store by progress than by democracy; or rather, since that is too crude a characterization of a subtle and careful attitude, he wanted democracy introduced along with the education required to make it work. Men should develop their aptitudes for government piecemeal rather than be asked to take over Juggernaut before they could steer it. Mill recognized that it was impossible to turn back social progress, nor did he wish to do so. But he felt that there was a grave danger that too much would be entrusted to state action and too little to individuals; if individuals were regarded as objects of administration, life could be comfortable, but its quality could never be high.

An example of the sort of policy he advocated to secure the

needs of the poor and uneducated without too grave a loss of liberty was that education should be made compulsory, but not be provided only, or even mainly, by the state. The state's part was to set examinations in necessary subjects, provide parents with information and the poorer parents with money; but the subjects taught, and the way they were taught, should be left to private initiative. A policy of this sort may be impracticable or too costly, but it cannot be said that it shows less of an insight into what education is about than does our present system.

Mill's defence of cooperation was, in a way, part of his attempt to set out what an education in self-controlled freedom should be. He thought that men who had no practice in industrial democracy were unlikely to make a success of political democracy, and that men who had secured the vote in political matters were not likely to make docile employees once they had tasted self-government. What Mill dreaded was that capitalism would be replaced by a bureaucratic state socialism of the sort which he thought Auguste Comte had advocated. His solution was what has sometimes been called 'market socialism': the means of production should be owned by those who used them; firms should belong to those who worked for them, and the distinction between owners and mere workers abolished. But this should not be state ownership; it should be a system of producer cooperatives, forced to compete with one another in an open market. Of course, some things, such as roads, lighting, various public works would be more efficiently provided by the state than by private suppliers, so Mill was not an all-out opponent of state initiative. It was, however, vital to keep up private initiative and vital to ensure that competition was not abolished along with capitalism. The tradition of the British left is more in Mill's line than in the line of continental socialism, largely because it has inherited his concern for individual freedom, and the pragmatic, utilitarian attitude towards the issue of state versus private initiative.

The other side of Mill's views was in some ways at odds with this concern for liberty, and especially with his advocacy of eccentricity in *Liberty*. The former attitude regards dissension as a sign of life, but the other side of Mill's views was a sense of loss at the decay of the traditional social certainties with their basis in a common religion, that lent coherence and point to the lives of all in society. Mill's own religious position was complicated and idiosyncratic. But his attitude to religion as a social force was simple and not uncommon. Religion had in the past supplied a framework in which everyone could see his place, know its justification, feel protected by it, and defer to the judgement of the wisest minds in his society.

As a young man, Mill set great store by the influence of the 'clerisy' – a term of Coleridge's – on the views of the whole society. The clerisy were to be a kind of secular clergy, composed of the educated and elevated classes; and one of the objections to utilitarianism in the form that Bentham and James Mill had left it in, was that it was not the sort of doctrine that such classes could preach. In this search for a common intellectual and moral bond to elevate society, Mill was in the tradition of French and German thought rather than that of English liberal politics. Mill accepted Comte's view that Christianity had provided such a doctrine in the past, but was now incapable of doing so, and must be replaced by some other creed. He was dubious whether this was yet true of England, where he thought Christianity had some life left in it – but he had no doubts that France had outgrown this stage of history.

In later life, I suspect, Mill became disenchanted with this search for what Durkheim called a *force civilisatrice*. He came to recognize that the dangers of intellectual repression were greater than the likely benefits of uniformity of opinion. But it may be argued that it was a valuable corrective to his fragmentary liberal upbringing to recognize the need of most men for some system of moral and social ideas that will both explain and justify their lives. Into one error at least Mill never fell. He always maintained vigorously the difference between factual expertise and moral virtue; the fact-value dichotomy that Popper places at the very centre of the scientific attitude was much in Mill's mind. The place of the expert in sociology is to tell us *how* we may achieve our goals. What he cannot tell us, and what we must decide for ourselves, is what goals we *ought* to achieve.

Although all this would assure Mill a place in the history of the social sciences, it would be as little more than a minor figure who happened to be influential by being in the main stream of two important traditions. What guarantees him a place as an original contributor to the social sciences lies in his work as a methodological writer. His criteria of what makes a science scientific have continued to pass into the intellectual equipment of every social theorist. When Weber, for example, tackled the issue of whether social science was really science at all, what the question meant to him was whether the social sciences satisfied the sort of conditions that Mill had said that they ought to satisfy. In France, Durkheim's *Rules of Sociological Method* showed the influence of Mill, both positively and negatively. And when Dilthey had earlier set out to show that the *Geisteswissenschaften*, or 'moral sciences' *did* proceed on different lines from the physical sciences, his terms were borrowed from Mill, and it was Mill's version of the unity of science which provided a major target for attack.

The achievement of Mill was to give concrete form to the demand that all sciences should fit a similar pattern. He was an unabashed believer in the uniformity of sound procedure and the uniformity of adequate explanations. So far as he was concerned, all explanations must fit one simple logical pattern. This involved the deduction of what was to be explained from the twin premises of one or more causal laws and the statement of a set of initial conditions. There is no question of other forms of explanation; either an explanation can be made to fit this pattern or else it is incomplete. A subject becomes more scientific as its laws become more general, cover a wider range of instances, and have fewer exceptions. In short, subjects become more scientific the more closely their logical structure resembles that of Newtonian mechanics – which long remained the empiricists' ideal of what a science should be.

What, therefore, distinguishes the 'natural' sciences from the 'moral' sciences, of which sociology is one, is not that the latter are *un*natural sciences. Human nature is just as natural as the nature of trees and rocks and stars. All are equally part of Nature. The difference is that the moral sciences involve the laws of mind as well as the laws of matter. To explain the fall of a stone to the ground we need only a simple physical law. But to explain how a slump or a boom occurs, we have to invoke human knowledge, wishes and fears. This sort of subject, that is to say, requires reference to psychological facts as well as to physical truths.

The precise nature of this reference is a matter of a good deal of argument even now, for Mill was one of those who denied the autonomy of sociology, and would, if pressed, have been forced to agree that it could in some sense be reduced to psychology. The precise sense in which he held this to be so is extremely elusive. The point of it is clearer; he wished to emphasize the truism that men in society do not cease to be men, that society is composed of men, and that what happens in society is what happens to particular men. That is to say, he was against what Popper has denounced as 'holism'. The other reason for his belief was that it seemed clear to him that it is impossible to obtain laws of social phenomena merely by observation, and equally impossible to obtain them from experiment. Yet, there certainly seemed to be valid societal laws; so they must be deducible from the basic laws of human behaviour, which form psychology.

Sociology is thus the most ambitious of a hierarchy of moral sciences. The first is psychology, whose laws are discovered by introspection, and by the observation of men in social situations, less those elements that can be attributed to social influences. Upon this basis we erect ethology, a kind of social psychology, which gives us the laws of the formation of national character. It is not clear whether the 'laws of the formation of national character' tell us how an individual American or Frenchman comes to be like he is, or whether they build up a picture of an 'ideal type' of American or Frenchman. But whatever the answer to this question, Mill was very enamoured of this projected science, and saddened by its lack of development. Its utility was to be that it could tell us such things as how the American trend to increasing democracy was likely to transplant in England.

On Mill's account of it, sociology has two aspects. The first is what we might call particular sociology, where we set out to answer the question of what effect a given change will have in a given society; we might inquire into the effects of abolishing the British monarchy for example, or of altering the law on murder. Such particular inquiries could be either predictive or retrodictive; that is we could explain what would happen in the future, or why what had happened turned out as it did. The second aspect is one to which Comte attached great importance, and to which one suspects that Mill did too. This is the discovery of how one state of society as a whole succeeds another state of society as a whole – a sort of societal natural selection is envisaged as in Comte's theory of the three stages, or Marx's rather similar theory. This is the study that Popper condemns as historicism, and which he thinks both logically ill-founded and morally pernicious.

Still, it does not do to exaggerate Mill's attachment to this kind of super-history. Predictability in theory is very different from predictability in practice, and Mill never expected more than a limited guide to rational decisions.

To my mind, Mill's attitude towards the social sciences has much to commend it. He was much less bewitched by the apparent successes of economics as a predictive science than his father had been, and indeed than many later political scientists have been. He saw clearly the amount of idealization and abstraction involved in economics; he was thus able to see the force of Macaulay's attacks on his father, and allow for their justice. But he saw equally clearly that crude empiricism was just as absurd as his father's abstract mechanicalism. Filial piety and good logic alike led him to proceed rather by loosening the tight bonds of economics in introducing more adequate assumptions about human nature than by assuming that historians were right to argue as they did.

And if one may venture a theory about the role of methodologists – and about Mill's role in particular – in social science, it is that they offer as the logical bones of social explanation both more and less than a description of what social scientists actually do. Less in that there is little reason to suppose that sociology will ever look like physics; more in that it sets a standard of explanatory adequacy by which sociology is tested. It sets up a

Holy Grail of scientific purity. It can never be grasped, but the attempt to gain it refines techniques, sophisticates explanation, sharpens criticism. As perhaps the most influential of methodological consciences Mill deserves a place with the founding fathers.

## FURTHER READING

WORKS

*Auguste Comte and Positivism* (Ann Arbor, 1962).

*A System of Logic Ratiocinative and Inductive* (Longmans Green, 1961).

(abridged) *John Stuart Mill's Philosophy of Scientific Method*, ed. E. Nagel (Hafner, 1961).

*Liberty, Utilitarianism, Representative Government*, ed. H. B. Acton (Everyman Library, 1972).

CRITICAL STUDIES

Gertrude Himmelfarb: *On Liberty and Liberalism* (Secker and Warburg, 1975).

J. M. Robson: *The Improvement of Mankind* (Routledge and Kegan Paul, 1968).

Alan Ryan: *J. S. Mill* (Routledge Author Guides, 1974).

Alan Ryan: *The Philosophy of John Stuart Mill* (Macmillan, 1970).

Pedro Schwartz: *The New Political Economy of J. S. Mill* (Weidenfeld and Nicolson, 1972).

Michael St John Packe: *The Life of John Stuart Mill* (Secker and Warburg, 1954).

Dennis Thompson: *John Stuart Mill and Representative Government* (Princeton, 1976).

# FRÉDÉRIC LE PLAY
## (*1806-82*)

### Ronald Fletcher

BORN in 1806 into a family of modest means, Frédéric Le Play died in 1882 a French Senator and a 'Grand Officier' of the Legion of Honour. His long life was one of many-sided accomplishment. He attained outstanding recognition as a mining engineer. His sociological studies, always undertaken in close association with his profession, were wide in scope; fertile in the ideas they offered, the methods of investigation they initiated, the social reforms they suggested; and exacting in the standards of rigour they employed.

Later in his life he applied himself energetically and generously to many kinds of public service. He forced politicians to take account of sociological study, and his administrative ability enabled him directly to influence industrial and social affairs – as, for example, in organizing the great Paris exhibitions during the last half of the century. His scholarship was part of his citizenship. His academic life was always rooted in practical affairs. He was a man of humanitarian concerns – a Roman Catholic it should be noted (since his beliefs were interwoven with many of the persuasions underlying his studies) but not given to narrow dogma.

Nowadays, Le Play is known chiefly, perhaps only, for his generalizations about the form of the family in society. Yet his designation as one of the 'founding fathers' is justified. His work goes far beyond considerations of 'the family' alone. It offers a mode of analysing societies in their entirety, and has much to say about every aspect of modern society and its problems.

The first few years of Le Play's life were spent in a small fishing community near the port of Honfleur – poor, and made the more insecure by the blockading activities of the British fleet during Napoleon's rule. The struggle for survival of the family in a harsh environment was, for him, a close reality. When he was five his father died and he was taken to live with an aunt and uncle in Paris. Here he was miserable in a tightly disciplined school (later he voiced much criticism of 'formal' education), but he enjoyed a happy home life and was much influenced by several guests of the household who were forever discussing the disruption of the Ancien Régime and their doubts and bewilderments about the kind of society that was in the making.

In 1815 Le Play's uncle died, and during the next seven years he again lived with his mother, studying the humanity courses at the Collège in Le Havre, and developing an absorbing interest in ecological studies (studies of the relationship between the mode of life of organisms and their surroundings). These were largely botanical but they involved him in detailed and extensive surveys of the neighbourhood.

Le Play then lived briefly with a friend of the family – a civil engineer – who encouraged him to take his studies further. Here again, Le Play enjoyed a broad cultural background: reading the classics, and Montaigne in particular (enough, in itself, to indicate the tolerance of his Catholicism). In 1825 he entered the École Polytechnique in Paris, and from then on his career was marked with high distinction. After two years he passed as the most outstanding student for the École des Mines, and, after two years there, he again passed at the head of the school.

A close friendship developed between Le Play and a fellow-student, Jean Reynaud. Reynaud was an ardent advocate of Saint-Simon and the new ideas of 'positivism', progress and social reform, and the two were involved in continual and passionate argument. Le Play was deeply sceptical about the idea of progress, and critical of what he thought were brash notions of justice, reform and the rational reconstruction of society by governmental means. The principles of social order had been long established in various forms of human community, he thought. It was absurd to think that they had remained undiscovered by mankind until the nineteenth century. There were vast changes disrupting traditional societies, which required urgent study and action, but these changes were not necessarily progressive. Le Play came to hold a cyclical theory of social change and was conservative about social reform. He believed that society, with its new industrial characteristics, could only preserve important human values and improve human life if men reached careful judgements from a knowledge of social facts and their interdependence in society as a whole. He was in the tradition which runs through much of French thought from Montesquieu to Durkheim.

Le Play and Reynaud decided to undertake a detailed survey of the mining districts of north Germany. Each had to undertake a scientific journey to complete his professional training, and this choice enabled them to study not only the technical aspects of these mining communities but also their social organization and how this was related to their environment. Their aims were: to observe accurately the organization of the communities; to participate as closely as possible in their family and social life in order to understand them fully and distinguish purely local factors from those general in mining communities; and to interview those who exercised authority.

The journey undertaken by these students reads, nowadays, rather like a sociological saga. Carrying a minimum of equipment, they travelled entirely on foot for seven months and covered more than 4,000 miles. This study established a few things firmly in Le Play's mind. He saw how his professional career could be linked with the pursuit of social studies and his aims of social service and reform. He was convinced of the intimate relationship between a community's social organization and the struggle for life which the natural environment forced upon it. An understanding of human society could only come from the same painstaking study of facts, the same pursuit of scientific method as in the natural sciences. A further persuasion was that travel was essential to comparative research in sociology. 'Travel is to the science of societies,' he wrote, 'what chemical analysis is to mineralogy, what fieldwork is to botany, or, in general terms, what the observation of facts is to all the natural sciences.'

For a long time, however, Le Play devoted himself chiefly to engineering, and sociology formed only his 'favourite recreation'. But his deepening distress about the social disorders of his time increasingly committed him to social study. After the revolutions of 1848, he decided to relinquish the Chair of Metallurgy, to which he had been appointed in 1840, and devote himself wholly to this. In 1855 he published *Les Ouvriers Européens*, and, on the recommendation of the Académie des Sciences, a society was founded in 1856 to pursue Le Play's methods. Some of his central ideas were these:

1. *Ecology* was the most significant factor for understanding the nature of a society. Within the environment, a number of families had to struggle for survival, security and happiness. *Occupations* were the basis of social organization. A community structure of traditions, institutions, laws and morality was based on these. No matter how complex the structure of society, its reality for most people rested on their occupations and the livelihood they derived from them, and was manifested in the nature of their family life.

2. The *family*, not the isolated individual, was the significant unit for understanding society. The institutions of society were closely related to, and were always organizationally focused upon, families and family relationships. The family was not only a focal unit for the individual's experience of the structure of society, but also for sociological investigation. Like Durkheim, Le Play took *social facts* to be the basic facts for sociological study, and thought that the nature and quality of the individual's experience could only be understood within this context.

3. The family organization of the *workers* must be studied in order to understand society as a whole. Some elites – absentee landowners, speculative financiers, for example – were cut off from the roots of community life. But the family life of the workers derived from their immediate relationships with their environment and its resources; and their traditions, customs, attitudes, would all reflect this. The workers were not only the majority, the masses, but the people whose material and moral life were one. This was the bedrock of society's structure.

4. On these assumptions, the best way into the understanding of societies was a detailed study of 'typical' families. He undertook a series of *monographs* of working-class families typically found among people in particular occupations. He then grouped these families in the types of society in which they existed and

showed these societies to be appropriate to specific ecological situations. Le Play wished his studies to be as testable as possible and sought some method of measurement. He took it that the most important pattern of any family's activities would be reflected in the regular budget they had worked out for their lives. The core of each monograph was a detailed budget of a 'typical' family, but it also included details of occupation, the grade within the occupation, the kind of contract existing between worker and employer. There were difficulties in this method of measurement, but Le Play always included relevant qualitative background factors: local geography, aspects of social and economic history, and the like.

His family monographs related to Russia, Morocco, Germany, Austria, France, Britain, Spain and eastern European countries. Simplified, his main generalization is this: in all traditional communities there are three important types of family and social tradition, rooted in three basic occupations.

On the large grasslands of the world, communities are nomadic – shepherds who follow their flocks to new pastures when necessary. The family and social organization is 'patriarchal', with a central authority, and is essentially conservative, clinging to firmly founded traditions. Women are subservient to men.

Secondly, in coastal areas, communities live by fishing. Fishing communities have a nomadic occupation in part, sailing in search of fish, but they require a fixed home. This kind of life makes for individual resourcefulness and a distribution of authority, skill and responsibility in the handling of vessels. It makes, too, for a division of authority between man and woman, since the woman is responsible for the continuity of the home. This gives rise to the 'stem' or 'stock' type of family, in which family property is left to a single male heir who remains responsible for the other members of the family – starting them up in life and helping them when necessary. Central security is blended with independence and flexibility. There is a blend, too, of stability (a core of conservatism) and adventurous initiative (an impulse to change and progressiveness).

The third type of family and society is found in forest areas among roaming hunting communities, and Le Play calls this the 'unstable' type. The family is a union of the sexes, growing and diminishing in size as children come and go, and having little continuity between the generations. Families live in the insecurity of the moment, and are, says Le Play, 'decadent' compared with the stable qualities of the other two types.

He argues that the conditions of industrial society make most families approximate to the 'unstable' type. We must remember that he was writing when the working people in European societies were suffering from the early calamities of unregulated industrial and urban change. He had various factors in mind. In particular, he believed that the French law of 1793, which abolished freedom of bequest and established a compulsory division of property in every generation, caused the disruption of the 'stem' family and its security. Mechanization stripped the individual of any personal distinction in his work. Men became factors of production; were employed or not as market forces fluctuated; and became 'nomadic', having no secure roots in one place. Few could afford their own homes, and were migratory in this additional sense of having to move from rented house to rented house as their fortunes changed. Home life was impermanent; family life was insecure. This engendered irresponsibility. Many married young, with no provision for their future. They had large numbers of children but could not care for them. Home life tended to be non-existent; children spilled into the streets and their fathers into public houses. Despite additional legal rights, the position of woman in the family and society had worsened. Driven out of the home into employment, she played a diminished part within the home.

The growing dominance of manufacturing industry and commerce meant a decline in values and morality. The criterion of profit had displaced the paternalistic obligations which gave stability and continuity in the traditional society. All this led Le Play to maintain that industrialization had brought a degeneration of family life, an instability and malaise in the whole nature of modern society.

After this diagnosis, some of Le Play's most interesting ideas came in his *La Réforme Sociale en France* (1864). On law and the family, he argued that everything should be done to increase home-ownership. Testamentary freedom should replace compulsory division of property, in order to strengthen the authority of the head of the family (in this he upheld British law as against the French). The law should not treat men and women as though they were on the same social footing.

On economic matters, he urged the rehabilitation of local agriculture and the elimination of landlord absenteeism. He thought that communistic kinds of ownership and management were doomed to failure (he quoted experiments in France after 1848). Joint-stock companies, too, might be necessary for large concentrations of capital, but these also suffered from size and impersonality. Le Play favoured small enterprises in which relations between employee and employer were personal and direct. He opposed voluntary and charitable associations because he thought they made societies' inadequacies chronic.

On education, he thought that children were subjected far too long to 'formal' education and artificially withheld from employment and engagement in social affairs. Education was not something to be handed over to schools and schoolteachers. Some work was positively good for children. Education for girls should be different from that for boys – but not, by any means, more narrow. It should focus on homemaking – not in any kitchen-sink fashion – but in such a way as to broaden out into scientific and cultural subjects. As wives and mothers, girls would then become a rich educative influence in home and society. Woman's place was in the home, Le Play said. But the home was the most important place not only for children, but also for the personal life and happiness of adults.

Finally, on the role of the state, Le Play thought that the only good government was one that sought to render itself unnecessary. Nothing was worse than 'rational' lawmaking and bureaucracy that rested on moral principles seen separately from a detailed understanding of social processes. The French property law of compulsory division, for example, was based upon the abstract principle of equality, and its consequence, Le Play said, was to ruin the family structure of France.

What is the value of Le Play's work today? There is still much value in his idea of a comparative study of family monographs –

though not necessarily with the same budgetary ideas that he used. If researchers in the various regions of Britain carried out monographs on an agreed basis, we would at once have something better than we now possess – a broad and useful knowledge of the family in our own society. Secondly, whether or not one agrees with Le Play's specific legal criticisms and proposals, his insistence on what amounts to the development of a sociology of law remains important.

He rightly insisted on rigorous scientific method, on the importance of a detailed acquaintance with social facts and on the constant reference of theories to the facts which they purport to explain. But his empirical studies did have theoretical orientation and, though specific and searching, were couched within a conceptual model of social systems as wholes. His work was a basis for academic societies and journals in France; for such pioneers as Patrick Geddes, Branford and the early Institute of Sociology in Britain; and it has had much influence elsewhere. It still deserves serious consideration.

FURTHER READING

WORKS IN ENGLISH TRANSLATION
*Family and Civilization*, ed. Carle C. Zimmerman (Harper, 1947).
Part IV, *European Studies*.

CRITICAL STUDIES
Sybella Branford and Alexander Farquharson: *An Introduction to Regional Surveys* (Le Play House Press, 1924).
Michael Z. Brooke: *Le Play: Engineer and Social Scientist* (Longmans, 1970).
Dorothy Herbertson: *The Life of Frédéric Le Play* (Le Play House Press, 1951).
Pitirim A. Sorokin: 'Frédéric Le Play's School' (ch. ii, *Contemporary Sociological Theories*), ed. F. Stuart Chapin (Harper and Row, 1964).
S. H. Swinny: 'The Sociological Schools of Comte and Le Play' (*Sociological Review*, vol. xiii, no. 2, April 1921).

# KARL MARX
## (1818–83)

### Donald G. MacRae

To write about Marx as a sociologist is to be hedged in with perils. The dangers which surround an enterprise are no true measure of its intrinsic worth, and even the Grail does not always seem an entirely adequate reward to the reader of Arthurian romance. One can write of most of the 'founding fathers' of sociology without too much ambiguity and with a sufficient candour and piety. One cannot write thus of Marx, for about him candour must go, so far as I am concerned, with scepticism and ambiguity. To write openly of Marx is to touch sacred things, expose oneself to the lightnings of orthodoxies both novel and venerable, and throw doubt on received opinions.

'What you adored, burn; what you burned, adore.' So Christianity enjoined the pagans, and so I would enjoin, at least as far as the first clause goes, sociologists. The influence of Marx on sociology has been great and is perhaps still increasing: in my judgement he was not a sociologist, and his influence has been unfortunate. I do not deny him his greatness as one of the major pioneers of economic history and institutional economics. I could not deny his greatness in that his ideas, however interpreted, are, eighty years after his death, among the decisive social facts of our time. All I wish to do is to examine his claims to sociological greatness, to having affected the history of sociology for the better, and to being a live and good influence on sociology in the present.

THE above paragraphs were written for *New Society* in 1963 and appeared in the first edition of this book in 1969. As the philistine 1970s draw to their close the situation is greatly changed: it is usual to hear, in Britain at least, the 'classics of sociology' described by Marx, Durkheim and Weber. It is assumed by the political left and right, by the decent and the malignant, that Marx's position in the mythology of our age is that of sociologist. This would have surprised Marx who looked down on Comte and hardly noticed his great contemporary Herbert Spencer. It would have disgusted the most practically effective of all Marxists, Lenin, who always groaned when he heard the word 'sociology', and who regarded his colleague Bukharin's fondness for sociology as at best an amiable weakness. (Stalin, who of course found no weakness amiable, had Bukharin shot).

How has this come about? Our knowledge of Marx has changed in two ways. In addition to the discovery of 'the young Marx' in the 1950s, we have had the discovery of 'the middle Marx' as represented in the *Grundrisse* and as reinforced by the ingenious, boring writings of the French Professor Althusser. I do not think that either of these, least of all the second, has made Marx appear more of a sociologist but they have both given new rhetorical resources to those who are concerned to argue for Marx's position as a major social scientist – not least because both are often obscure and the reputation of Marxism as both containing and revealing mysteries is a large part of its success as an ideology, and ideology in great need of repair after the Stalin period.

But not only our knowledge of Marx has changed: so have our circumstances. The blasted hopes of the utopian 1960s and the felt discontents of the 1970s both make the Marxist style in social diagnostics seem more appealing for understandable reasons which, if not necessarily ungenerous, are certainly not purely intellectual. In addition Marx bulks larger through the grinding successes of régimes totalitarian in content, progressive in rhetoric and Marxist in official ideology. Advancing power is very attractive to those in the path of that advance.

But most important, and only in part explicable by way of the above points, is fashion, that fashion that is the conscious creation of men. In the 1960s when sociology expanded in most countries in education and in prestige, a very large number of people adopted sociology – and not, I shall suggest, completely without reason – as a way of pursuing Marxism by other means. The discovery of new aspects of the old Marx and of new Marxist teachers – Gramsci, Korsch, the Frankfurt school, the new Left (in England, genuinely impressive), all aided this fashion which, like all fashion, requires a constant element of novelty to make it interesting, provocative and successful.

Sociology had tried to be as value-free as possible: now with

Marxism it admitted the propaganda of values – the new vocabulary of 'commitment', of 'alienation', of 'exploitation' and of 'hegemony' proclaimed the fact – and of course the propaganda of values was also the propaganda of a kind of social hope. Thus could sociology be directly politicized. Yet none of this can alter the tasks of critical knowledge and inquiry – and Karl Marx is the legitimate object of both criticism and inquiry.

Now when Marx preceded Spencer into a grave in Highgate Cemetery his fame was that of an economist. Disputes about his correctness turned on his technical economics – theory of value, of crises, and so on – and these disputes continued for a long time but largely died out in the late 1930s. His contributions to economic history were sifted and absorbed, his contribution to institutional economics was (and is) neglected, and his great learning in the historiography of economics was almost forgotten, but is now being rediscovered.

Between about 1910 and 1950 – all these dates are arbitrary, but not, I think, useless – his fame was as a philosopher. Dialectical materialism was studied and expounded as the method of science and all knowledge that was reputable. Except in Russia this is no longer a burning topic – in any sense – and since about 1945 we have had, after Karl I and Karl II, Karl III who is (we are told) both a sociologist because of his early philosophical writings (mainly unpublished or obscure in his lifetime), and a philosopher because of his sociology. It is with Karl III that we will ultimately be concerned here.

I am not arguing that this account of Marx's reputation justly mirrors what should have been; merely that it happened, and that this is significant. It results largely – not altogether – from the investment of faith which men made in Marxism, and from the fact that Marxism was rich enough, one vein all but exhausted or shown to contain only fool's gold, for others to be explored. One could, indeed, offer a Marxist interpretation of this history, but it would not be very profitable or appropriate here.

It would be helpful had we space here to explore the personal and intellectual biography of Marx from his birth in Trier in 1818 into a family alienated at once from Judaism and from provincial German society, to his death in London in 1883 after thirty-five years exile in an England with which he could never be bothered to identify himself, and in which he had been the comfortable pensioner of Engels – a more complex, original and deeply ambiguous man than his biographer, Mayer, suggests. In this long exile Marx played ineffectual politics, wrote an enormous amount of good journalism and excellent, savage, learned letters, and left us the torsos, the fore-studies and afterwords, of uncompleted books. His work seems to me distinct from that of Engels, not always congruent with it, but yet always closely related to it. It is like the symbiosis by which one species of crab conceals and arms its claws by mounting on them sea anemones which gain from the crab's mobility and share its appetite.

This appetite was almost as universal as the nineteenth century of which Marx was so gigantically representative. Marx could have been an actor in the human comedy of his favourite novelist Balzac, characterized by a monomaniac avidity for knowledge, for the interconnexion of things, and for that ambiguous power which prophetic minds possess and which is always flawed by an obsessive need never to be wrong. But for one thing, as was said, he had no conscious appetite, and that was to be a sociologist in the sense in which the word was used by his contemporaries Comte and Spencer.

Partly, indeed, he could not be a sociologist, for sociology is a form of inquiry, and he already knew. More profoundly he could not be one, for he was concerned not with the social but with what underlies and explains the social; that is, in his judgement, with the economic order. And lastly, he did not need to be one, for he was concerned above all with a philosophic anthropology and his favourite tense was the future. Yet none of this prevents our extraction of something very like a sociology latent in his work, and – though I would not entirely agree – it can be argued that this was until recently the most satisfactory and fruitful general sociology available. More importantly it was for long, and is for many, the only easily available body of social thought, and it carries with it a promise of relief from the burdens of want, fear and hope, and the justification for wrong and error if they are committed in its name.

One can sum up this latent sociology in something like the following terms. The appearance of society is not its reality. Despite reservations and hesitations, the structure of society consists of an economic reality and social epiphenomena, surface phenomena which only rarely affect the underlying reality. This basis for most of history is that of economic exploitation of the many by the few. Politics is the violence and chicane of the few. Religion is the sorry consolation of the many. The family is the embodiment in little of the exploitation which is the class-system. Art is the mask of corruption and the reassurance of the mighty that their world is one of beauty and peace – or, Marx was a romantic and inconsistent, it is the cry of despair from the heart of the many and the rending of the veil of illusion by individual genius. Science is the technical basis of economic power and interest. Philosophy is ideology – for to Marx ideology, which had been the science of ideas, is the corruption of ideas by advantage and desire.

Society is change. Sometimes Marx – often Engels – writes as a kind of technological determinist to whom technology includes not merely the material techniques of economic production, but also the techniques of economic organization – 'the relations of the means of production'. Five great modes of social being successively embody the dynamics of society (this is largely Engels). First was the sparse Eden of primitive communism – a concept so odd and difficult that in a short article one must avoid it out of mere prudence. Second is slavery – the economy of the ownership of the exploited. Third is feudalism – agrarian exploitation without the burdens of ownership to hinder exploitation. Fourth is capitalism with exploitation made impersonal by the market and production maximized by the machine and the routine of the factory. Fifth will be socialism, society without exploitation, without ideology, with no breach of appearance from reality, no let to the self-realization of man.

Society is class, and class is opposition, the constant war of those who have on those who have not. But class is complex: the polarization is seldom complete, and, to change the metaphor, through its interstices new exploiting classes have emerged, the gods have defeated the titans, and exploitation takes new forms.

Only with the last stages of capitalism will there be naked confrontation of the few and the many because of the specifically economic dynamics of capitalism which (1) concentrate power in fewer and fewer hands, (2) produce – absolutely, or relatively? – ever greater impoverishment, (3) result in ever more violent economic crises of poverty in the midst of potential plenty.

The consciousness of class has represented itself in many ideological forms, but in the end it emerges clearly in scientific, that is, Marxist socialism. The end of capitalism comes in a true consciousness of social and human reality – the veritable end of ideology. The mechanism of this change, as of all change, is force and revolution. Dissonance can be resolved only by dissonance. Until this resolution tension and conflict, veiled or open, *are* society.

Parts of this are worked out with profound research, vehemence and wit. Other portions are sketched, while yet others are briefly asserted and abandoned. There are, as in all human work, lacunae and ambiguities. And there are, of course, contradictions. It is this that has given Marxism much of its strength, flexibility and appeal as a political ideology. But this is not all.

If Marx is a 'founding father', I would suggest the following reasons. He is deadly serious about the importance of the social as he understands it – that it is *not* the social in Durkheim's sense or, for that matter, in mine, is not the point. This seriousness is necessary to any sociology, and in the same ways the countervailing sociology of Weber would have been impossible without taking the Marxist seriousness seriously. To those who like or need an emotional charge before undertaking scientific work this commitment is attractive and has been important.

As I have often said, Marx stresses the non-obvious. Social appearance is not always reality. If it were, common sense and a little statistics would suffice instead of real sociology. Very often Marx is right, wholly or in part, in ascribing concealed, unconscious group-interests to historic acts and professions. One form of awareness sociologists should encourage in themselves is of the covert working of interests in social relations, manifesting themselves in thought and expression.

But more specific than this admittedly important and valuable drawing of attention to the possibility of latent factors and interests in society was Marx's work on economic institutions. Here, as in much of volume one of *Capital*, he is concrete, specific and original. He stresses that these institutions have a temporal shape and his concept of the economic includes much that a modern sociologist would treat as social. However one might modify or reject Marx's account of the primitive accumulation of capital of his famous section on the working-day in the factory, these remain indelibly in the mind as examples of knowledge and research brought into life by passion. Sociologists have too much neglected economic institutions. So too have economists save when concerned with their formal and/or financial aspects. To this Marx is a constant corrective. In Marx we see clearly the possibility of something better than and different from a philosophy of history: a historically specific sociology. But it is a possibility we see, a potentiality for which Marxism is no sufficient basis. If there is ever to be an 'economic sociology', then Marx, along with Veblen, Weber and Sombart, will be one of its founders.

And again in Marx there is one antidote to what should be incredible: the fact that much sociology has been, and some still is, based on the assumption that harmony and changelessness are the normal characteristics of society. How anyone in the traditions of the Western world could believe this of the human condition in society is hard to conceive. Nonetheless, some sociologists have apparently believed it, and at the least Marx, emphasizing tension, opposition, hatred and contempt, fraud and force, and the mutability of all sublunary things, reminds one of the harder facts of social life.

On the writings of Marx and Engels is founded most of the enterprise of the sociology of knowledge, so grand in its aspirations, but so nugatory in most of its achievements. There are other elements, consciously or unconsciously, present in the sociology of knowledge, deriving from late-nineteenth-century neo-Kantianism. And there is an alternative, though historically-related, tradition in the Durkheim school which seems to me more fruitful and more genuinely sociological. For all that, the Marxist study of ideology and the work that has arisen from it on the social conditioning, distribution, and relations of ideas is perhaps Marx's most solid claim to be a founding father of one constituent of our discipline. It is a claim that leads us, alas, to the endless ocean of the relativity of all knowledge.

It is not my intention to deny that there has been a very considerable Marxist tradition of social and above all historical research, and that it has often been stimulating and sometimes convincing, or that its practitioners have not brought to light much evidence which might otherwise have been neglected. The pages of a journal like *Past and Present* in England are continuing evidence of this, and of its values. Other examples are not hard to find. This, of course, is usually Marxism in a weak, diffuse sense. For a stronger sense one is often directed to such a figure as Lukács or some more recent writers in German. About them I have reservations. And I often wonder why Marxist apologists make so little of Lenin's *Development of Capitalism in Russia* or of the learned, dull and condemned Bukharin. But none of this is to the point if one believes sociology to be possible and, in fact, to exist – imperfectly of course, for finality is not the task of true learning and science, though it was the implied claim of the Marxists.

It is just to remark that some Marxists since Marx have found a ploy which allows them the authority which Marx always claimed and yet avoids the absurdity of claiming either a final knowledge or, what is in fact much the same, access to a final methodology. This is the tactic of stressing the polymorphous perverse creativity of the 'superstructure' whereby the underlying predestinarianism of the 'base' is abolished or postponed. There are texts to justify them in Marx, explicitly in Engels, and the tactic is central to Mussolini's victim, Gramsci. The genuinely brilliant Perry Anderson, a most illuminating scholar, is expert in the use of this tactic in modern Britain.

The trouble is that the general sociology we have sketchily imputed to Marx is not true. We know too much about social structures, too much about history, too much about social change, too much – which is inevitable, but Marx *did* stake his case on the future – about what has taken place since March 1883, to accept this. We have too many workable concepts for social analysis for this system still to be useful or relevant. It is evident 'that all previous history' is not the 'history of class struggles', even if we interpret this as a methodological impera- tive: *always look for class struggle in what seems significant; all that is or was significant is class struggle*. And how inadequate are Marx's conception of slavery or feudalism; how much man experiences and devises that is outside these categories. There are social truths, many of them, in Marx, but that does not make him a sociologist. Communists should themselves perhaps be ready to accept this, and continue to reject sociology as decadent bourgeois ideology much as they did in the brave days of Stalin. Even non-communist Marxists could consistently adopt this position.

But in fact they will not do so. Marx is one of those culture heroes who must be kept alive and up to date. Recently sociology was fashionable because of its promise and its mystery at least as much as for its truth and its attainments. We have therefore lately had what I called Karl III, essentially a modern artefact, but more than that, for the availability of the docu- ments has revealed a partly unfamiliar young Marx. It is perhaps not unfair to wonder why the real Dr Marx of Chalk Farm forgot or rejected him, and to think he was right. But he, the young Marx, is now the accepted Marx except to old Bolsheviks like Kuusinen or their modern avatars like Althusser. And as I said, this Marx is claimed as a sociologist.

Here, alas, we come to 'alienation'. Men are alienated from each other by the economic order – which is, of course, often true – and they are alienated from their necessary economic labour and the commodities they produce by that labour. No doubt, and no doubt by living in a world of 'objectivity' we are also all metaphysically alienated. No doubt many of us would be happier were we not merely human, but made perfect and whole by some deliverance, of which the proletarian revolution is but one apocalyptic instance. Religion is full of such promises. And doubtless labour is not its own reward, nor man at home with man. Nor is it false to hold that all relationships are ever in danger of involving the exploitation of man by man. What else? The old joke is true: that is what happens under capitalism;

under socialism, of course, it is just the other way round ...

But what has this to do with sociology? It is interesting as philosophical anthropology, but that is another activity. The doctrine of alienation is related to the most dangerous and least rewarding aspect of the French revolution: the terrifying injunction to fraternity. To speak very personally and seriously, I approve both liberty and *much* equality; I regard it as an essential liberty that I am not promiscuously called 'Brother'. I welcome the division of labour and the diversity, even the anomie of advanced society. But in these positions I am not a sociologist, and this is not the business of sociology, which is essentially the knowledge and understanding of social structures and their transformations.

At best we can find in Karl III, taking him as a social scientist almost uncontaminated by the later researches of the real Marx, a contribution to social psychology, which has some bearing (though not a central one) on the study of political sociology and stratification. It seems to me that this contribution, stressed by Lenin, was already clear from the later Marx, and that it neither greatly alters the balance sheet nor seriously offers any clear orientation to modern sociology.

To those, on the other hand, who see sociology as a commitment to political action this will all be less than just. But it is not difficult in fact to know when one is acting as sociologist, when as citizen. The knowledge of the former will often bear on the latter, and the concern of the citizen may help some in the choice of areas of social research without corrupting their work. But the two are different.

Within sociology the issues are all open, and the logic is not the either/or of Marx, but a multi-valent both/and. Sociology, *labor improbus*, has been whipped to the oar by diverse passions – generous, angry, invidious. But these passions are not its content. One does not judge Kepler by his hermetic aspirations, but by his science. Marx deserves such a judgement. He has not had it, and he will not have it so long as he is thought of as primarily a sociologist. He did social research and he has inspired it. He is a culture hero, a great fact of our age. For sociology he is, and this is not a dismissal, a most interesting historical figure.

FURTHER READING

WORKS IN ENGLISH TRANSLATION

*Capital*, ed. Frederick Engels, tr. Fowkes (Penguin, 1976).

*A Contribution to the Critique of Political Economy* (Moscow, 1970).

*Economic and Philosophic Manuscripts of 1844*, ed. Dirk J. Struik and tr. Martin Milligan (Moscow, 1977).

*Manifesto of the Communist Party*, tr. Moore (Penguin, 1967).

*The Poverty of Philosophy* (Lawrence and Wishart, 1956).

*Grundrisse* (Penguin, 1973).

Marx-Engels: *Selected Works*, two vols. Moscow (Foreign Languages Publishing House, 1955).

Marx-Engels: *Selected Correspondence 1846–95* (Moscow, 1975).


CRITICAL STUDIES

Louis Althusser: *For Marx* (Paris, 1966; tr. Allen Lane, 1969).

Shlomo Avineri: *The Social and Political Thought of Karl Marx* (Cambridge University Press, 1968).

Isaiah Berlin: *Karl Marx* (Oxford University Press, revised 1978).

Tom Bottomore: *Marxist Sociology* (Macmillan, 1975).

E. H. Carr: *Karl Marx: a study in fanaticism* (Dent, 1934).

Anthony Giddens: *Capitalism and Modern Social Theory* (Cambridge University Press, 1971).

Henri Lefebvre: *The Sociology of Marx* (Paris, 1966; Allen Lane, 1968).

George Lichtheim: *Marxism: an historical and critical study* (Routledge and Kegan Paul, second edition, 1964).

David McLellan: *Friedrich Engels* (Fontana, 1977).

David McLellan: *Karl Marx: his life and thought* (Macmillan, 1973; Paladin, 1976).

David McLellan: *The Thought of Karl Marx: An Introduction* (Macmillan, 1971).

Franz Mehring: *Karl Marx: the story of his life* (Allen and Unwin, 1936).

Robert C. Tucker: *Philosophy and Myth in Karl Marx* (Cambridge University Press, 1961).

Edmund Wilson: *To the Finland Station* (Secker and Warburg, 1941; Fontana, 1974).

# FRIEDRICH ENGELS
## (1820–1903)

### John Rex

THERE is probably nothing quite like the collaboration of Marx and Engels in the history of literature or politics. Many of their works were written jointly; and, in the case of those which were not, the actual author discussed the work with his partner while it was in progress and had his approval for its publication. Moreover, there developed between them a mutual trust and respect which is the more remarkable in that they disagreed with and distrusted almost every one of their literary and political contemporaries.

It might seem that to attempt a separate exposition of the ideas of Engels is a waste of time; and it might well be if our interest were simply in the history of Marxism. In that case what mattered would be the body of Marxist ideas which took root in history. If, however, our concern is with those ideas in Marxism that might illuminate the problems of contemporary sociology, things are different. We then have to sort out some of the strands which were amalgamated, sometimes with loss of conceptual clarity, in the working political doctrine of Marxism. Even if Engels were not important in himself, it would be useful to assess his contribution in order to arrive at a clearer picture of the original ideas of Marx.

Engels was born in the German town of Barmen in 1820 and was the son of a manufacturer of deep pietistic convictions. Such higher education as he received was acquired while working in an export office in Bremen and during his year of military service in Berlin. In Bremen he became interested in the so-called Young Hegelians through reading Strauss's *Life of Jesus* and while in Berlin met many of them. On completing his military service, he was sent by his father to work for his firm in Manchester, but stopped off in Cologne to meet the Hegelian editor of the

*Rhenische Zeitung*, who like himself had been much impressed by the communist ideas of Moses Hess.

At this meeting, in 1842, it seems that Marx was not much impressed by Engels. He was himself a far more thoroughly trained philosopher and was at that stage wrestling with three separate philosophical conceptions: the Hegelian dialectic as mediated by Feuerbach; the theories of Hess; and the importance for world history of the new class, the proletariat, which had emerged in the French revolution. Engels probably appeared to him as little more than a romantic dilettante, not very different from other young 'critical theologians' he had met in Berlin.

Central to Marx's thinking at this stage was the work of Feuerbach whose ideas he was developing in a profoundly sociological direction. It is important to understand this development in order to grasp exactly the difference which his partnership with Engels was to make.

Feuerbach produced a naturalistic version of the Hegelian dialectic. Instead of seeking to understand history as a process in which Abstract Spirit expresses itself in material objects and then seeks to regain itself through human cognitive activity, Feuerbach suggested that man was the only subject of history and that ideas, including the idea of God, were simply human products. He further argued that, if man was to understand and realize himself, he must rid himself of the notion of an external and alien God.

Marx sought to develop these ideas further. If man was alienated in his idea of God, were there not other more important forms of human alienation? What about money or the state, both of which were really human creations but came to exercise an external control over man? Further, Marx felt that Feuerbach, like Hegel, placed too much emphasis upon thinking, whereas the important fact in history was not man's thought but his action. The real key to history was therefore to be found in the action rather than the thought of those historical actors who were trying to overcome their alienation through revolutions – i.e. the working class.

Marx's own thoughts on this matter were jotted down in his *Theses on Feuerbach*. But by the time they had been written, Marx had already met Engels again (in 1844) and entered into a working partnership with him. Marx had moved to Paris and had joined

Ruge in editing the only edition of the *Deutsch-Französische Jahrbücher*. He contributed two articles himself and also included a review of Carlyle's *Past and Present*. But most important of all he received from Engels a piece called *A Critique of Political Economy*. He had already recognized that, if the social relations of production were all-important, it was vital that he should master and criticize the bourgeois theory of production. Engels now seemed to be pointing the way.

By this time Engels was busy gathering the materials in Manchester for his great book, *The Condition of the Working Class in 1844*. In doing so he met the real live proletariat in their industrial hovels, while Marx was still speaking of them as 'the instrument of philosophy'. It is difficult to imagine two discussions of the working class more distinct than those to be found in Marx's *Critique of the Hegelian Philosophy of Right* and Engels's book.

But the greatness of *The Condition of the Working Class* (published in 1845) lay not in its empirical description. Had Engels been merely an early Booth or Rowntree, Marx might have had little time for him. What interested Marx most was the theory which explained observable conditions. For Engels suggested that the misery of Manchester was to be explained by the simple fact of a system of class relations within which labour was sold as a commodity like any other. And he showed how this same system of class relations was leading to specific and successive stages of proletarian organization. This seemed to Marx to be the veritable 'secret of the earthly family', the key to understanding social development which he had thought about in theory but could now see exemplified in history. He immediately decided to adopt Engels as a pupil who would teach him about capitalism.

The ensuing important Marxist works are *The Holy Family* (1844) and *The German Ideology* (1846). The old Hegelian Karl Marx is still to be seen in *The Economic and Philosophic Manuscripts of 1844* and in his denunciation of Proudhon in *The Poverty of Philosophy* (1847), and these works remain helpful in understanding original Marxist sociology. But Marx was excited by the new prospect of his partnership with Engels and *The*

*German Ideology* was intended to settle his accounts with Hegelianism and begin afresh.

What emerges in *The German Ideology*, stated clearly in Marx's letters after 1846, and receiving its fullest exposition in Marx's *Preface to the Critique of Political Economy* (1859), is a theory subtly but significantly different from that contained in the *Theses on Feuerbach*. In the *Theses*, production appears as a free human activity and the social relations of production, being a human creation, are subject to human alteration. The only nature to which they refer, as Lichtheim has pointed out, is human nature.

In the new statement of the materialist conception of history, social evolution becomes part of natural evolution. The social relations of production cease to be seen entirely as the product of human agency and become instead the inevitable consequence of a certain mode of production – i.e. the particular stage of technological development. Thus revolution can occur only when the existing social relations of production are incompatible with, or 'become a fetter on', production. The only choices left open to the theoreticians of the working class are tactical ones. The Marxist problem is to decide when technological and economic conditions are ripe for revolution.

This new doctrine of capitalist development and class struggle was worked out jointly by Marx and Engels and became the theory held by considerable sections of the working class after the publication of the *Communist Manifesto* of 1848. The *Manifesto* itself is a remarkable document which we understand too little because we have read it too much. In fact it blends the theoretical and historical ideas of the two authors and the traditions from which they came in a quite remarkable way and it contained enough ambiguity to provide a working basis for co-operation with Blanquists, Proudhonists, Lasalleans, British trade unionists and German Social Democrats in the years that lay ahead, even though Marx in his political writings might take occasion to denounce the political illusions of his allies.

In fact, the tactical compromises which Marx and Engels necessarily had to make in their political writings were not conducive to clear and consistent sociological thinking, and only the theologians of the socialist movement would wish today to take these writings as of first importance. Probably more important were those writings not concerned with immediate issues, and Marxists must be grateful that in the years of defeat and disillusion both Marx and Engels turned to theoretical questions.

Of greatest importance during these years was Marx's *Capital.* Engels had first directed Marxism into the sphere of political economy; but it was now Marx, living partly on Engels's money, who sat in the British Museum ransacking government documents to bring up to date Engels's account of the condition of the proletariat and tortuously working out an adequate economic theory which would justify the economic assumptions on which they had worked. The first volume of *Capital* – the only part published in Marx's lifetime, in 1867 – was a formidable book, but it left a train of formidable economic problems. Its main problem was that it didn't appear to explain actual price movements or why some firms prospered more than they should have done according to the theory of surplus value. In the end it was left to Engels to edit Marx's manuscript of the third volume in which he tried to solve some of these problems.

During this period Engels completely subordinated himself to Marx, even to the extent of writing some of Marx's pieces for the *New York Herald-Tribune* for him while allowing Marx to claim the authorship and the fee. But one finds in Engels's correspondence a wide-ranging interest in religious, political and military history and a growing interest in prehistory. Perhaps one of the most important outcomes of this was the Marxist recognition of a socio-historical type called the 'asiatic mode of production' which stood outside the general line of development from ancient, through feudal and capitalist, to socialist society. The recognition that oriental societies were not subject to the same laws of historical development as those of Europe was to be of great importance in twentieth-century Marxism.

Engels's interest in prehistory led him, after Marx's death, to incorporate the evolutionary ideas of the American anthropologist Morgan into Marxism. They certainly fitted well. For Morgan had apparently shown that both the family and the state were nothing other than means of defending property. It was a wonderful example of the superstructure being determined by the economic base, and Morgan's work was all the more acceptable because of his speculation that man would eventually have more than a mere 'property history'. Little wonder that Engels's rewrite of Morgan in *The Origins of the Family, Private Property and the State* should have become orthodox Marxist reading.

There is, too, Engels's *The Peasant War in Germany* (1850). Every sociologist of capitalist society must at some time have dealt with the Reformation, and Engels set out to assess the role of Luther and Thomas Munzer in the German Reformation. The work has none of Weber's subtlety; but perhaps that is its merit, because the political involvement of religious leaders is often pretty direct. This work supplements much else that has been written on the sociology of the Reformation and is perhaps the one Marxist study in which religion appears both as 'the cry of the oppressed creature, the heart of a heartless world' and as 'the opium of the people'.

Marx died in 1883 and Engels was left as his intellectual and political legatee. Engels's speeches and newspaper articles gain in importance and he remains politically active right up to his death in 1895, most notably in advising Kautsky on the 'Erfurt programme', on the basis of which the Social Democratic Party in Germany was to play a new parliamentary role. But of more central and long-term significance was the theoretical writing in which he attempted to sum up the method which he and Marx had been using. His *Anti-Dühring*, which had been published before Marx's death and approved by Marx, went into new editions. He also worked on a retrospective intellectual biographical work, *Ludwig Feuerbach and the Outcome of the Classical German Philosophy*, and on some notes about scientific method, published after his death as *The Dialectics of Nature*. These works constitute a third Marxist philosophy and sociology which for better or worse has also become official Marxist doctrine (the first being Marx's own thinking, the second that of the Marx–Engels collaboration).

The new doctrine contrasts sharply with that of Marx's *Theses*, despite the fact that these were published for the first time as an appendage to Engels's *Ludwig Feuerbach*. In the *Theses*

Marx straddled the materialist–idealist distinction and was explicitly anti-deterministic in the sociological ideas which he expounded. This is what Marx would have called 'dialectical materialism' in 1845.

The 'dialectic' which Engels now opposes to Dühring is nothing like this. The difference, as he sees it, between Dühring and the Hegel–Marx tradition lies solely in Hegel's and Marx's understanding of change and the laws of change in nature and society. This may separate Engels from Dühring, but it hardly separates Marxism from most modern science and philosophy. In its search for deterministic laws of progress and in its belief in unilinear development this later Marxism differs little from much nineteenth-century positivism.

Dialectics in this sense adds little to science or to sociology and it is difficult to see why any such general philosophy is needed. It hardly helps to be told that a variety of things and processes – ranging from plant reproduction to the equation $-a \times -a = a^2$ – are all examples of the negation of the negation. And when Engels replaces Marx's definition of materialism in terms of its emphasis on 'sensuous human activity' with a Dr Johnson-like assertion that there are really things out there, we seem very far from a specifically Marxist philosophy of science.

A strong argument can be put that Engels had in fact assimilated Marxist sociology to a general materialistic evolutionary theory which was widespread in nineteenth-century England. Clearly he had not lived for so long in Manchester for nothing. But the sad thing about it all for sociologists is that Engels not merely proposes a revision of original Marxist sociology. He abolishes the need for sociology and for history altogether. The partial determinism of Marx's 1859 *Preface to a Critique of Political Economy* is now made complete. Man and his class struggles are all simply the continuation of nature's dialectical progression.

Such a doctrine is not of very much use in understanding either the social development of capitalism or of those forms of society which succeeded it. It could, however, provide an ideological superstructure for Marxist democrats in the west where no revolution happened, and for communist Russia where Stalin set about constructing a superstructure which would fit the process of industrialization on which Russia had embarked.

Yet to say that Engels was a poor systematic sociologist, or even that he sold out Marxist sociology to a kind of evolutionary positivism, is not entirely to deny his greatness. Marx was essentially a man of the study, the library and the committee room. Had he worked entirely on his own, had Engels not continually stimulated him by his writings and his arguments, even the rich sociological insights of Marx's early work – not to mention *Capital* – might have been lost to us; and we should not still be discussing Marxism today.

### FURTHER READING

#### WORKS IN ENGLISH TRANSLATION

*The Condition of the Working Class in England in 1844* (Allen and Unwin, 1892).

*The Origin of the Family, Private Property, and the State* (Chicago: C. M. Kerr, 1902).

*Socialism: Utopian and Scientific*, ed. E. Aveling (London, 1892).

#### CRITICAL STUDIES

William Otto Henderson: *The Life of Friedrich Engels* (Frank Cass, 1976).

Steven Marcus: *Engels, Manchester and the Working Class* (Weidenfeld and Nicolson, 1974).

Gustav Mayer: *Friedrich Engels: A Biography* (Chapman and Hall, 1936).

# HERBERT SPENCER
## (1820–1903)

### John H. Goldthorpe

'WHO now reads Spencer? It is difficult for us to realize how great a stir he made in the world ... He was the intimate confidant of a strange and rather unsatisfactory God, whom he called the principle of Evolution. His God has betrayed him. We have evolved beyond Spencer.' This quotation from Crane Brinton stands at the beginning of Talcott Parsons' massive study, *The Structure of Social Action* – the book which for more than two decades now has been the *pons asinorum* for students of sociological theory. In this investigation of the intellectual revolution which gave birth to modern modes of sociological analysis, Parsons takes the demise of Spencer as his starting point and sees the crucial question as – who killed Spencer and how? This is representative of the attitudes which present-day sociologists display towards Spencer. He is recognized as a figure of considerable historical importance. But he would not be regarded as being, like Durkheim or Weber, a thinker of great contemporary relevance and value.

In general, this view is as easy to explain as it is to justify. But it is still possible to feel that the total abandonment of Spencer to the historians of ideas is as yet somewhat premature. For even as he was being led on into ultimate error and confusion by his false God, Spencer was made to grapple, in an often instructive way, with a number of basic sociological issues – and issues which not a few of his successors have evaded rather than confronted.

Spencer was born at Derby in 1820, the son of a Nonconformist schoolteacher of decided and somewhat eccentric views. Because of his father's mistrust of conventional educational methods, the young Spencer received an irregular and unorthodox schooling, chiefly from an uncle who was an Anglican clergyman with a strong interest in the natural sciences. Under the latter's tuition, he gained a firm grounding in mathematics and elementary physics but his historical and literary education was almost entirely neglected. Plans for Spencer to go up to Cambridge failed to materialize, chiefly because of his own reluctance, and at the age of seventeen he decided to make a career for himself in the quickly expanding profession of railway engineering. He achieved quite rapid success in this field and published papers on the design of bridges and related geometrical problems.

However, during early manhood, Spencer's intellectual interests grew quickly, and engineering soon came to appear limited in the opportunities it offered a versatile and independent mind. In the course of his work, Spencer had acquired a knowledge of geology and through this was led on to the biology of his day, the work of Lamarck, in particular, making a great impression upon him. At the same time, though, he had developed an overriding concern with social, political and economic questions and began to write for various periodicals on such subjects as education, church and State, 'the proper sphere of government', and so on.

In 1848 these journalistic efforts were crowned with some success when Spencer was offered the sub-editorship of *The Economist*, at that time one of the leading organs of radicalism. This post enabled Spencer finally to abandon engineering and gave him both the time and a favourable atmosphere in which to advance his own thinking. Three years later he published his first book, *Social Statics*, which was essentially an extended essay in social theory constructed around his fundamental beliefs in individual responsibility and *laissez-faire*.

As soon as he was able, he left *The Economist* and lived as an independent scholar. His work became all that was meaningful in his existence, and he worked unremittingly until the period of chronic illness and nervous disability which preceded his death in 1903. He never married ('I was never in love') and spent most of his later life in genteel boarding houses and hotels. He had scarcely any intimate companions and recognized his own incapacity for feeling any strong attachment to relatives or friends. But this, he believed, was the price he had to pay for his intellectual commitment.

In 1852, in a paper entitled 'A Theory of Population', Spencer put forward some of his early ideas on the development of human society and claimed that of major importance in this process had been 'the struggle for existence' and the principle of 'the survival of the fittest' – a striking anticipation of the theory of natural selection which Darwin and Wallace were to apply some six years later to the organic world generally. Following on this Spencer then produced a second book, *The Principles of Psychology*, in which he sought to apply an evolutionary approach to mental phenomena.

Finally, as the culmination of this most creative and crucial phase of his work, Spencer took his evolutionism to its ultimate point in a celebrated essay of 1857 – 'Progress: its Law and Cause'. In this he advanced the thesis that the idea of evolution was of *universal* applicability; that it was the key to the understanding of phenomena of *all* kinds, whether inorganic, organic or 'super-organic', that is to say, social. The most general laws of all the separate sciences, Spencer argued, could, in principle, be subsumed, and thus unified, under the one supreme law of 'evolution and dissolution'. This law provided, therefore, a systematic, genetic account of the entire cosmos; or, as Spencer put it, 'an account of the Transformation of Things' and of 'the ultimate uniformities they present'. All secular change within structures of whatever kind went on through a process of *increasing differentiation* on the one hand and *increasing integration* on the other. The unevolved structure was internally homogeneous and its parts cohered only loosely; the evolved was heterogeneous yet tightly knit. And this held true in Spencer's theory whether the process being considered was the formation of the earth out of a nebular mass, the evolution of species, the embryological growth of an individual animal, or the development of human societies. No wonder that Darwin should say of him, 'He is about a dozen times my superior!'

Once he had taken up this uncompromising position, the remainder of Spencer's life was largely devoted to its justification and defence, primarily in the form of his monumental *Synthetic Philosophy*. His *Principles of Sociology*, published in several parts between 1876 and 1896, formed but one element in this greater enterprise, along with the companion volumes on psychology, biology and ethics; and it is an important feature of Spencer's sociology that it constitutes in this way an integral, and quite consistent, part of a wider 'system'.

To begin with the negative side, Spencer's sociology was perhaps most fundamentally flawed because of its highly 'naturalistic' character; because, that is, of Spencer's reluctance to draw sufficiently firm analytical distinctions between the realms of the organic and 'superorganic' and because of his concern to integrate biology and sociology virtually to the point of fusion.

In the first place, Spencer insisted on drawing very close analogies between societies and organisms. The similarities, in his view, were such that in analysing the structure of societies and the functioning of their institutions biological parallels were of primary value. Spencer was in fact generally prepared to take established ideas in the field of biology as ready-made instruments of sociological understanding. However, his arguments in this respect became largely self-defeating through being carried to obviously ridiculous extremes.

For example, at one point Spencer represents the shift within a society from road to rail transport as being an evolutionary advance directly intelligible in terms of the difference between the vascular systems of higher and lower animals – even down to the detail that the dual track corresponds to the veins and arteries. Similarly, the introduction of the electric telegraph was seen as the analogue of the evolution in the organic sphere of a more developed nervous apparatus. Nerve fibres and telegraph wires were both classified by Spencer as 'internuncial agencies' and were therefore to be treated as generally comparable phenomena.

Secondly, and, of course, in complete consistency with his idea of societies as 'superorganisms', Spencer then sought to gain vital support for his system as a whole by showing that the evolution of societies, considered as entities, was a process essentially akin to that of the evolution of species. His aim here was not only to demonstrate that the *pattern* of change was the same in the two cases – increasing differentiation and integration – but also that this change was brought about through directly analogous *mechanisms*. Thus, although Spencer recognized that social change could result from a plurality of factors, his theory of social evolution contained two major emphases, both reflecting the biology of his day.

On the one hand, under the influence of Lamarckian ideas, Spencer claimed that within human societies a process of mutual modification was continually going on between the various institutions of social control and the characteristics of individuals. Thus, societies tended to become progressively more integrated, and by consensus rather than by constraint, even while the division of labour (differentiation) was increasing.

On the other hand, though, following his principle of the 'survival of the fittest' and the Darwinian extension of this, Spencer also stressed the part played in the evolution of societies by social conflict and, most notably, by war. Particularly in the earlier stages of social evolution, Spencer argued, warfare and conquest had been of crucial importance in the formation of larger and more complex social systems and at the same time in strengthening their internal cohesion. With the emergence of industrial societies, Spencer was prepared to accept that 'From war has been gained all that it had to give.' But he continued to regard conflict in other forms, and primarily in the economic field, as being a major evolutionary force which should not be impeded.

Here again it is fairly apparent that Spencer's attempt to derive sociology from biology is fraught with error. And, ironically, it is the sounder of Spencer's biological notions – the more Darwinian rather than the more Lamarckian – which are the most obviously inapplicable to human society. Even among Spencer's contemporaries, thinkers such as T. H. Huxley were able to expose the inadequacies and misconceptions of what the latter described as 'the gladiatorial theory of existence'. Was not man essentially different from other animals in that to an ever greater extent he created his own environment and, moreover, continually refashioned this so as to provide a changing *milieu* for his own development? Was not man also different in being a moral animal and was not human society a moral community? What meaning then could be given to the idea of the survival of the fittest in a societal context? And were not economic conflict and competition, at least, themselves *dependent upon* some accepted and relatively permanent framework of order?

Many later critics have elaborated these points and there have been major objections raised against various other aspects of Spencer's theory: for example, against the underlying assumption that all societies must necessarily follow the same sequence of evolutionary stages; against Spencer's tendency, in spite of himself, to fuse the idea of evolution with that of progress; and perhaps most serious of all, against the dubious 'social morphology' through which Spencer sought to provide empirical confirmation for his deductive arguments. As Bergson was one of the first to observe, the vast classification of the forms of institutions and societies which Spencer carried out generally supports his evolutionary ideas – but for the simple reason that the principles of classification that were used were derived from these ideas at the outset. Spencer's method, in other words, was perfectly circular.

But it is still possible to make out a case for regarding a knowledge of Spencer as part of a sociologist's education. This case, one would suggest, rests chiefly upon the relevance of Spencer to important and still current issues in sociological thinking relating to what would now be termed 'structural-functional' analysis.

It was Spencer who first systematically used the terms 'structure' and 'function' in ways approximating to their present sociological usage. His penchant for a biological style of thinking led him to develop earlier 'organic' conceptions of society on more sophisticated lines and, further, to consider what such an orientation implied for the nature of sociological inquiry.

Essentially, Spencer arrived at the idea of society as a kind of self-regulating system which could best be understood through the study of its constituent parts and their pattern of interdependence, and through the analysis of the contributions which each part made towards the maintenance of the whole. In this way he initiated a mode of sociological explanation which was elaborated further by Durkheim and by social anthropologists such as Radcliffe-Brown, and which has since been applied more widely and with probably a greater degree of success than any other thus far. Spencer's own attempts to put his insights to use in an empirically based sociology proved of little value; but his more programmatic statements are none the less of continuing interest in that they emphasize certain cardinal points in the 'functionalist' position which are perhaps too readily neglected in the current reaction against this.

First, it is important to note that Spencer did not merely suggest that in society different institutions will in some way be inter-related. His major interest was, rather, in the way in which certain institutional forms showed a tendency to co-exist from society to society while others were seemingly incompatible. For example, he observed that in highly 'militant' societies the status of women was generally very low; that in societies with a despotic form of government there was elaborate ritual in social inter-course; that as societies became increasingly industrial, coercive institutions tended to decline – and so on.

In other words, Spencer not only reformulated the idea of societies as systems but also, and much more importantly, he directed attention to the problems of discovering how far and in what ways variation in the structure of social systems might be patterned and limited. Problems of this order undoubtedly still arise in sociological theory at the present day – as, for example, in ongoing debates on the 'logic' of industrialism. And, one would suggest, they are ones which still lend relevance to a func-tionalist approach.

Second, and in consequence of his ideas on the 'patterning' of social systems, Spencer was always anxious to stress the degree of 'resistance' which such systems could offer to attempts to induce changes in them, as, for example, through legislation. The point he repeatedly made in this connexion was that if in fact there can be a science of society – if social phenomena do exhibit regularities and conform to 'laws' – then it must follow that men cannot shape society entirely according to their desire and will. Certain bounds will exist to what can be achieved through pur-posive action at any given stage in a society's development.

This argument was, of course, extremely valuable in supporting the *laissez-faire* political views to which Spencer was com-mitted, and he delighted in finding instances where governmental intervention in economic and social affairs had misfired and had produced results quite different from those envisaged. Today, it is apparent that Spencer greatly exaggerated his case and seriously underestimated both the ability of government to play a constructive and creative part in social change and also the necessity for this in a highly complex and dynamic form of society. But nevertheless, his awareness that social systems will not be radically changed by mere legislative tinkering and his concern with what have been called 'the unintended consequences of intended social actions' remain much to the point. They could, for example, be profitably shared by many present-day Benthamites and 'piecemeal social engineers' who appear to believe that no sociological theory – and certainly none of a functionalist kind – can have any significance for their mission.

Third, and finally, Spencer is of interest in his efforts to avoid being forced by his system into a completely 'necessitarian' position; that is, into a position in which he would have to assert the futility of all attempts at reform or deliberate social change of any kind. In part, he saved himself in that purposive action was incorporated into the 'Lamarckian' aspect of his evolutionism: as institutions changed the character of individuals, they in turn, or their children, would seek to mould institutions into closer conformity with their evolving needs.

But further, Spencer was drawn towards the idea of what he termed 'rational reform'. By this he meant something rather similar to what R. H. S. Crossman called 'science-based government', though with the main emphasis on the need for expertise in the sociological field. In other words, Spencer was ultimately prepared to extend his previous argument and to claim that a social science was the one means of making effective social action possible – even while its existence implied that at any one time hard alternatives would have to be faced and certain limits recognized. Thus, the case of Spencer serves to refute again the old charge that a functionalist is inevitably a conservative. But it illustrates the valid point that in the functionalist view society is not a pipe for anyone to play on.

## FURTHER READING

WORKS

*Education – Intellectual, Moral and Physical* (Watts, 1929).

*Facts and Comments* (Williams and Norgate, 1902).

*First Principles*, sixth edition (Williams and Norgate, 1900; Watts, 1937).

*The Man Versus the State* (Williams and Norgate, 1885).

*The Principles of Ethics*, two vols. (Williams and Norgate, 1892).

*The Principles of Sociology*, three vols., third edition (Williams and Norgate, 1893).

*Social Statics* (Chapman, 1851).

*The Study of Sociology* (D. Appleton and Co., 1873; Williams and Norgate, New Library Edition, 1894).


CRITICAL STUDIES

J. W. Burrow: *Evolution and Society: a study in Victorian Social Theory* (Cambridge University Press, 1966).

Ronald Fletcher: *The Making of Sociology*, vol. 1 (Nelson, 1971).

J. D. Y. Peel: *Herbert Spencer: the Evolution of a Sociologist* (Heinemann, 1971).

Jay Rumney: *Herbert Spencer's Sociology* (London, 1934; Atherton, New York, 1966).

Werner Stark: 'Herbert Spencer's Three Sociologies' (*American Sociological Review*, vol. 26, no. 4, August 1961).

David Wiltshire: *The Social and Political Thought of Herbert Spencer* (Oxford, 1978).

# EDWARD TYLOR
## (1832–1917)

### Godfrey Lienhardt

SIR EDWARD TYLOR'S reputation has been eclipsed during this century by that of another knight of cultural anthropology, Sir James Frazer, his junior by some thirty years. Tylor is not listed, for example – as are Frazer, Sir Henry Maine and Herbert Spencer – in the useful guide to significant yearly publications, *Annals of English Literature 1475–1950*, and it is Frazer's work that has been diffused through creative literature in the writings of T. S. Eliot and others.

Yet it was certainly Tylor who dominated, shaped and con-solidated anthropology in Britain for the first fifty years of its development. After his *Researches into the Early History of Mankind and the Development of Civilisation* (1865), anthropology really was 'Mr Tylor's science' as Max Müller and others called it. His other substantial book *Primitive Culture* (1871) was des-cribed in the *Pall Mall Gazette's* review of *The Golden Bough* as standing with that work and Herbert Spencer's *Principles of Sociology* 'among the main foundations of the new science of human belief and human institutions'.

Both Andrew Lang and R. R. Marett referred to Tylor as their 'father, Parmenides', and D. H. Lawrence, speaking for the discerning general reader, recommended *Primitive Culture* to Lady Ottoline Morell and John Middleton Murry as 'a very good, sound substantial book, I had far rather read it than *The Golden Bough* or Gilbert Murray.' Tylor was also well known in the wider world of scholarship, becoming a fellow of the Royal Society before he was thirty and continuing to receive honours for the rest of his life. He became Keeper of the Pitt-Rivers Museum and later Professor at Oxford.

And though anthropologists still often couple 'Tylor and Frazer' as the Tweedledum and Tweedledee of their subject's history, most would probably agree with D. H. Lawrence that

Tylor's work is more substantial than Frazer's, and stands the test of time better than that of any other Victorian anthropologist except perhaps Sir Henry Maine.

All Victorian writings in the subject are, of course, outdated and offer more to the historian of ideas than to modern students of anthropology. But if Tylor's contribution also must be assessed for the most part historically, his individual gifts are outstanding. For his period he had remarkably few philosophical, religious or racial obsessions; and as the first great synthesizer and sifter of ethnological knowledge it was he who largely created the universe of discourse inherited, through Frazer and Malinowski, by the senior living generation of British anthropologists.

Edward Burnett Tylor was born in 1832, the son of a Quaker brassfounder in whose business for a short time as a young man he learnt something of working life outside the groves of academe. For him as for other Dissenters, many of Quaker stock like himself, the new science of ethnology was of more than scientific importance. With their sense of Christian responsibility for peoples then commonly treated by Europeans as creatures of a different and inferior species to themselves, they sought in ethnology a scientific basis for the philanthropic principles expressed notably in the founding of the Aborigines' Protection Society in 1837. This moral interest, if not religiously grounded, has characterized much anthropological writing in the present century.

Further, the Dissenters' religious disabilities saved them from a too conventional education with its emphasis on the established church and the Greek and Latin classics as ultimate arbiters of moral and intellectual value. Their sympathies were not trained to the same exclusiveness as those of others of their class, with their prolonged schooling in national self-esteem. Hence, though Tylor, like all the rest at that time, takes the existence of 'higher' and 'lower' peoples for granted, he never lapses into the condescension and sensationalism with regard to 'savages' that mar the studies of Darwin and Frazer, not to speak of the arrogant Sir Richard Burton and his like. His claim to a sense of community with the most 'primitive' men rings true and just at a time when Trollope in *Barchester Towers* was depicting a contemporary society where even close Italian connexions set a family of British gentlefolk rather below the salt.

It may then have been an advantage to Tylor as an anthropologist that he was largely self-educated, though not, it should be added, in labouring penury. And for his achievement in the subject he was later to profess, it is particularly relevant that this self-education included early in his life a spell of foreign travel more exciting than the European tour. At the age of 24, travelling in the New World for his health, he was diverted by a chance meeting with the archaeologist Christy on the way to Mexico, where they spent some months together.

His first book, *Anahuac: or Mexico and the Mexicans ancient and modern* (1861) is a record of that journey. It opens with a paragraph showing the bent of Tylor's mind at that time:

In the spring of 1856, I met with Mr Christy accidentally in an omnibus at Havana. He had been in Cuba for some months, leading an adventurous life, visiting sugar plantations, copper mines and coffee estates, descending into caves, and botanizing in tropical jungles, cruising for a fortnight in an open boat among the coral reefs, hunting turtles and manatis, and visiting all sorts of people from whom information was to be had, from foreign consuls and Lazarist missionaries down to retired slave dealers and assassins.

There, in the father of British anthropology, is exposed the romantic temperament for which anthropologists are occasionally slighted by pundits of the 'hard' sciences. There is bound perhaps to be something rather odd about a science born, to all intents and purposes, in a Cuban omnibus.

But the passage shows also the value set upon direct and varied experience that inspired the fieldwork characteristic of Tylor's successors, and without which knowledge of peoples outside our own backyard would now be flimsy indeed. And travelling as he was in a land of endemic revolution, without the helping hand of a British colonial government, Tylor may well have had an insight into difficulties of research not commonly experienced again by anthropologists until colonial independence.

In ranging from speculations on the history of an ancient non-classical civilization to studying prisons, cockfights and labour conditions, *Anahuac* also prefigures Tylor's later insistence on the ideal comprehensiveness of anthropological study. 'Narrow it down, Mr Tylor!' his academic advisers urged for the syllabus at Oxford, but he held to his view that a narrow scholarship was not worthy of the Science of Man. How and if to 'narrow it down' remains a problem in elementary teaching.

In *Primitive Culture* Tylor himself faced this problem, and in a way not very different from that of today. He writes in the preface:

In discussing problems so complex as those of the development of civilization, it is not enough to put forward theories accompanied by a few illustrative facts. *The statement of the facts must form the staple of the argument* [my italics] ... Should it seem to any readers that my attempt ... sometimes leads to the heaping up of too cumbrous detail, I would point out that the theoretical novelty as well as the practical importance of many of the issues raised make it most inadvisable to stint them of their full evidence.

The great interwar field-monographs – such as Malinowski's *Coral Gardens and their Magic*, R. Firth's *We, the Tikopia* and E. E. Evans-Pritchard's *Witchcraft, Oracles and Magic among the Azande* – have been constructed on these lines; and though anthropologists have recognized the futility of merely amassing ethnographic detail (not, I hasten to say, characteristic of the books mentioned), this has been less a denial of its value than a plea for a more adventurous approach to thinking about it, as in Edmund Leach's *Rethinking Anthropology*.

For Tylor this particular intellectual disquiet of our postwar studies did not exist. His *was* the new thought that he confidently expected to lead to a new society. He was absolutely assured of an underlying evolutionary order in all human development; and though he recognized more than many did that there had been long halts and shameful retreats in the great march of mind (of which the spiritualism of the time seemed to him a disgracefully cowardly withdrawal) he had no doubt that every human fact was stationed somewhere along the route.

If this philosophy of progress provided him with an organizing principle for the vast range of information which is still a strength and an embarrassment to anthropologists, it also directed his thought into a highway that came abruptly to a dead end with the First World War. Whether or not the general course of history has been one of progressive social improvement now concerns anthropologists as little as the conflict between biblical and zoological or scientific versions of human origins which then fired Tylor's arguments; and it is here that Tylor seems less a father than a fuddy-duddy.

But, also, Tylor's approach to humankind went with a greater regard for what then seemed humble human achievements than the High Bayswater vision of Herbert Spencer, and it led him to a conception of culture which – it seems strange now that this should be so – was new when he formed it:

> Culture or Civilization, taken in its wide ethnographic sense, is that complex whole which includes knowledge, belief, art, morals, law, custom and any other capabilities and habits acquired by man as a member of society. The condition of culture among the various societies of mankind, in so far as it is capable of being investigated on general principles, is a subject apt for the study of laws of human thought and action.

Tylor's use of 'culture' in this sense derives explicitly from his readings in German 'cultural-history', but it was he who began to give it its neutral anthropological sense. (His usage might be contrasted with that of, say, Matthew Arnold, for whom 'culture' was the opposite of the 'barbarism' that Tylor found so worthy of serious attention.)

So, after *Primitive Culture*, which opens with the passage quoted above, it became possible to speak of the 'cultures' and 'civilizations' of peoples who had been commonly considered to lack either. Upon this simple reorientation of the meaning of a word much subsequent anthropological work depended.

In America and at least in the early stages of teaching in Britain, 'cultures' are still the broad entities studied by anthropologists, as the title of a recent introduction to social anthropology, John Beattie's *Other Cultures*, suggests. Daryll Forde's *Habitat, Economy and Society* also shows what instructional use the concept can be put to. But for many years in Britain particularly, the term has also been thought ultimately to obstruct analytic thought and comparison, providing only for a descriptive integration of the material. The study of structural relations, abstracted from the whole cultural reality, has permitted greater intellectual advance.

Nevertheless structural anthropologists necessarily still draw upon Tylor's notion of culture. It is centrally important, for example, to the main theses of Lévi-Strauss, and it is assumed in much of that pioneer work on political structure, Evans-Pritchard's *The Nuer*. Others of Tylor's main interests, too, if the mental parallax of his own period be allowed for, may have more in common with modern trends than would have been expected when Malinowski and Radcliffe-Brown governed theoretical anthropology.

Durkheim, representing the tradition of French sociological thought that is a major influence in theoretical work now, rightly rejected Tylor's individualistic and intellectualist interpretations of symbolic activity – his idea, for example, that primitive man arrived at religious belief by faulty reasoning from effect to cause. But Tylor's still deeper concern with language, meaning, modes of thought and communication has in part lived on in recent writings. Linguistic analysts – Whorf, for example – might well find as much of the real spirit of their investigations in Tylor as in his more sociologistic successors. Again, Robin Horton (in articles in *Africa* and the *Journal of the Royal Anthropological Institute*) and Lawrence and Meggit (*Gods, Ghosts and Men in Melanesia*, 1965) are only three modern fieldworkers who urge the value of a more sophisticated version of Tylor's theories of 'primitive' thought; while such observers of the 'expressive' character of symbolic action as John Beattie or V. W. Turner have in Tylor a Victorian prototype.

At a time when a version of Lévi-Strauss's *La Pensée Sauvage* has been translated into English (misleadingly enough as *The Savage Mind!*) it is worth quoting at some length a passage from Tylor upon a related topic. Stripped of its rationalism, it does open a vein of inquiry that has since been most profitably worked by Malinowski, Evans-Pritchard, Lévi-Strauss and many of their followers.

Tylor is considering the etymologists' account of the 'meaning' of words:

But explanations of this kind have no bearing on the practical use of such words by mankind at large, who take what is given them and ask no questions ... there is a great deal to be said for the view that much of the accuracy of our modern languages is due to their having so far 'lost consciousness' of the derivation of their words, which thus become like counters or algebraic symbols, good to represent just what they are set down to mean ... when it comes to exact argument, it may be that the distinctness of our apprehension of what a word means is not always increased by a misty recollection hovering about it in our minds, that it or its family once meant something else. For such purposes, what is required is not so much a knowledge of etymology, as accurate definition, and the practice of checking words by realizing the things and actions they are used to denote.

Problems of meaning are crucial to anthropologists with their dependence on translation; this indeed may be what differentiates them from straight sociologists more than either realizes. And here in Tylor, it seems to me, is the germ of an idea that Lévi-Strauss has approached from a different angle in his recently translated book -- the idea that there are two broadly different, and for Lévi-Strauss complementary, forms of apprehension and systems of knowledge.

On the one hand there is 'wild' thought, creating its image of the world by means of associations suggested by concrete experience of living. Here, the proliferations of meaning that Tylor associates with etymological explanation are the essential feature. On the other hand there is 'domesticated' thought, analytic in a quite different way, and depending for its effectiveness on so to speak breeding out the wild etymological strain. It says something for Tylor's intellectual vitality that he would have understood some of Lévi-Strauss's work, different as his attitudes towards the facts might have been.

R. R. Marett's *Tylor* (1936) gives a good account of the 'theoretical contributions' with which he is conventionally accredited: the invention of the term animism, 'a belief in spiritual beings', for the root of all religions; his use of comparative methods, with attempts at statistical correlations; his stress on material culture; and so on. But others have done this much better since his time. What really still recommends him is the spirit and tone of his scholarship, and the breadth of vision that enabled him to see large issues in anthropology that have continued, if in a different way, to engage attention.

And practical services to the subject are not to be ignored. Tylor certainly laid good foundations in Oxford where he taught. Some years ago, Sir John Myres recalled Tylor's last, unfortunately clouded, years:

He resented the rejection of his project for a degree examination in anthropology. It was an unholy alliance, he said, between Theology, Literae Humaniores and Natural Sciences. Theology, teaching the True God, objected to false gods; Literae Humaniores knew only the cultures of Greece and Rome; Natural Sciences were afraid that the new learning would empty their lecture rooms. And the archvillain was Spooner of New College, whom he never forgave.

But Tylor got his own back. Until quite recently students of social anthropology in Oxford were filling every room of 11 Keble Road – once Warden Spooner's own home.

### FURTHER READING

WORKS

*Primitive Culture*, 2 vols (Murray, 1891).

*Anthropology*, 2 vols (Watts, 1930).

*Researches into the Early History of Mankind and the Development of Civilisation* (Murray, 1865).

CRITICAL STUDIES

E. E. Evans-Pritchard: *Theories of Primitive Religion* (Clarendon, 1965).

Margaret T. Hogden: *The Doctrine of Survivals. A chapter in the history of scientific method in the study of man* (Allenson and Co., 1936).

Abram Kardiner and Edward Preble: *They Studied Man* (Secker and Warburg, 1962).

Godfrey Lienhardt: *Social Anthropology* (Opus Books, Oxford University Press, 1966).

Robert R. Marett: *Tylor* (Chapman and Hall, 1936).

Brian V. Street: 'Sir Edward Burnett Tylor' in *Encyclopaedia Britannica* (fifteenth edition, 1974), vol. 18, p. 808.

# CHARLES BOOTH
## *(1840–1916)*

### T. S. Simey

THE name of Charles Booth is well known to social scientists and social historians, but it may be doubted whether many who are well established in their craft have taken the trouble to read his books. Yet he was, in his own way, a sociologist of originality. Indeed, he was more than this, because he was equally great as a man of affairs. He founded and managed a large and prosperous shipping line, and he was a partner in a merchant business which dealt on the international market in skins, developing something approaching a monopoly in the manufacture of 'patent' leather, and ultimately ventured into the building industry. Any of these activities would have sufficed for a normally active and responsible man.

In his business, he made a substantial contribution to the growing economic prosperity of the period. But he had no stomach for Victorian complacency, and the 'insight' of a Freudian would no doubt find the cause of his lifelong dyspepsia in this phrase. The gigantic labours of his survey work were carried out in the evenings and late at night, when business affairs were over; the daily round of a university department would have been child's play to him.

He was far more at home with working-class people, with whom he lodged for long periods when he was carrying out his Inquiry, than with the upper classes and the rich. He was very much an odd man out in 'Society', and it was this, perhaps, which made it possible for him to probe into Victorian society so deeply and so accurately.

The inner story of Booth's life can best be told in terms of a struggle between the intellect and the feelings. His early Unitarianism, and the close physical association in the Liverpool of his day between rich and poor, gave him an unshakeable identification of the most personal kind with the ordinary people, and a really genuine sympathy with them in their sufferings. The interaction in his mind between reason and emotion was at times so powerful as almost to reach the point of explosion, and perhaps destruction.

But he ultimately achieved, after much suffering, a *modus vivendi* in the strictest sense of the term. If Booth's feelings drove him on to almost superhuman feats of endeavour in his survey, it was his rational understanding of what he was about which kept his purposes alive, and his ultimate aims were never deflected by any trace of sentiment.

His work is sometimes criticized because it had so direct a bearing on social policy as to appear to be descriptive rather than analytical; some have thought that this must have weakened, if not destroyed, its 'objectivity', and that it could not have been 'scientific'. Moreover, it had no relation to the abstract theorizing of the day, and this has led some to question whether he could be said to be any sort of sociologist at all.

Whatever truth there may be in this, however, there can be no doubt that the tradition he established of the discovery of social realities by hard and honest work is a most valuable one. Sociology would be a much poorer thing without it.

Booth's main contributions to the social sciences were made in the years between 1887 and 1903, seventy years ago and more. It might be expected, therefore, that it is only the historian of sociological thought who would be inclined to pay a tribute to his memory; the twentieth century has made rapid advances in the social sciences, and a considerable degree of shifting of interest has taken place. It is hardly probable, on the face of things, that work done so long ago would still be considered significant by those responsible for social researches today. Yet we can find Peter Townsend, writing in *Conviction* in 1958, that when as a young man he had immersed himself for a time in the struggles, uncertainties and squalor of working-class life, he emerged with a 'deeper respect' for Booth, and a corresponding disrespect for the academic sociology of today. For him and many others like him, Booth's work still has a quality of immediacy about it; it seems to deal with real people, issues, and remedies in a real way. Why, we should now ask ourselves, is this so?

Booth's work was done at a time when it had come to be assumed by nearly all those in positions of power and influence, including those whose lives were lived with any degree of security or affluence, that every man had a fair chance of making his own way in the world, and caring adequately for his family, if he would work with true diligence, and spend and save responsibly. Those who did not do so were to be blamed for their moral short-comings; they could not be helped in the mass by making gifts to them in cash or kind to supplement their earnings, for this would merely lead to the undermining of self-reliance and the exacerbation of poverty, rather than to any improvement in social welfare. The argument was a general one, stated in *a priori* terms with great force and conviction both in popular sermons and in the Reports of the Charity Organization Society. It was hard to contradict in the same language, for it had the support of the 'common sense' of the period. Experience showed, however, that it could be countered by an appeal to the facts, and it was in this way that Booth made his contribution both to our public life and to sociology. His self-imposed task was, first of all, to examine the problem of poverty, for him the Problem of all Problems, which for many years robbed him of his peace of mind; for, as a wealthy industrialist and man of business, he found it impossible to reconcile the fact of Liverpool's poverty with the affluence of its upper and middle classes.

Prominent among the schools of thought that have developed during and since the last quarter of the nineteenth century was that of so-called British sociological empiricism, and Booth's claim to fame rests on the part he played in its foundation. The impact of the earlier effects of the Industrial Revolution on the public mind, especially on those persons concerned with the poor law and public health, had resulted in the publication of a large number of reports by newly created government agencies, commissions of inquiry and the census organization, and the presentation of papers to the newly formed statistical societies, literary and philosophical societies, and the like. The origins of the new empirical school are thus to be found in the work of such administrators and researchers as William Farr, Edwin Chadwick, Sir John Simon and Sidney and Beatrice Webb, rather than in that of social philosophers such as Bentham (as distinct from his followers), Comte and Spencer.

A large mass of information became available concerning the true nature of the conditions under which life was led in our society, together with much which threw light on the growth of industry and commerce, the system of education (or lack of it), the public health, the state of the poor, and social and cultural conditions generally. Much of it, as in the case of Chadwick's reporting on poverty and public health, was tendentious; but much also, as with Farr's work in the General Register Office, and Sir John Simon's on public health statistics, was accurate and highly influential. Such people were able to give a reasoned account of one aspect or another of the nation's social or economic life, based on information that had been collected for routine purposes of administration; established methods could be relied on to gather supplementary information to fill out what was already available, if this was found to be insufficient.

By the last quarter of the century, therefore, it became possible to base a new sociology on inductive rather than deductive reasoning. The first important event in the development of the empirical sociology that was thus founded in England was the publication of Booth's paper on poverty in the *Journal of the Royal Statistical Society* in 1887, followed by his first comprehensive work on the same subject, *The Labour and Life of the People*, in 1889–91. As a practical man of business, Booth was much more anxious to understand how the industrial system of his times functioned, and to determine the nature of its impact on social conditions, than to propound all-embracing theories designed to explain why things had happened as they had, and what would therefore come to pass in the future.

He had been made suspicious of *a priori* speculation of this kind when he had sought to discover how much light the theoretical economics of his day had thrown on problems of everyday business, and his experience had led him to lean over backwards to avoid tendentious argument or superficial speculation. He had come to have no use for a 'big theory', and he had eventually arrived at the conclusion that facts could be organized within a 'large statistical framework', which would then make it possible to formulate 'the theory and the law, and the basis of more intelligent action' in the world which was familiar to him. Over and over again, he asserted that he wished to 'let the facts speak for themselves', a remark that provoked an echo in the mind of his successor Seebohm Rowntree, who followed his example as an empirical sociologist when he asserted that 'I did not set out upon my inquiry with the object of proving any preconceived theory, but to ascertain actual facts.'

Booth's true position was midway between an interest in facts for their own sake – as the rather overworked phrase used so much today has it – and a concern for the welfare of individuals who could only be regarded by him as persons, and certainly not as 'facts' in the more narrow sociological sense. He knew why he wanted to know more about the society in which he lived, and he knew what he wanted to study. His lack of interest in abstract theory has unfortunately led many people to undervalue his work, for it is too often by the complexity and extent of a man's theorizing that merit as a sociologist is judged today.

His attitude to fine-spun philosophizing was typically British; remote as this must be from everyday affairs, he took no interest whatever in it, and he ignored it altogether. His inquiry has therefore been generally regarded as a catalogue of facts rather than as a scientific work, and his reputation has suffered accordingly. Beatrice Webb, for instance, credited him with the 'scientific impulse', but not with the practical capabilities of a working scientist, and he has usually been remembered as the author of the *Poverty Survey* which was so influential in the old-age pensions campaign, an epoch-making event at the turn of the century, rather than as a sociologist.

He has been greatly misunderstood, for this among other reasons, and his importance as a sociologist correspondingly underestimated. There is, on the contrary, no doubt that he pointed out the way along which much of the sociological work of our own century has been carried out. However much he allowed himself to remain out of touch with the theoretical sociologists of his day, he carved out his own territory in the world of ideas in which he felt himself at home, though he never displayed it to others, or even encouraged others to explore its depths. He endeavoured to reconcile a faith in individualism with the fact of poverty; the acceptance of the values he held compelled him, however, to re-examine relevant facts. He was ultimately compelled, as a result, to admit that the facts concerning poverty as he discovered them made it necessary to transform part of the social world around him, so as to diminish part of its misery. The interplay between fact and value, and the interaction of induction and deduction, was of fundamental importance in his system of thought, and the outcome profoundly influenced both his own life, and that of the society in which he lived.

It was, in his own language, a 'way of looking at things' not a 'doctrine or argument' that he endeavoured to present to the world. His struggle to achieve this highly individual point of view did not lead him to any final solution for the problems which he had sought to solve, for he saw his researches only as establishing the 'character, extent, and symptoms' of the social ills he thought should be cured, and some of their implications. 'May some great soul,' he wrote, 'master of a subtler and nobler alchemy than mine, disentangle the confused issues, reconcile the apparent contradictions in aim' and 'melt and commingle the various influences for good into one divine uniformity of effort.'

The essential characteristics of Booth's work were its timeliness, its practicality, and its accordance with the canons of scientific inquiry. It is not to be disposed of as the 'working through' (as those addicted to psychoanalytic explanations of human conduct and experience might suppose it to have been) of the frustrations of an inhibited mind, or the compulsive behaviour of a man whose life was overpowered by feelings of guilt. It was, on the contrary, the result of the acceptance by an able man of affairs, with an ability for the rational analysis of situations and tendencies that amounted to genius, of a personal responsibility to understand the true nature of the society which he had done much himself to create, and to study the ways in which its harshnesses could be alleviated, and the level of welfare enjoyed by its members raised to the highest point. The task which he set himself was at one and the same time of great utility, and a substantial contribution to learning.

The completion of Booth's Inquiry in 1903 might have been expected to mark the beginning of a new era of sociological work, in which empirical research would have assumed a leading, if not a dominant, place. Instead of the new era dawning, however, the spectacle that presented itself was that of a false dawn. This is attributable to many causes, which are part and parcel of the ethos of the age at the end of the century. 'Academic' sociology, in the person of L. T. Hobhouse, parted company from 'practical' sociology, in that of Patrick Geddes. The doctrinaire thinking of Bentham was restated as a conservative creed by Charles Loch; it became the foundation of the anti-statism of the Charity Organization Society, and ultimately of yet another system of thought in which belief was much more important than demonstration.

Hobhouse, as a man of ideas, seems to have had no interest in Booth's work, which made no contribution to the understanding of the relationships between social life and the working of the human mind, to the clarification of which his own life was primarily devoted. It is important to remember that Hobhouse was the leader of sociological thought in this country for many years, and this may explain the neglect of Booth's work by his colleagues. Moreover, Loch, with his extreme views on the necessity of relying on individual initiative, and protecting society from being undermined by the operations of publicly controlled agencies, was bitterly critical of Booth. As he provided British social workers with their philosophical foundations until his thinking was replaced after the First World War by the hardly less dogmatic faith of Freud, this may explain the fact that Booth's Inquiry was soon forgotten by them.

In recent years, philosophical speculation (or what has been termed 'grand theory') has absorbed the energies of many sociologists; the accumulation of facts ('for their own sake') that of many others. The former have tended to develop a more or less sterile scholasticism; the others have endeavoured, without much success, to demonstrate that wisdom can be regarded as the product of the use of not very sophisticated statistical techniques. Neither has taken much interest in, or has had much to say about, the realities of social conditions in a rapidly changing world. Neither has as yet produced anything comparable with what Lord Beveridge called Booth's 'passion to understand'.

Charles Booth must be regarded as having laid the foundations of a new kind of sociology, and as having created some of the most useful methods whereby it can be developed. Many of the issues which his work raised are still alive today: in particular the extent to which sociological researchers can and should be directed towards the examination and solution of problems of public concern, and the question whether sociological theories can be satisfactorily propounded *in vacuo*, or whether they require testing in the light of the evidence before they can be regarded as anything more than hypotheses.

Finally, there is the issue, a very real one in America perhaps more than in Britain, of the most effective way of dealing with the troubles of individuals in an industrial society. Should these be alleviated by having social workers treat them as such, or could they not be prevented from arising at all if the necessary alterations in the social structure could be made, as in the case of the poverty of the aged and old-age pensions? All these are matters of great importance, and it is impossible to deal with any of them fully or adequately without reference to Booth's work. Nothing could be a greater tribute to the importance of his work in the modern world than this. Lord Beveridge himself assured me that it was Booth who gave him the ideas on which his Report was based. Is it likely that any contemporary sociologist will make a similar contribution to his age?

#### FURTHER READING

WORKS
*Life and Labour of the People in London*, 17 vols. (Macmillan, 1903).

CRITICAL STUDIES
Belinda Norman-Butler: *Victorian Aspirations: The Life and Labour of Charles and Mary Booth* (Allen and Unwin, 1972).
Thomas S. and Margaret B. Simey: *Charles Booth, Social Scientist* (Oxford University Press, 1960).

# GEORGES SOREL
## (*1847–1922*)

### Neil McInnes

GEORGES SOREL was born in Cherbourg in 1847 into an old Norman family of Roman Catholic bourgeois. He was thick-set, ruddy and blue-eyed, like many Normans, and when in later life he wore a pointed silver beard he cut an impressive figure in his black frock-coat with the Legion of Honour button in the lapel. From his origins he drew firm prejudices about respectability and chastity, which never varied even when his political ideas became such as to shock people of his class. Though he lost the faith early, he retained respect for, and a keen interest in, the Catholic Church because he held, unlike other Marxists, that though religion was an illusion its future was assured, so freethinkers must reckon with the impressive institutions in which it was organized.

Brought up in Cherbourg with his cousin, the historian Albert Sorel, Georges was sent to the École Polytechnique in Paris, the college that trains many of France's engineers, mathematicians and soldiers. He joined the roads and bridges department and worked as a civil engineer for twenty-five years in Corsica, in the Alps, in Algeria and finally in Perpignan. Competent and devoted, he reached the grade of first-class chief engineer at forty-five and received the official decoration that consecrates loyal service. Thereupon, to everybody's surprise, he resigned and retired, refusing the pension that was his right, the better to safeguard his independence.

His mother had died, leaving him enough to live quietly with his wife (they were childless) and he resolved to live in Paris and read books. He invested his money in Russian bonds, like so many other French *rentiers* of the day, though his attitude was different to theirs when the bolshevik revolution led to the repudiation of those debts. His wife died in 1897 and, saying he had always loved her *con la forza del primo amore*, Sorel made something of a cult of her memory, dedicating his major works to her and insisting on the role that a wife plays in the achievements of a creative thinker. Actually, Sorel had never married her. She was a servant girl who had cared for him when he fell sick in an hotel once, and his family's objections to Marie's proletarian origins were too strong even for Sorel's rigid ideas on marriage and chastity.

While still in service in the provinces, Sorel had written two books of pure erudition. One, on the Bible, argued that the Old Testament should be read as the political literature of a revolutionary peasantry. The other, on the trial of Socrates, suggested that the philosopher probably well deserved to be put to death, for he had helped spread mysticism and immorality at the expense of sound Athenian traditions. Though curious, these uneven productions gave no inkling of the sort of work Sorel was to do in the thirty years between his retirement and his death at seventy-five.

From his cottage in Boulogne, a suburb of Paris, poured a mass of papers, reviews and rambling books full of original ideas about the philosophy of science, the history of thought, theology, social theory and Marxism. He had discovered Marx's work soon after arriving in Paris, and he became editor of a magazine, *Le Devenir Social* (1895-7), which introduced theoretical Marxism into France. At the same time he cooperated with Benedetto Croce and Antonio Labriola in preaching Marx's ideas in Italy. Italy was always his second intellectual home (though he never visited it, or even left French territory for that matter), and much of his work has been published only in Italian. Sorel soon came to reject Marxism's pretension to be scientific, and he joined with Croce, Edward Bernstein, Thomas Masaryk and Saverio Merlino in touching off the revisionist crisis among the Marxists.

All the other revisionists drew, explicitly or tacitly, reformist conclusions from their critique of Marxism. If Marx was wrong in his predictions of capitalism's increasing oppression and ultimate overthrow, they concluded, one must abandon revolutionary activity and theory for reformism. Sorel did just the opposite. He transferred his allegiance from orthodox, nominally Marxist socialism to the most revolutionary wing of the French labour movement, the anarcho-syndicalists. He said that because Marxism was not a science, it was not necessarily dead and useless. It was not science that changed the world but myth, and the anarcho-syndicalists were using Marxism precisely as myth. It was in accounting for the mythical character of extremist social doctrines that Sorel elaborated one of his most influential theories.

Though he became instantly world-famous for his theory of anarcho-syndicalism in the *Reflections on Violence* (1908), Sorel lost faith in that movement within a few years. On the eve of the 1914 war he was associating with extreme right-wing groups, such as the monarchists and nationalists around Charles Maurras, and with a Catholic revivalist group around the poet, Charles Péguy. Throughout the war, which he saw as the clash of predatory empires, Sorel remained silent and alone, but he emerged again after the bolshevik revolution to devote his last, failing energies to the defence of Lenin's cause.

He radically misunderstood it, like many others in the west during the confused first years of the Soviet regime. He thought the Russian revolution meant the transfer of power away from central authority to the workers' and peasants' soviets, and was thus a step toward anarchist, federative self-rule of the sort prophesied by Proudhon rather than by Marx. Having survived both his capital and his notoriety, Sorel died in Paris in 1922, poor and isolated but sure that the Russian revolution marked the beginning of a new era, one in which the bourgeoisie of the western 'plutocracies' would be ruined and humiliated. Croce said that Marx and Sorel were the only original thinkers socialism ever had.

Sorel saw himself as a philosopher first and last – though not only of socialism. He spent more time on the philosophy of science and the history of Christianity than on the labour movement. In his philosophy of science, he argued that there was no determinism in nature, only hazard and statistical probabilities, 'no laws, only limits'. Exact science was still possible, but it referred to man-made mechanisms, such as experimental equipment and productive machinery. In those limited areas men did violence to lawless nature by shutting out hazard and chance interference, thereby creating determinism. Their works, however, were ever threatened by malevolent nature, whose chance, waste and entropy invaded man-made machinery the instant men relaxed their efforts to ensure regular operation of their creations. Science, engineering and industry were all part of a vast enterprise of dis-entropy, the rebellion of a part of nature against its sense-less confusion and running down.

Himself an engineer and mathematician, Sorel set out this theory in much technical detail, carrying it to its most startling implications – maintaining, for example, that geometry was about architecture not nature, because its figures and proportions existed only where men created them. The pragmatists at that time were emphasizing the practical element in the acquisition and verifica-tion of knowledge; and the Marxists were arguing the connexion between intellectual activity and mechanical, economic work. Sorel's theory was a combination of the extremist versions of those two doctrines.

His theory of culture was precisely parallel. History, too, was lawless confusion and meaningless succession. Cultural and social creations were ever threatened by relapse into disorder and barbarism. Against a chaotic background of perpetual decadence, men occasionally struggled heroically to set up limited areas of law, order and historical significance. To make any sense of history, they had to impose a hard discipline on themselves, doing violence to their own nature, rejecting the claim of so-called 'social science' that history had its own laws and could make sense without our intervention. They would only make that effort jointly, in a social movement that consented to cut itself off and aspired to live according to a new morality.

That morality could only be an 'ethic of the producers', not in the sense that it had to be a workers' morality or even to have any economic reference, but in that it took the good life to be a cooperative, creative enterprise undertaken in a self-reliant spirit. In contrast there was the 'ethic of the consumers' which saw the good, not as a way of going on, but as something to be obtained and enjoyed – like welfare, prosperity, the classless society or happiness. Sorel said that enterprises undertaken in the consumer spirit – like slave revolts, peasant uprisings, Jacobinism, anti-semitism and twentieth-century welfare-state socialism –

were all inspired by envy and would all fall under the sway of adventurers (usually intellectuals).

A producers' movement might be concerned with religious, artistic, scientific or industrial activities, and Sorel spent much time describing examples of each of those types: the early Christian religious communities, the architects who created Gothic, the scientific community which creates and invents (not discovers) science, and, finally, capitalism and syndicalist socialism as successive and equally admirable varieties of the industrial producers' movement.

All such movements dismiss plans for future felicity as utopia, while they concentrate on the present task of creating the independent institutions that embody their morality of productiveness and solidarity. Revolutionary socialism was a movement of that sort because it was not concerned, as reformist socialism was, with such consumer interests as living standards and social conditions. Rather, it was a movement of revolt against a ruling class that had become unenterprising, cowardly, incompetent and hypocritical. It was not the only youthful, vigorous movement that aspired to take over from a decadent bourgeoisie – hence Sorel's early interest in Mussolini and in right-wing extremism – but it looked for a time to be the most promising among them.

Until some such movement could wrest pre-eminence from the bourgeois who remained in the high places but were too weak to rule, until some new morality could sweep away ideology and official wisdom, western society's history would be meaningless, a mere string of predatory wars abroad and, at home, inglorious deals between parliamentary pressure groups. For it was only when a heroic morality dominated an age that its history made sense, showed regular sequence and was liable to scientific study. For example, Marx could frame the historical 'law' of capitalism's inexorable supersession by socialism, not because there was any such trend in history (as Engels imagined when he compared it with the laws of motion), but because that would be the inevitable upshot of a clash between a ruthless, enterprising capitalist class and a vigorous, independent workers' movement. But once the capitalists, untrue to their morality, were willing to follow the humane urgings of do-gooders and reformers, and once the workers were willing to be bought off with consumer goods and bourgeois favours, then Marx's 'law' no longer held. And not only Marx's law: no law held of such a society; it was meaningless, and it would lurch from explosions of envy to craven peace, drifting toward the 'ruination of all institutions and all morality'. In his 1907 account of a lawless society, which had the sub-title, *Capitalist decadence and socialist decadence*, Sorel anticipated many of the features of nazism and totalitarian democracy, not omitting to forecast the momentous future reserved for anti-semitism.

One understands now why he greeted Lenin's revolution with such passion. One sees, too, to what extent he was correct in doing so, however grotesque his errors of detail, for the new movement of bolshevism, and the west's necessary reaction to it, indeed made sense of subsequent history, making it more 'one story' than it otherwise might have been.

It is not Sorel's philosophical system that has preserved his name and relevance so much as two notions that can be taken from it and find more general application. These are the notions of myth and violence. In the face of tenacious misunderstanding, Sorel insisted that he found both of these things going on in society and did not favour or preach them but sought to account for them. In reality, his attitude to both was not quite so detached and scientific: he found people being hypocritical about violence and he found them being intellectualistic about myth. He attacked that hypocrisy and that intellectualism, saying that not all violence was deplorable and myths could not be debunked by clever people. So inevitably he seemed to be apologizing for violence and defending myth, but it is fair to concede that he did so only to the point needed to get people to understand them better.

Sorel found a myth being put about by revolutionary syndicalists, and he recalled other mythopoeic movements from the past. He in no way urged political activists to perform the feat of adopting extremist doctrines while knowing them to be false. He noted, and was the first to do so, that the ambiguity is in the social facts themselves: one finds movements spreading views of the future without trying to establish those prophecies as scientifically plausible, because they do not care whether they will turn out to be correct or incorrect forecasts. They care for these visions of the future only as inspiring pictures of what the world would be like if one day their ethic won all men's allegiance. Such visions are myths, a present morality stated in the future tense.

The case in point was the 'general strike'. The syndicalists said socialism would conquer the day all the workers came out on strike at once, thus paralysing the capitalist state. Parliamentary socialists replied that for the workers to strike all at once and to defy the state, they would need to be socialist heroes to a man and the state ripe for overthrow. But in that case socialism would have arrived and the workers need not even bother to come out on strike. The general strike therefore was not a *means* to socialism, because it assumed socialism as given. Quite so, said Sorel, and that is why it is the kernel of the socialist faith. It is not a socio-logical theory that can be met with arguments.

Not only is intellectualist criticism of such myths socially ineffective, added Sorel, it is presumptuous – because the in-tellectuals do not know any more than the myth-makers what the future holds. Their 'social science', on which they base their 'scientific' forecasts, is totally bogus because there is no regularity in history except when great, violent myth-making movements put it there. It is the myth-makers who fashion the future, be-cause their myth epitomizes the aspirations of an enthusiastic mass and thus could well foreshadow something like itself, some-thing sublime. On the contrary, the sociologists' scientific blueprints for the future foreshadow nothing but ridiculous dis-appointment: the rule of intellectualist planners and the spread of the consumer mentality among the dupes who wait for the coming good times. The future is unknowable, and there are two attitudes we may take toward it: myth and utopia.

Myth deserves respect as the product of intense social wills that may well decide the future, whereas utopia deserves scorn as the divagations of intellectual charlatans. Sorel leaned on Bergson for the dogma that the future is radically and totally unpredictable. On other and more logical views of futurity, intellect reclaims some of its rights to discuss the predictions contained in social myth, yet Sorel's contribution to social theory stands.

Violence, too, Sorel found in the social facts, for it was

frequently resorted to by the revolutionary syndicalists, especially in the great strikes at the start of this century. He set out to answer the charge that any movement resorting to violence was, *ipso facto*, condemned as evil and retrograde. That meant questioning the confident Edwardian belief that civilization necessarily required peaceful settlement of all disputes and that, as humanity progressed, it moved nearer social and international peace.

Sorel replied by drawing on the histories of Christianity and French republicanism to show that great progressive movements had sometimes welcomed violent confrontations, when that helped them signify clearly their rejection of compromise. Violence in such cases was not stupid or due to lack of arguments and above all not immoral; it was a sign of moral health, it was a way of scaring off lukewarm supporters and it gave an earnest of the determination to break with the past.

Violence here meant every stance of no-compromise – right from a 'violence of principles' and the adoption of vehement attitudes, to literal headbreaking and bloodshed. When believers insist on parading the least acceptable part of their doctrines (as when Christians, in the heyday of science, stick to the literal interpretation of the miracles and of the assumption) they are discouraging their 'reasonable' friends, who find them extremist.

At the other end of that range of vehement attitudes was actual physical violence, whether courted, provoked or practised (the distinction is often fine and generally hypocritical). Such violence was never typical of social relationships but it was a logical extremity from which no rising movement would shrink, notably in certain unfavourable circumstances. The classic case, said Sorel, was early Christianity which could have easily secured toleration within Roman polytheism at the cost of a few concessions, which reasonable folk recommended. Instead, it enthusiastically sought violent persecution in order to mark its differences with paganism.

Twentieth-century democracy, he went on, was infinitely more dangerous to independent moralities than polytheism had been to Christianity, because elected parliaments were reputed to be the perfect market for the reconciliation of all social demands. Democratic prejudice made it seem barbaric to evade quasi-judicial procedures of representation and arbitration, by resorting to direct action. Yet the functioning of democracy's market in social demands depended on the assumption that all movements wanted the same things, things that could be translated on to a common scale of political power and budget subsidies – a typical consumer's notion. So a movement that wanted to intimate unequivocally that it did not just want more of what other people got but wanted to live independently outside the system of favour-brokerage would have to resort to direct action and must envisage violence. And, to the scandal of men of good will, that violence might often be directed not at its supposed enemies but at the peacemakers sent to persuade the movement to conform.

This anatomy of violence shocked respectable people and caused some morbid fascination among proto-fascists. Yet Sorel did not preach indiscriminate violence. He said that violence is ubiquitous in society and shows no sign of disappearing, but that we are tolerant of it in the forms of warfare and law-and-order enforcement, reserving our horror for oppositional violence. We should, rather, look to see in each case whose violence it is and ask whether it is not associated, as so often in the history of civilization, with a progressive and heroic morality that is ruthlessly forcing recognition of its independence and its rejection of mediocrity.

He noted that such movements usually construct sanguinary legends about how much violence they have experienced. The workers exaggerated police brutalities and the church had not really been nourished by the blood of so many martyrs. Such bloodthirsty traditions are true only symbolically; the grain of truth in them is a few violent clashes that proved a readiness to go to extremes. Such violence had revealed the movement to its enemies, and sometimes to itself. 'Real violence means going to the end of one's ideas,' said Sorel, adding that there was no reason to 'confound violence with senseless, sanguinary brutalities. For me, violence is an intellectual doctrine, the will of powerful minds who know what they are doing.'

And, finally, Sorel argued that we delude ourselves if we imagine that civilized men will ever reach a stage where violence will no longer be used to advance estimable causes. Violence will not be outgrown; it is not a barbarous atavism; it is not, absolutely and in itself, brutish. It can be lucid, noble and applied to the defence of high purpose; it can serve the cause of a new civilizing faith.

Thanks to the examples of national liberation movements, antifascist resistance and campaigns for racial equality, our day is rather less sweeping in its condemnation of violence than were the imperialist bourgeois of Sorel's day. Since some of those movements implicitly invoked Sorel in their apologies for violence, his reflections contributed to that evolution. The fascists made more frequent and explicit appeal to Sorel, but there is not a line in his work to condone systematic violence or violence applied otherwise than by a progressive morality of liberty.

### FURTHER READING

WORKS IN ENGLISH TRANSLATION

John L. Stanley (ed): *From Georges Sorel: Essays in Socialism and Philosophy* (Oxford University Press, 1976).

CRITICAL STUDIES

Pierre Andreu: *Notre Maitre, M. Sorel* (Bernard Grasset, 1953).

Michael Charzat: *Georges Sorel et la Révolution au XXe siècle* (Hachette, 1977).

Paul Delesalle: Bibliographie Sorélienne (Leyden, 1939: first published in *International Review for Social History*, vol. iv, pages 463–87).

Michael Freund: *Georges Sorel. Der Revolutionäre Konservativismus* (Vittorio Klostermann Verlag, Frankfurt, 1932).

Richard Humphrey: *Georges Sorel: Prophet without Honor. A Study in Anti-Intellectualism* (Harvard University Press, 1951).

James H. Meisel: *The Genesis of Georges Sorel* (Michigan University Press, 1951; Athena, 1966).

F. F. Ridley: *Revolutionary Syndicalism in France* (Cambridge University Press, 1970).

Victor Sartre: *Georges Sorel. Élites Syndicalistes et Révolution Prolétarienne* (Éditions Spes, 1937).

# VILFREDO PARETO
## (*1848–1923*)

### John H. Goldthorpe

VILFREDO PARETO was born in 1848, the son of an Italian aristocrat and his French wife. He was trained as an engineer and began his professional life in the Italian railway administration. After a few years, however, he left state employment, which he had never found congenial, to become managing director of an important group of iron mines owned by one of the leading Italian banks. In this new position Pareto became inevitably involved in current controversies on the issue of free trade versus protectionism and was soon actively engaged in the free-trade cause, taking a leading role in public debates and political campaigns.

In the course of participating in the controversy, he became intellectually captivated by the problems of pure economic theory which arose out of the practical issues and which were, in his view, vital to the understanding of the latter. Moreover, he was surprised and dismayed to find that most of the economic thinking of his day was of a highly unscientific character if judged by the standards of the physical sciences to which he was accustomed. As then his interest in business and politics waned, largely in consequence of the defeat of free trade, it became increasingly Pareto's ambition to devote himself to an academic life and to show the way to a new kind of economics which, by being more securely based on genuine scientific method, would provide more accurate and reliable guides to action.

On the death of his father in 1882, Pareto's inheritance gave him the opportunity which he sought. He was able to withdraw from business life and concentrate entirely on his academic pursuits. By 1893 he had achieved sufficient eminence in his field to be invited to the chair of economics in the University of Lausanne. In this post, which he held until his retirement, he established himself as one of the foremost theoretical economists of his generation and as perhaps the most important of the contemporary exponents of mathematical economics. Totally absorbed in his work, Pareto now lived virtually as a recluse. In his villa at Céligny he shut himself off from the troubles of the world, and, when not engaged in preparing lectures or writing, he diverted himself with the art of viticulture and with breeding Angora cats, large numbers of which always surrounded his person. His only return to the political field came after the triumph of Mussolini in 1922. Disillusioned with the ineffectiveness and corruption of Italian political liberalism, Pareto was inclined to look with favour on Fascism, and he was eagerly recognized by Mussolini as one of the great intellectual progenitors of the new regime. He was made a Senator of the Kingdom of Italy and invited to contribute to Mussolini's personal periodical, *Gerarchia*. However, by the time of his death in August 1923, less than a year after Mussolini's accession, Pareto was already at odds with the regime on the questions of personal and academic freedom. Though often labelled as a Fascist, it would perhaps be truer to say that he remained to the last a liberal *malgré lui*.

Pareto's interest in sociology, which developed only in the later years of his life, arose directly out of his work as an economist. He believed that as economics grew more scientific – as variables became more rigorously specified and the relationships between them expressed with mathematical precision – the field of economics had necessarily to become more narrowly and sharply defined. In his view, in fact, the concern of economics could properly be limited to one single aspect of human action: that is, action in so far as it was of a logical kind and was directed towards the acquisition or allocation of scarce resources. This assumption of logicality, or rationality, was, in Pareto's view, a necessary basis for the development of any advanced economic theory.

At the same time, however, Pareto's wide experience as administrator, businessman and politician had left him under no illusions about the part played in human affairs by *non*-logical or *non*-rational action. This, he recognized, was extensive and often decisively important. And because this was so, economic theory could never be expected to work out precisely in real life. Like any other kind of scientific theory, it held good only under conditions which in the real world could be no more than approximated. If then, Pareto argued, social science was to develop so as to give man the kind of understanding and control of society that he had of nature, a scientific economics needed to be *complemented* by a scientific sociology and psychology. The special concern of these disciplines would be with the study of those non-logical elements which economics strategically neglected.

In his last major work, *A Treatise on General Sociology*, Pareto set himself the task of laying the basis of the kind of sociology he believed necessary. This great book is in fact an attempt towards a general theory of non-logical conduct. It begins with several chapters devoted to making clear the scope of such a theory. Here Pareto defines the category of non-logical action as a residual one covering all forms of action which do not result from correct observation and reasoning: non-logical action stems not from the application of a scientific approach but rather from a 'state of mind' or from what Pareto termed 'sentiments'.

Following this, Pareto seeks to demonstrate the degree to which non-logical action is predominant in social life. For this purpose he takes as evidence the great number of doctrines and ideologies which have wide acceptance and to which men continually relate their actions, but which have no adequate observational-cum-logical (scientific) foundation. For example, Pareto includes here all political and moral philosophies, all forms of religious belief, all systems of metaphysics and so on. Such bodies of thought, he argues, all fail in one way or another to conform to the standards required of a scientific theory – they 'transcend experience', or they involve value judgements, or they may contain serious factual errors or flaws in argument. And yet, Pareto stresses, their prevalent influence in human affairs is a matter of common experience.

Though merciless in exposing the non-scientific elements in systems of thought, Pareto was not, one should note, primarily concerned to ridicule or condemn the theories which fell short of his exacting standards, nor the non-logical actions associated with them. His aim was rather to leave little doubt that action determined *purely* by 'process of reason' was of a decidedly rare and special kind. Moreover, Pareto emphasized that the truth of a theory or the logicality of an action should not be confused with their social utility. For example, quite unscientific forms of thought, such as myths, and entirely non-logical action, such as ritual, often had functions of great importance, particularly in maintaining the solidarity and morale of groups or indeed the cohesion of whole societies.

Having thus indicated the extent and social significance of the non-logical, Pareto's next concern was to reveal its sources and components. The various kinds of non-scientific theory to which he had drawn attention were not, he maintained, in themselves the basic *determinants* of non-logical action. Such action and the theories relating to it were *both* to be regarded as being primarily the product of sentiments. The interrelationship between action, theory and sentiments can be shown diagrammatically as in diagram 1. Though A, B and C are in a state of mutual inter-dependence, A influences B and C far more than it is in turn influenced by them, and more than B and C influence each other.

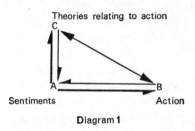

Diagram 1

To think that C was the chief determinant of B was, Pareto held, to fall victim of the rationalist fallacy. Non-scientific doctrines and ideologies do not constitute the mainsprings of human action; they serve rather to give the appearance of logicality – that is, to rationalize – the action which stems from sentiments.

The claim that C is much more an effect of A than a cause of B is, moreover, the basis for the next part of Pareto's analysis. Through examining further the nature of non-scientific thought Pareto believed that he could show how certain elements recurred from one non-scientific theory to another. These constants or 'residues' could then, in his view, be taken as direct manifestations of sentiments and were thus to be regarded as the key to the understanding of non-logical action.

Consistently with this he devoted a large part of his treatise to their description and classification. For example, one class was that of the 'residues of combinations'. Here Pareto referred to the abiding tendency among men to connect things together though they have no knowledge of any logical or scientifically established link between them: the believer in magic relates certain ritual acts to, say, the making of rain; the astrologer links the individual's horoscope to his future life: just as today bad weather is attributed to sputniks or H-bomb tests. A further class of residues Pareto termed the 'residues of the persistence of aggregates'. Here he had in mind those tendencies towards conservatism in thinking which lead men to retain complexes of beliefs and attitudes long after any rational basis for them has disappeared: customs and traditions survive even though manifestly anachronistic; prejudices and stereotypes which grow up in regard to ideas, people or things persist in spite of being scientifically exploded.

The residual elements were then the constants in non-scientific theories. Complementary to these, in Pareto's analysis, were the variable elements which he termed 'derivations'. The latter were the specifically rationalizing elements in such theories. Their function was in fact to provide justification for the sentiments expressed in the residual elements by giving these at least the semblance of logic or scientificity. Derivations were thus generally exercises in sophistry or self-deception. Pareto delighted in arguments to show that the same residue could give rise to a multiplicity of derivations, usually taking his examples from the comparative study of morals. He noted, for instance, that 'A Chinese, a Moslem, a Calvinist, a Catholic, a Kantian, a Hegelian, a Materialist, all refrain from stealing; but each gives a different explanation of his conduct.' In other words, each justifies in his own way the residual need which all have in common to maintain integrity of personality, i.e. to preserve their self regard (diagram 2).

The discussion of residues and derivations completes the

analytical part of Pareto's sociology. In the last section of his Treatise he turns to synthesis: to an attempt, in fact, to show how the distribution of residues among the population of a society is related not only, as one might imagine, to its intellectual and spiritual life, but also to the state of its economy and, most importantly, to the character of its ruling elite. The theory which

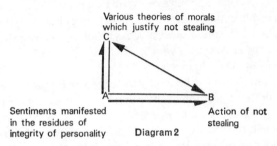

Various theories of morals which justify not stealing

Sentiments manifested in the residues of integrity of personality

Action of not stealing

Diagram 2

Pareto advances here is that the changing balance of the two key residues – those of 'combinations' and 'persistence' – forces the history of human societies into a cyclical pattern.

In one era the men of combinations, the 'foxes', are in the ascendant. This is a time characterized by experiment, innovation and enterprise, but also by intellectual uncertainty, economic swindling and political fraud. It is ended by a reaction on the part of the men of persistence, the 'lions', who rise up and sweep away the foxes, if necessary by force.

Then ensues a period of stability and conservatism accompanied by a resurgence of faith and national feeling. But, because of their expertise and resource, the men of combinations can never be dispensed with for long. Slowly they infiltrate into the ruling elite and, little by little, this reverts back from an elite of lions into an elite of foxes. Thus, the wheel has come full circle and is ready to turn again. For Pareto, societies were systems in a state of continually shifting, but ultimately unchanging, equilibrium: he rejected alike the liberal creed of unending progress and the Marxist dream of Utopia through revolution.

The theory of the circulation of elites is probably the best known part of Pareto's treatise, and from it has stemmed a tradition of political sociology centrally concerned with questions of the formation of elites, their interaction, and above all with the problem of the relationship between the elites and the mass. In recent years probably the most striking example of this tradition to have appeared is C. Wright Mills' *The Power Elite*, a controversial study of the dominance exercised by an alleged consortium of industrial, political and military groupings in modern America. Though making no explicit reference to Pareto, Mills reveals in this work an urge to expose political myths and a contempt for the importance of ideas in politics – save as legitimations of the *status quo* – which, whether consciously or not, are wholly Paretian in character.

It would, however, be wrong to suggest that it is through the theory of the circulation of elites that Pareto exercises his greatest influence on the sociology of the present day. What remains in evidence in the work of Mills and others is really only the spirit of the theory, not its content: the latter is largely ignored. It is in fact the analytical rather than the synthesizing parts of Pareto's *Treatise* which have generally proved the more lasting in their influence; and the area in which this has been chiefly apparent is, interestingly enough, that of industrial rather than political sociology.

In this respect the crucial link between Pareto and the present is created by the famous Hawthorne studies carried out by members of the Harvard Business School between 1927 and 1932 and generally regarded as the most important of the pioneering social research projects conducted in the industrial field. The focus of the research was on the determinants of worker morale and performance. As it progressed, what chiefly emerged was that assumptions currently made in this connexion were to a large extent unsound.

In the first place, it became clear that, contrary to the views of the industrial psychologists, there was no direct and necessary connexion between improvements in the physical conditions of work – lighting, length of hours, rest pauses, etc. – and improvements in operatives' productivity. Then, in subsequent studies, it was also shown that, contrary to the faith of the economists and scientific management experts, financial incentive schemes in no way guaranteed maximum worker effort. Such schemes could be entirely frustrated by operatives deliberately restricting output according to their own idea of what constituted a 'fair day's work', despite the fact that this might cause them financial loss. In other words, the research demonstrated that workers acted neither as simple organisms responding blindly to changes in their physical environment, nor yet as 'economic men' coolly calculating the best way of maximizing their earnings – even though they might claim various economic justifications for their restrictive practices.

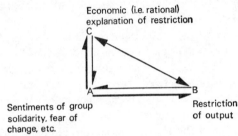

Economic (i.e. rational) explanation of restriction

Sentiments of group solidarity, fear of change, etc.

Restriction of output

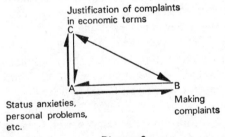

Justification of complaints in economic terms

Status anxieties, personal problems, etc.

Making complaints

Diagram 3

In appraising and organizing their largely unexpected findings, therefore, the Harvard team were in need of some new way of thinking about worker behaviour. This need they met to an important extent by adopting a Paretian viewpoint. In part, this was a historical accident: it so happened that at the time Harvard was experiencing a Pareto vogue. But it was also the case that Pareto's theory, particularly in its anti-positivist and anti-rationalist emphases, was in many respects well suited to the purpose in question. Those aspects of worker behaviour which were not explicable physiologically or in terms of economic rationality could be attributed to sentiments, and claims that such behaviour *was* economically rational need not then be taken at their face value.

For example, restriction of output could be interpreted as a manifestation of the work group's sense of solidarity and fear of change, and explanations given by workers in terms of guarding against rate cutting or unemployment could be regarded simply as rationalizations. Similarly, many worker grievances, though phrased in economic terms, could be treated as symptomatic of status anxieties or personal psychological difficulties (diagram 3). These non-rational aspects of worker behaviour could be set in contrast to the policies and practices of management; the latter being understood as means to the business ends of the enterprise devised in a strictly rational way. And thus, in the incompatibility which was shown up between the workers' 'logic of sentiment' and management's 'logic of cost and efficiency', a basic source of industrial conflict was revealed.

The influence of the Hawthorne studies in giving direction to subsequent social investigation in industry has been immense, and in much of this research their Paretian style of analysis has been taken over, though often, no doubt, unwittingly. It is, however, interesting to note that in recent years criticism has mounted of the basic assumption of the Hawthorne studies that worker behaviour stems largely from sentiments, while that of management is essentially rational. Research has suggested that many shop-floor practices, even if non-rational in economic terms, may nevertheless be rational in other respects: for example, in giving workers more control over the work situation. At the same time, it has become increasingly recognized that management itself offers ample opportunities for the study of myths, ideologies, non-scientific theories and non-logical conduct. Pareto would never have doubted it.

## FURTHER READING

### WORKS IN ENGLISH TRANSLATION

*The Mind and Society: A Treatise of General Sociology*, ed. A. Livingstone, tr. A. Bongiorno and A. Livingstone, four vols. (Dover, 1963).

*The Ruling Class in Italy before 1900* (Vanni, New York, 1950).

*Vilfredo Pareto: Sociological Writings*, selected and introduced by S. E. Finer (Pall Mall Press, 1966; Blackwell, 1976).

### CRITICAL STUDIES

S. E. Finer: Introduction to *Vilfredo Pareto: Sociological Writings* (Pall Mall Press, 1966; Blackwell, 1976).

Andrew Hacker: 'The Use and Abuse of Pareto in Industrial Sociology' (*The American Journal of Economics and Sociology*, vol. 14, no. 4, July 1955).

George C. Homans and Charles P. Curtis: *An Introduction to Pareto: His Sociology* (Knopf, 1934).

James H. Meisel (ed): *Pareto and Mosca* (Prentice-Hall, 1965).

Fritz J. Roethlisberger and William J. Dickson: *Management and the Worker* (Harvard University Press, 1939; Science Eds., 1964).

C. Wright Mills: *The Power Elite* (Oxford University Press, New York, 1956).

# SIGMUND FREUD
## (1856–1939)

## Laurie Taylor

As Professor Marie Jahoda ruefully observes in her sensitive book, *Freud and the Dilemmas of Psychology*, there is little uncontroversial which can now be said about Freud. Even the standard details of his life and death are the subject of debate as critics tumble over themselves to correct the sympathetic, almost protective tone of Ernest Jones's standard three-volume biography.

It may, for example, be just about agreed that he was born in 1856 in Freiberg, Moravia, and died in 1939 in London; but controversy has already arisen about whether he was really the child of his father's second or third marriage, and about the exact nature of his own death, and his unconscious and conscious attitudes towards it. And no longer is it just the nature of his intellectual debates with critics and revisionists (Reich, Jung, Adler) which absorbs the biographers of his middle years. Increasingly the emphasis is on his personal friendships, his jealousies, his vindictiveness.

Many of these contributions seem to rest upon the idea that accurate details about Freud's own sexual repressions, anti-feminism or aggressive urges will enable us to detect the weakness of his theoretical ideas. This 'genetic fallacy' appears more understandable when it is recognized that much of the bio-graphical argument has occurred in the United States. Psycho-analysis in that country has now become inextricably linked with clinical practice, and therefore with notions of adjustment and balanced living. How appropriate then that the originator of such therapeutic prescriptions should himself be exposed as a suitable case for treatment. Physician, heal thyself.

But this therapeutic emphasis gives a misleading view of the Freudian enterprise. There may be good commercial and professional reasons for some to insist on it as central, but there is little evidence that Freud regarded it in such a light. Certainly it does not help us to understand his distinctive contribution to social science.

It is, of course, true that Freud's initial concerns were wholly medicinal and therapeutic. His early work with Charcot in Paris on the use of hypnosis in the treatment of neurosis, and his collaborative work with Breuer on hysteria (*Studies on Hysteria*, 1895), were straightforwardly directed towards the removal of patients' symptoms. But the move away from this stage was a very calculated one.

I took a momentous step. I went beyond the domain of hysteria and began to investigate the sexual life of the so-called neurasthenics who used to visit me in numbers during my consultation hours. This experiment cost me, it is true, my popularity as a doctor, but it brought me convictions which today, 30 years later, have lost none of their force.

It is these lifelong convictions, rather than the establishment of the practice of psychoanalysis, which constitute Freud's claim to be a founding father of social science. They are claims about the social creation of human beings, about what the French marxist, Louis Althusser, has called 'the long forced march which makes mammaliferous larvae into human children, masculine or feminine subjects'. They are hypotheses about the structure of our psychic life, the relationship between conscious and unconscious realms of experience, between childhood attempts to understand the world, and adult representations of that world.

Freud does not always frame his discoveries in such universal terms. Indeed his greatest insights often appear in relatively circumscribed 'psychological' texts rather than in such self-consciously 'sociological' works as *Future of an Illusion* or *Civilisation and its Discontents*. It is this modesty, coupled with a readiness to tolerate contradiction and ambiguity, which also makes it difficult to assess his precise contribution to particular social theories. Quite dissimilar theorists can often claim with some legitimacy that their respective writings are directly based upon Freudian sources.

*The Interpretation of Dreams* (1900) marks the emergence of Freud as a social theorist. Talcott Parsons echoes many other writers in describing the book as 'one of the great landmarks in the intellectual development of the twentieth century'. Freud certainly always regarded it as his most important work, for though it contained many concepts which were to undergo revision, it introduced the enduring fundamentals of his work, and together with *Three Essays on the Theory of Sexuality* (1905) provided the basic ideas which would weave their ways in and out of so much social theorizing, if not clinical practice: the significance of the unconscious, the phenomenon of repression, the role of childhood sexuality.

Freud asserted, on the basis of clinical observations and his own self-analysis, that dreams provided us with evidence of the existence of a dynamic unconscious. They were the 'royal road to a knowledge of the unconscious activities of the mind'; opportunities for the expression and fulfilment of unconscious wishes. Such wishes were disguised within the actual dream by such devices (also unconscious) as condensation and displacement. The transformations effected by this 'dream-work' were essential in that the unconscious wishes were invariably ones which had been initially repressed – forced out of consciousness. They were characteristically infantile and sexual.

Each of these elements was to be considerably amplified. The language and grammar of the unconscious was elaborated by an analysis of lapses of memory, slips of the tongue (*The Psychopathology of Everyday Life*, 1901), humour (*Jokes and Their Relation to the Unconscious*, 1905) and taboo (*Totem and Taboo*, 1912). Ideas on the relationship between consciousness and the unconscious were extended in *The Ego and the Id* (1923), and Freud's findings on infantile sexuality were coordinated in the 1915 revision of the *Three Essays on Sexuality*. Finally, the instinctual theory was given a new dialectical basis by the introduction of the death wish in *Beyond the Pleasure Principle* (1920). Some more specific aspects of these developments will emerge as we trace the use made of Freud's ideas by other social theorists, as will disagreements about exactly what he said, and about the nature of his fundamental discoveries.

Herbert Marcuse's critical chapter on the neo-freudians in *Eros and Civilization* (1955) is a good introduction to the debate on Freud's contribution to social science. Marcuse's main attack is on the 'cultural and interpersonal schools' of psychoanalysis, upon writers like Erich Fromm, Karen Horney and Harry Stack Sullivan, who are accused of abandoning the tough core of psychoanalysis – the fundamentals of *The Interpretation of Dreams* (the role of sexuality, function of the unconscious), and the notion of the death instinct.

Marcuse argued the neo-freudians were being misleading when they asserted they were 'sociologising' Freud by stressing possible cultural variation between societies in the degree and nature of repression, or by the emphasis on the different personalities which resulted from varying social conditions. The neo-freudians might demonstrate the links between psychic states and capitalism, stress the relationship between personal neurosis and economic exploitation, talk knowingly of marxism and alienation, but their concentration on the idea of the whole personality, on such values as responsibility, inner strength and integrity, showed how thoroughly (in Marcuse's view) they still clung to traditional capitalistic virtues.

They misinterpreted Freud by placing the individual in conflict with his environment, instead of recognizing that the conflict occurred *within* the individual, and was a fundamental feature of 'socialization' into every society, a necessary repressive feature of all human life. Their claims to have 'de-biologized' Freud in the name of sociology were also misleading, according to Marcuse. They had simply failed to understand that Freud's version of our biological nature was already thoroughly sociological. Overall, they had managed to construct a theory whose tone was loving, progressive and hopeful, whereas Freud had remained 'cold, hard, destructive and pessimistic'.

Marcuse's own updating of Freud in the rest of *Eros and Civilisation* did, however, reveal that he also was prepared to shift the meaning of freudian ideas when it suited his own theoretical purposes. His concepts of *surplus repression* (the additional restrictions on sexuality which resulted from economic and political domination) and the *performance* principle (the contemporary form of Freud's 'reality principle') were arguably legitimate extensions rather than revisions of Freud's ideas. But this was hardly true of his case for the 'resexualization of the body' as a weapon against capitalism, and as a way in which the instinct of destructiveness might be countered. (Freud certainly never allowed for a victory of Eros over Thanatos.) But at least Marcuse's particular revisionism, his un-freudian optimism about the prospects for an early 'sexual revolution' were quickly to be qualified by his own analysis of actual events. In 1966, in a new preface to *Eros and Civilisation*, he regretted the 'optimistic, euphemistic, even positive' nature of his earlier thought.

It has been pointed out that the 'unacknowledged hero' of *Eros and Civilisation* is Marx, for though his name is never mentioned it is evident that Marcuse uses the notion of 'instinctual repression' as a conscious parallel to the idea of 'economic exploitation', in order to effect an alignment between marxism and psychoanalysis. He does, however, make one reference to another self-declared marxist who had made explicit claims to be engaged in the same task – Wilhelm Reich. But one highly critical paragraph sufficed.

At first glance, this cursory treatment seems strange. For Reich's writings make it quite clear that he was as concerned as Marcuse with the corruption of freudian thought by the ego-clinicians of bourgeois society, and he had been just as intense about the need to restore its original revolutionary character. In 1937 Reich wrote: 'Psychoanalysis once worked at the roots of life; the fact that it did not become conscious of its social nature was the main factor in its catastrophic decline.'

Reich's version of this 'social nature' relativized Freud's terms to such an extent that it is no surprise to find the neo-freudians occasionally claiming him as one of their number. The Oedipus complex, for example – that constellation of repressed ideas about the family drama in which the child imagines himself to be immersed – was not regarded by Reich as a universal process which ended the child's bisexuality and gave rise to the super-ego, but as a particular pathological effect of the patriarchal family structure. Neither was the unconscious 'absolute, eternal or unalterable'; it was shaped by particular social circumstances.

In all these reformulations of Freud, Reich also worked with an uneasy dialectic – the opposition between nature and culture. Social institutions could be radically transformed along marxist lines in such a way that culture became no longer repressive, and human nature (which Reich conceptualized in idealistic terms) emerged from its long history of containment. This was a form of biological essentialism which had no appeal to Marcuse: 'sexual liberation *per se* becomes for Reich a panacea for individual and social ills.'

But Reich's work on the family does provide us with an interesting example of how two quite different theorists may both claim common freudian origins. Reich saw the family as an institution which ensured patriarchal domination, and the oppression of women and children. Its principal function was

that of serving as a factory for authoritarian ideologies and conservative mental structures . . . it is the conveyor belt between the economic structure of conservative society and its ideological super-structure; its reactionary atmosphere must needs become inextricably implanted in every one of its members.

This notion of the family as a factory for shaping children is also explicitly adopted by a social theorist who could hardly be further away from Reich's peculiar blend of marxism and biological essentialism – the systems analyst, Talcott Parsons. Even a superficial reading of Parsons's *Family, Socialisation and Interaction Process* demonstrates the two men's very different use of freudian ideas. Whereas Reich regarded the childhood process of acquiring values and beliefs as a subversion of an ideal libidinous human nature, Parsons saw it as an admirably sophisticated mechanism for the production of appropriately motivated members of society. And if Reich was inclined to 'over-biologize' Freud by insisting on some ideal unconta-minated substratum, Parsons was reluctant to let any biological or irrational residues mar the surface of the smooth cultural products created by the familial system.

Parsons claimed to find warrant for this in Freud's later work on personality: in works like *The Ego and the Id*, in which the emphasis was no longer so much on the various territories of mental life (the unconscious, preconscious and conscious) as on the structural dimensions of personality (ego, id and super-ego). According to Parsons's reading, even aspects of the id became socialized during childhood, and the super-ego became a functional repository of cultural values. Small wonder, perhaps, that other American sociologists – in particular, Dennis H. Wrong in his essay 'The over-socialized conception of man in modern sociology' – began to complain about the attenuation of Freud's ideas. To Freud, Wrong reminded his readers, 'man is a *social* animal without being entirely a *socialized* animal'.

Many of these disagreements about *What Freud Really Said* (the slightly irritable empiricist title of a recent book by David Stafford-Clark) are reflected within the feminist debate about Freud. There have, for example, been several attempts to condemn the 'biological reductionism' of his theory, which is said to have led him to an absolutist characterization of women as passive and dependent. 'Of all the factors that have served to perpetuate a male-oriented society,' Eva Figes wrote in *Patriarchal Attitudes*, 'the emergence of freudian psychoanalysis has been the most serious.' Juliet Mitchell has responded at length to this view, in *Psychoanalysis and Feminism*, with the powerful argument that there is no simple choice to be made in freudian theory between biology and culture, as 'psychoanalysis is precisely a theory about the ways in which culture is assimilated and handed on'.

Mitchell accuses several leading feminist writers, de Beauvoir, Friedan, Figes, Greer, Firestone and Millett, of sharing 'a strong protest against the fact of an unconscious mind': they make the mistake of translating aspects of mental life into social reality. As Christopher Lasch summarized the argument in a review of Mitchell's book:

Femininity is not innate, but neither is it the product of 'cultural conditioning'. For psychoanalysis the important point is not that women are victimised (as they are) by sexual stereotypes perpetrated by men in their own self-interest but that in any culture the process of becoming a woman requires the repression of the active and phallic side of women's sexuality, a repression so thorough, and so little accessible to conscious understanding or control, that passivity comes to resemble a fact of nature, an inherent attitude of womanhood.

Some of the recurrent disagreements about Freud arise from a tendency to relate his work to dissonant methodological and theoretical paradigms. His technique, for example, is mistakenly regarded as predictive rather than post-dictive; his names for psychic processes (id, ego, super-ego) tend to become distinctive entities; his accounts of childhood are regarded as references to actual events rather than as the elicited memories of such events. This confusion is not without some warrant. Ideas about what should count as evidence, and how we should treat Freud's statements, are continually complicated by his tendency to move uneasily between dynamic, economic, topographic, structural, genetic and adaptive approaches to his subject matter.

This was not, perhaps, surprising. He was pioneering a new science, and had to endure what Althusser has described as 'theoretical solitude'. He had

to be himself his own father, to construct with his own craftsman's hands the theoretical space in which to situate his discovery, to weave with thread borrowed intuitively left and right the great net with which to catch in the depths of blind experience the teeming fish of the unconscious, which men call dumb because it speaks even while they sleep.

Althusser's rolling metaphor is also a fanfare for a contemporary approach to Freud which does not so much seek to resolve the contradictions within Freud, or to rectify the theory on the basis of new data, but rather, by drawing on the science of linguistics, to make the contradictions themselves the subject of study.

This enterprise is particularly associated with the writings of the French theorist, Jacques Lacan. The real subject of psychoanalysis, Lacan argues, is the unconscious, and the discourse of the unconscious. This discourse is structured like a language, and its grammar can be unravelled with help of such freudian terms as *condensation* and *displacement*. Writers like Lacan are not denying the biological basis of instincts. They are arguing that we may only have access to them through their various linguistic manifestations, by the examination of the 'features of systematically distorted communications'. Thus, even the surface plausibility of Freud's own writings can be parted so as to reveal attempts to disguise and draw attention away from his own fundamental discovery of the unconscious. In other words, Freud's own theory of repression was itself constantly and necessarily threatened with being itself repressed.

Obviously, Lacan and his admirers take great exception to the whole American school of ego psychology. It is not simply that this school denies the significance of the unconscious, or under-estimates the role of biological forces, but also that it mistakenly reintroduces the conscious subject as the central figure of psychoanalysis. According to Lacan, the real 'subject' does not take the form of an ego which somehow sits in the centre of con-sciousness: it is 'de-centred' from consciousness. Lacan's ego is not an amiable agent of synthesis or adaptation. Quite the contrary: it is the victim of its own 'illusion of strength.' The ideas of wholeness and integrity, which inform so much of ego-psychology, are the very neurotic symptoms – 'the synthesis compulsion' – which typically afflict the ego. The recent tendency, seen in the work of Erikson and others, to prefer the term 'identity' to 'ego', compounds this anti-freudian movement.

An emphasis on psychoanalysis as a guide to the understanding of distorted communication has also appeared in the writings of the German social theorist, Jurgen Habermas. Whereas Habermas's predecessors in the Frankfurt school of sociology (Adorno, Horkheimer, Marcuse) primarily turned to Freud for answers to questions about the way in which the belief structures of capitalism became lodged within individual psyches, Haber-mas takes a more literal approach to the texts.

Psychoanalysis is regarded as a new form of hermeneutics, a way of understanding distorted messages; not just dreams and slips of the tongue, but also the distortions in communication which are imposed by the present institutional constraints on free discussion. So we find Habermas regarding the analytical conversation between physician and patient not as a specific therapeutic practice, but as a model of the 'ideal speech situation' – a situation in which people come to an agreement not because of constraints on the discussion, but because of the gradual removal of obstacles: displacements, condensations, repressions, reifications.

The psychoanalyst's task of restoring autonomy to his patients, of making them understand their position in the world, is therefore, Habermas argues, similar to that which should be performed by the social theorist. Only when we have created a community in which all public discussion is freed of communicative distortion will we be able to talk of an ideal society.

This concentrated survey of Freud's impact on social science has necessarily only provided a number of map references. It has omitted many of the details of the disagreements between 'fundamentalists' and 'revisionists', and has failed to distinguish some of the basic epistemological differences between them (positivist, structural-functionalist, structuralist, hermeneutic), as well as simply excluding a number of important social theorists (Lévi-Strauss, Ricoeur) who did not fall within the course of the argument. It has also neglected Freud's own 'sociological' contributions (his pessimism about revolutionary socialism in *Civilisation and its Discontents*, and his rejection of religion in *The Future of an Illusion*), on the grounds that these have not only failed to stimulate social theorists in the same manner as other sections of his writings, but also that they are only more 'sociological' if judged by the crude criterion of their explicit subject matter.

Freud – despite the impatience of empiricists who do not like his methods, clinicians who distrust his therapeutic techniques, professional analysts who have transformed his work into a religion of adjustment, and theorists who rebel against his pessimistic determinism – shows no signs of going away. He is as influential among social theorists as at any time in the last thirty years (some would say more so). A new journal, *British Ideology and Consciousness*, which is devoted to a discussion of many of his ideas, provides the following explanation of his enduring significance for social scientists:

With Copernicus the earth moved from its position of centrality in the universe, with Darwin man moved from his position of centrality in the eye of the creator, with Marx the individual human subject moved from its position of centrality in history, and with Freud consciousness moved from its position of centrality in the structure of the psyche.

### FURTHER READING

WORKS IN ENGLISH TRANSLATION

*Complete Psychological Works of Sigmund Freud* (Hogarth Press, 24 vols., 1953–74).

*The Pelican Freud Library* (Penguin, 1974–  ).

CRITICAL STUDIES

Louis Althusser: 'Freud and Lacan' in *Lenin and Philosophy and other essays* (New Left Books, 1971).

Penelope Balogh: *Freud: a biographical introduction* (Studio Vista, 1971).

Bruce Brown: *Marx, Freud and the Critique of Everyday Life* (Monthly Review Press, 1973).

Marie Jahoda: *Freud and the Dilemmas of Psychology* (Hogarth Press, 1977).

Herbert Marcuse: *Eros and Civilization* (1956; Sphere, 1969).

Juliet Mitchell: *Psychoanalysis and Feminism* (Allen Lane, 1974).

Paul Robinson: *The Sexual Radicals* (Temple Smith, 1969; Paladin, 1971).

Lancelot Law Whyte: *The Unconscious before Freud* (Tavistock, 1962).

# THORSTEIN VEBLEN
### *(1857–1929)*

## J. A. Banks

HISTORY has dealt harshly with Thorstein Veblen; for surely there is no other sociologist of his generation whose words are so often quoted but whose works are so little read. Conspicuous consumption, ostentatious display, trained incapacity, the higher learning, predatory culture, absentee ownership, discretionary control – these are just a few of the terms which he bequeathed to the use and wont of everyday social analysis. Master of the telling adjective, Veblen filled the role of gadfly in the American academic world of the late nineteenth and early twentieth centuries. His juxtaposition of ironic epithet and innocuous noun caused even those who were least disposed to listen, to sit up and question the trend of values in modern civilization. The empirical content of his writings, as we should understand it today, was slender to the point of emaciation. But as an *interpretative* sociologist he has had few equals.

The capacity to seize upon the significant features of an issue, to elucidate and to illuminate, however insubstantial the empirical description, may have derived at least in part from Veblen's perpetual failure to adjust to the circumstances which surrounded him. Rosenberg calls him 'the stranger', the marginal man *par excellence*, who was at home in neither town nor country. Born to an immigrant farming family in Wisconsin, he spoke the language and followed the cultural interests of rural Norway for the first seventeen years of his life, attending the local school where English was taught, but without having very much contact with English-speaking neighbours. Possibly he always hated farm work; certainly his parents, like most hard-working immigrants, held high aspirations for his future. At seventeen he was sent to Carleton College Academy to study religion and moral philosophy with a view to entering the Lutheran ministry; but after graduation the only post he could obtain was that of a teacher of mathematics in a Norwegian college in Madison. This college failed after he had been there a year and he went on to struggle through the next five years, first at Johns Hopkins and then at Yale, where he was awarded his PhD in 1884 for a dissertation on the ethical grounds of a doctrine of retribution.

During these years he met three notable scholars who in different ways influenced his transition from philosophy to institutional economics and sociology: the liberal economist John Bates Clark at Carleton, the pragmatist philosopher Charles Pierce at Johns Hopkins, and the evolutionary sociologist William Graham Sumner at Yale. Yet no post which he could, or would, accept offered itself for another seven years; and he spent the first four of them living off his family, and the remaining three living off his father-in-law, having married the daughter of a railroad king in 1888. Perhaps he would have remained relatively content in this life, reading and ruminating, writing articles which did not find a publisher, but the railway fortune disappeared in 1891, and Veblen went off to Cornell where he was fortunate to receive a grant to study economics for a year, before taking up a tutorship in the subject at Chicago.

Veblen was now in his thirty-fifth year and another eight years were to pass before he was promoted to assistant professor, after the publication of his first book, *The Theory of the Leisure Class*, in 1899. He was not a good teacher, in the conventional sense. He was often incoherent, even inaudible, and when asked to repeat what he had just said, he would reply that it was not worth repeating. He made it a standard practice never to give above a c grade, not because he had contempt for his students, but as a gesture against the invidious distinction of persons which the ritual of examinations fosters.

His move to Chicago was the first time he had ever really been to a great industrial centre and he found it ugly. His relations with his wife deteriorated to the extreme of divorce in 1911, not before the scandal which their incompatibility occasioned caused him to move from Chicago to Stanford (1906) and from Stanford to retirement for a time in Idaho (1909). In 1911 he was offered a lecturing post on a low salary at the University of Missouri where he stayed until 1918. A short period in Washington as an employee of the Food Administration was followed by eight years in New York, first as one of the editors of *The Dial* and later as a member of the New School for Social Research; but already by 1922 he was looking for a new post, and eventually in 1926 he went to Palo Alto where he died three years later.

Even in his day, American academics were far more accustomed to changing their universities in the course of their careers than has been the case in this country, but Veblen's frequency of removal was unusual. Moreover, it was generally understood that they moved up when they moved on. Veblen's unhappy migration took a very different form. At no time did he rise above the rank of associate professor. The fault was as much in himself as in his circumstances. In a very real sense, as Riesman has put it, he conspired to his own exploitation. It was to the benefit of his generation that his books were often a product of this academic maladaptation, but the mischief itself was frequently produced by his own inability to cope.

In many respects Veblen never emancipated himself from his agrarian background and the values his family held. His books show an intense appreciation for the virtues of workmanlike performance and for labour-saving machinery, which he undoubtedly derived from his father. He saw no point in drudgery as such, no worth in routine toil; but like his father, who is said to have preferred machines to men, he clearly thought 'industrial' employments to be superior to 'pecuniary' ones, and engineering to be superior to business, no matter how much American society evaluated them differently. *The Instinct of Workmanship and the State of the Industrial Arts*, his favourite work, comprises an elaboration of the argument that there exists in mankind a tendency towards craftsmanship as an end in itself, developed by reference to a cultural heritage, the stock of technical knowledge possessed by the community. All societies, even the very primitive, overlay this 'instinct' with obscuring alternatives. However, in his more optimistic moments, which admittedly were rare, Veblen seems to have believed that in the long run the industrial arts always prevailed.

In this sense he was a technological determinist, holding that 'the adoption of new industrial ways and means, whether in the way of specific devices and expedients or of comprehensive changes in methods and processes' is followed by 'a growth of conventional usages governing the utilization of the new ways and means' – modifying the society, whether it develops them itself or borrows them from abroad. Even the control of industry by predatory businessmen and absentee owners could be explained in these terms. 'What threw the fortunes of the industrial community into the hands of the owners of accumulated wealth was essentially a technological change, or rather a complex of technological changes, which so enlarged the requirements in respect of material equipment that the impecunious workmen could no longer carry on their trade except by a working arrangement with the owners of this equipment; whereby the discretionary control of industry was shifted from the craftsmen's technological mastery of the ways of industry to the owner's pecuniary mastery of the material means.' Power, property and technology were the mainsprings of social change.

*The Theory of the Leisure Class*, subtitled *An economic study of institutions*, was in his day the book for which Veblen was best known, admired or detested. Of all his works it is the one most referred to, and quoted from at the present time, as an example of his sociology. Yet it is a book which he himself referred to contemptuously as 'that chestnut', and it is far more often esteemed for its ironic style than for its content. Indeed, there is a very real sense in which the style obscures the content. His perception of the significance of the debilitating effect of the Victorian corset, for example, although penetrating and unforgettable, directs attention away from the main theme of his argument, which is not simply that such uselessness was created *deliberately* to demonstrate the pecuniary strength of the middle and upper class Victorian paterfamilias. Rather was it Veblen's intention to emphasize the power on all Victorians of conventional forms – Sumner's 'folk-ways' – and, like Marx, to show how they developed in response to the evolution of a class system based on coercion, military power and private ownership.

From this point of view, the meaning of the book is best

approached by a consideration of what is meant by the term 'theory' in its title and in the title of Veblen's second full-length study, *The Theory of Business Enterprise*, published in 1904. For, although he clearly wished to draw some attention to the fact that he personally was trying to understand the nature of the class system and of business, more emphatically the 'theory' which is most pronounced in both books is the set of values which members of the leisure class and businessmen used to justify their ways to their fellow men. In contemporary terms, Veblen's main concern was to document in detail the ideology of those with power in society, especially in the society of his time. More generally, in *The Theory of the Leisure Class* he wished to make manifest how this ideology of the ruling class, through emulation and invidious comparison, became the ideology of an epoch. But the memorable nature of the ironic passages and the intriguing quality of the illustrations have masked the book's main drift.

For this reason *The Theory of Business Enterprise*, which in the stock phrase is a much less brilliant book, is nevertheless probably a better guide to Veblen's interpretative powers than *The Theory of the Leisure Class*. In its opening sentence it sets out that relationship in modern society which for Veblen spelled a conflict situation conducive to social change. 'The material framework of modern civilization is the industrial system, and the directing force which animates this framework is business enterprise'. Of course, he was aware that power was possessed by the latter, not the former. 'Industry is carried on for the sake of business, and not conversely ... The adjustments of industry take place through the mediation of pecuniary transactions, and these transactions take place at the hands of the businessmen and are carried on by them for business ends, not for industrial ends in the narrower meaning of the phrase.' Yet the important issue for Veblen was not simply that businessmen had different goals from the men they controlled. It was also that the machine process which is fundamental to the modern industrial system requires and fosters habits of mind at contrast with those essential to business success. The engineers, chemists, metallurgists, electricians – all who invent, produce, operate and maintain modern machinery –

follow 'a reasoned procedure on the basis of a systematic know-ledge of the forces employed'.

Businessmen, and all whose occupations are devoted to the making of money, function on the basis of pecuniary transactions involving 'shrewd investments and coalitions with other business-men' by reference to market values. And businessmen even find it advantageous from time to time to disrupt the workings of industry in order to increase profits or avoid losses, whereas technologists work to see that the industrial system 'bears the character of a comprehensive, balanced mechanical process' so that every form of maladjustment must be put right.

In this analysis, it should be clear that Veblen owed little to Marxism, for all that he was well acquainted with Marx's writings and made considerable use of them. His cast of thought was too pessimistic to allow him to accept Marx's romantic radicalism, and he nowhere saw the outcome of a possible struggle between business and industry, pecuniary and technological interests, as the dictatorship of the proletariat leading to a classless society. The working class, to be sure, were compelled to develop habits of thought similar to those of scientists and engineers. 'What the discipline of the machine industry inculcates in the habits of life and thoughts of the workman is regularity of sequence and mechanical precision, and the intellectual outcome is habitual resort to terms of measurable cause and effect, together with a relative neglect and disparagement of such exercise of the intellectual faculties as does not run on these lines.' But this similarity of thinking between workers and technologists was not interpreted by Veblen as inducing any sentiments akin to class consciousness.

Towards the end of *The Theory of Business Enterprise* there is some indication that he considered the 'natural decay' of the businessman's ascendancy might be speeded up by community policies with something of a socialist bent, but even in saying so Veblen pointed to the extent to which the 'quest of profits' leads to a predatory national policy; and the glorification of international warfare, which was associated with such a policy, was more likely to result in dynastic despotism than to a society of the common man. By the time he came to write his last book,

*Absentee Ownership and Business Enterprise in Recent Times* (1923), this possibly had become a virtual certainty except for the conviction that the businessman was likely to remain firmly in the saddle.

The pecuniary and industrial pursuits, it should be understood, are rather polar types than clear-cut dichotomies. It is, therefore, possible to regard them as standing at the extremes of a continuum from pure pecuniary to pure industrial occupations. Thus, those managerial posts which fall towards the pecuniary pole, while they have predominantly cost-accounting characteristics, will nevertheless temper them with some productivity consciousness. Unskilled workers, similarly, may be deemed to show more concern for the pecuniary aspects of work than should be the case with skilled tradesmen. Moreover, even at the extremes, Veblen left room for some element of the other. A businessman, for example, was said to be motivated by 'something of the instinct of workmanship'. In this respect he is 'moved by ideals of serviceability and an aspiration to make the way of life easier for his fellows ... Businessmen are also, in a measure, guided by the ambition to effect a creditable improvement in the industrial processes which their business traffic touches.' Veblen, as always, was concerned to weigh up both the positive and the negative aspects of the values which prompt action, even though he never doubted on which side the balance lay.

This is particularly noticeable in Veblen's *The Higher Learning in America: a memorandum on the conduct of universities by businessmen* (1918), a study which has come to be regarded by many American sociologists as his most enduring monument, possibly because it is based on 'participant observation'.

In a university, scholars and scientists share a rather special instinct of workmanship, what Veblen called 'idle curiosity, a disinterested proclivity to gain a knowledge of things and to reduce the knowledge to a comprehensible system'. However, they also share the task of instructing students, and it is through this that they are open to influence, and even control, by politicians and businessmen, especially since the universities have come to be organized fiscally as corporate bodies.

The administration uses the intellectual distinctions of academics as part of its bargaining power in the market competition for students and donors. Businessmen, for their part, exercise influence through the governing boards in their role as trustees. Both the academic bureaucrats (whom Veblen called 'captains of erudition') and the businessmen ('captains of finance') recognize the virtues of idle curiosity. But learning, for them, is a commodity to be bought and sold in standardized lots; and the emphasis on teaching to the detriment of research inculcates businesslike qualities in academics.

It is here, indeed, that Veblen's interpretative writing is most likely to be useful to the contemporary sociologist, not so much for the penetrating manner in which he describes the erosion of scholarly values, but for the emphasis he gives to size, scale, and to the function of educational institutions as places of socialization in the modern world. Of course, he does not use this language, but the ideas are clear enough. Veblen antedated William Whyte's *Organisation Man* by nearly forty years. Conscious himself of the constraining influence of university rituals and ceremonies, and of the decisions of committees engaged in 'sifting sawdust', he uttered a protest on behalf of the solitary man, the maverick who wanted to get on with his own work in his own way, be this research or teaching. Such a conception is clearly capable of generalization beyond the organizations of higher learning to all organizations, just as Veblen's analysis of the ideological basis of engineering and business is open to extension to all occupational roles whatsoever. In this respect Veblen deserves to get far more attention from industrial sociologists and from organization theorists than he has so far been accorded.

One final point should be emphasized. Many of Veblen's ideas have become so much part of the general currency of sociology and of general social criticism that we have forgotten it was Veblen who first gave them point and emphasis. Status-consciousness and social emulation, in some respects a major enduring theme of *The Theory of the Leisure Class*, had been written about long before Veblen put pen to paper, but it was he who showed how they were related to other values in society and how they led to certain consequences such as the development of advertising in modern times. Bureaucratic attitudes had similarly been commented upon with respect to civil service performance before he came on the scene, but it was Veblen who most surely demonstrated how they operated in other fields – in business and in education.

### FURTHER READING

WORKS

*The Portable Veblen*, ed. Max Lerner (Viking, 1958).
*The Theory of the Leisure Class* (Mentor, 1954).
*The Higher Learning in America* (Hill and Wang, 1957).
*The Theory of Business Enterprise* (Kelley, rept. of 1904 ed.).

CRITICAL STUDIES

Stanley M. Daugert: *The Philosophy of Thorstein Veblen* (King's Crown Press, New York, 1950).

Joseph Dorfman: *Thorstein Veblen and his America* (Viking, 1934; Gollancz, 1935).

Douglas F. Dowd (ed.): *Thorstein Veblen: a critical reappraisal* (Cornell University Press, 1958).

John A. Hobson: *Veblen* (Chapman and Hall, 1936).

Carlton C. Qualey (ed.): *Thorstein Veblen* (Columbia University Press, 1968).

David Riesman: *Thorstein Veblen. A critical interpretation* (Scribner's, 1953).

Bernard Rosenberg: *The Values of Veblen: A critical appraisal* (Public Affairs Press, Washington, D. C., 1956).

David Seckler: *Thorstein Veblen and the Institutionalists* (Macmillan, 1975).

# ÉMILE DURKHEIM

## (1858–1917)

### John Rex

WHY should there be a special science called sociology? Why not simply a science of human behaviour in general? Is the behaviour of social groups not ultimately reducible to the behaviour of the groups' individual members? Questions such as these are bound to occur to anyone approaching sociological literature for the first time. But much of that literature fails to answer these questions. It is concerned with a ragbag of problems, which might equally well be dealt with by a biologist, a psychologist, an economist, or a statistician. It looks for no special class of determinants, it asks no special questions, it brings no special insights to the facts under review.

The student who feels this way cannot do better than to turn to the work of one of the great masters of sociology, Émile Durkheim. Durkheim was an Alsatian Jew who was born in 1858 and grew up in a turbulent period of French history, marked by the defeat of the Franco-Prussian war, the setting up of the Third Republic and the weakening of traditional educational institutions dominated by the church. Himself an agnostic, Durkheim devoted himself to the search for a new secular and scientific social ethics which would serve to bind the new French society together. For a period of nearly thirty years he addressed himself to the teachers of France, first as Professor of Social Science in Bordeaux and then as Professor of the Philosophy of Education and of Sociology in the Sorbonne. And the theme of his teaching was always that attention should be devoted not simply to the characteristics of individuals but to the specifically social bonds which united men in society.

In his *Rules of Sociological Method*, Durkheim sets out to distinguish the specifically social element which it is the task of the sociologist to study. He shows how, along with the purely individual, biological and psychological determinants of human

behaviour, there are others, which do not arise from the constitution of the individual. As he says:

When I fulfil my obligations as brother, husband or citizen, when I
execute my contracts, I perform duties which are defined externally to
myself and my acts in law and custom. Even if they conform to my own
sentiments and I feel their reality subjectively, such reality is still
objective, for I did not create them.

Obligations, contracts, duties, laws and customs are thus isolated
as a specific subject matter, and their distinguishing features are
that they are 'exterior' to any individual and that they exercise
constraint over him. If we confine ourself to facts of this kind we
shall be studying 'society'.

Sometimes, however, individuals are constrained by external
facts which are rather more vague and difficult to study. If one
wishes to study the legal determinants of human behaviour one
has data ready to hand in written legal codes. But if one seeks to
study the effect of a crowd on its members, or vague social trends
such as fashion, it is not quite so clear what kind of evidence one
should seek. Durkheim believed that it was important that such
social trends should be studied. Indeed he probably felt that they
constituted the major part of the subject matter of sociology. He
therefore argues that if the social fact has no independent observable existence of its own, it is the sociologist's job to give it
one. He should do this by discovering statistical rates which
should be taken not merely as a counting of separate individual
phenomena but as indices of social currents.

The empirical application of these ideas is to be found in two of
Durkheim's greatest works: *The Division of Labour in Society*
and *Suicide*. In the first, his doctoral thesis, Durkheim argues that
social order cannot be explained, as the English utilitarians
sought to explain it, in terms of the enlightened self-interest of
individuals. There must, as it were, be something there, apart
from purely individual tendencies binding individuals together
into social wholes. This 'something' is a form of social solidarity.
In simple societies this form of social solidarity rests upon
collectively held sentiments and ideas. In advanced societies it
rests upon the division of labour which is not just an expedient
device for increasing human happiness, but a moral and social

fact whose purpose is to bind society together. Both forms of social solidarity, however, have this in common. They are expressed in legal codes and it is to the comparative study of these codes that Durkheim directs our attention.

In *Suicide*, which still stands as a model of the specifically sociological use of statistics, Durkheim begins by showing that the available statistics do not seem to support any hypothesis which attributes suicide to individual causes. What matters is the rate of suicide and this (which varies only slowly) is indicative of a kind of society whose very structure compels a minority of people towards self-destruction. In a society having the first kind of social solidarity discussed in *The Division of Labour* the trend is towards 'altruistic suicide'. In a society of the second kind suicide tends to be 'egoistic'. What Durkheim has done for suicide, could be done in relation, say, to patterns of marriage and divorce, delinquency or industrial unrest. By contrasting the statistical rates of these phenomena in different social groups we should be able to discover the strictly *social* concomitants of variations in the rate.

Because Durkheim inherited the tradition of nineteenth-century positivism, he did not confine himself to the empirical study of sociological data for its own sake. He was concerned to extract from empirical material a positive guide to action. And he believed that in showing what were the essentials of social order he was also showing what were the conditions of human happiness.

The great enemy, as he saw it, of an adequate positive ethic was the tradition of English utilitarianism culminating in the sociology of Herbert Spencer. The utilitarians believed that human happiness could be increased by a continuous increase in the size and number of individual lots of pleasures. It seemed to Durkheim, that, far from this being the case, human happiness could only be assured if the pleasures of the individual were limited by socially approved norms. In circumstances in which these norms collapsed, the individual found himself in the state of personal disorganization which Durkheim called 'anomie'.

The notion of anomie crops up both in *The Division of Labour* and in *Suicide*. In *The Division of Labour*, Durkheim recognizes that the division of labour does not in fact always produce social order. In many cases differentiation of function is actually accompanied not by reintegration but by conflict. This state Durkheim calls 'the anomic division of labour'.

He goes on to argue from this that what is needed to overcome anomie and reintegrate our social order is the organization of men into occupational groups, whose professional ethics will not merely integrate each group within itself, but also relate it to the other groups in the larger society.

The ambiguities of Durkheim's position here together with his evasion of such problems as the economic basis of class conflict, have made it possible for him to be hailed as the prophet, both of guild socialism and Fascist corporativism. But he does have the merit of having formulated what must be the central question of modern social organization, namely, 'When the old social order based upon kinship and the tribe breaks down, what will be the elements from which the new social order will be built up?' In suggesting that the occupational group might be such an element, moreover, he offered an alternative to the individualistic and family-centred ideal which has played such a large part in English sociology.

In *Suicide* we again encounter the possibility of anomie. For along with the forms of suicide which are, as it were, inherent in forms of social order, there is another kind of suicide, 'anomic suicide' which follows from the collapse of social norms. And here Durkheim recognized that the collapse of social order is accompanied by actual personality disorganization. The individual who commits anomic suicide is sick and he is sick because his society has collapsed.

The recognition of this fact in *Suicide* forced Durkheim to explore new ground. For, despite his insistence to the last on the distinctiveness of social facts, he found it less and less possible to argue that such facts are solely and simply 'external' to the individual. That which is external is also a constitutive element of the social personality. It was to the problem of the intimacy of the relation between the social and the personality system that Durkheim addressed himself in his lectures on education and in his greatest work, *The Elementary Forms of Religious Life*.

This last is, like most of Durkheim's work, of complicated

origin. As a Jew, brought up in a Catholic educational tradition and ending up as an agnostic, Durkheim had undoubtedly pondered long on the question of the validity of religious belief and he wished to defend publicly the shocking thesis of the equation God = Society. But having devoted himself so long to the problem of the nature of social facts he was equally interested in discovering why social norms should have the morally constraining quality which they do. And finally, he was, as we have said, concerned with the relationship between the social system and the social personality of the individual.

What Durkheim purports to show under the first head is that on important social occasions among primitive people when the whole clan or tribe has gathered, an atmosphere is generated which is attributed to supernatural origins, but which, in fact, is simply due to the collective excitement of the crowd. This atmosphere carries over into the ordinary 'profane' life of the people. So that all the symbols of society's presence take on a sort of supernatural quality.

Now there is much in this, and anyone who has participated in great national rituals will recognize the similarity between our feelings about purely social and religious symbols. But it has often been asked whether this really proves Durkheim's point. Why do social symbols have the quality they do? Crowd excitement by itself seems a weak explanation. Would it not be equally true to say that the social has a divine origin as to say that the divine has a social origin?

What is much more important, however, is the effect of this argument on Durkheim's conception of the relation between society and the individual. The conception of social order as a mere expedient will not do. But nor will that of society as a purely external fact. As he says, society awakens in us not only 'the idea of a physical force to which we must give way of necessity' but 'that of a moral power such as religions adore'. Or again, 'When we obey somebody because of the moral authority which we recognize in him ...' we do so 'because a certain sort of physical energy is immanent in the idea we form of this person, which conquers our will and inclines it in the indicated direction'.

For anyone who accepts these formulations, the nature of sociology is transformed. It ceases to be simply a matter of head counting. What we have to do, if we accept them, is to study man always as a member of a moral community. The first question which we have to ask of any society which we are studying is 'What are the moral communities which compose it?' – a question which leads on the one hand to the understanding of the dynamics of the society and on the other hand to an understanding of the kind of man which the society produces.

Durkheim also made notable contributions to the special empirical fields which he investigated, particularly to the study of suicide and primitive religion. On the subject of suicide he discovered that the rate was higher among soldiers than civilians, higher among Protestants than Catholics and higher in times of both boom and slump than in times of economic stability. From these and other discoveries he was to draw his theoretical conclusions, but it is important to notice that the theoretical conclusions rested upon empirically tested and therefore retestable hypotheses. Thus even today when some of his conclusions may be rejected, his method is not and his hypotheses remain fruitful.

Similarly in his study of Australian religion Durkheim confronted the puzzling reported facts of the situation with a clear hypothesis. The fact that totemic species served both as the badge of the clan and as objects of religious reverence seemed to him explicable only in terms of the notion of the social power generated by the great clan festivals. Whatever doubts we may have today about this rather sweeping hypothesis it remains one of the most insightful hypotheses in the field.

Durkheim's influence both as a general theoretician and as a contributor to specific fields of empirical study has been lasting. Before his death in 1917 he had founded a school in France and for more than a generation the writers who contributed with him to *L'Année Sociologique* continued to apply his methods and to explore his hypotheses further. Georges Davy who succeeded him in his Sorbonne chair set out to trace the evolution of more advanced social forms from the simple totemic complex which Durkheim had studied in Australia. Mauss illuminated his studies of gift giving and of primitive religion with Durkheimian insights into the significance of particular customs for the maintenance of the social system as a whole. Halbwachs investigated further the hypotheses about the causes of suicide and was led from this to a careful analysis of the family as a social institution. Through these and other writers the Durkheimian tradition survived and remains perhaps the liveliest force in French sociology.

Outside France, Durkheim's ideas made headway very slowly. In England the administrative approach to social problems of the Fabians was no more hospitable to his emphasis on social wholes than had been Utilitarianism. It was only in the 1930s that the two great teachers of social anthropology, Malinowski and Radcliffe Brown, were to turn to his work for the theoretical foundations of the method which they called 'functionalism' (i.e. explaining strange social customs in terms of the contribution which they made to the maintenance of the social structure). But even they had little impact on the sociologists concerned with modern society.

In America, too, the first reaction to Durkheim's thought was a philistine one. He received little serious consideration before the mid 1930s when his ideas seem to have been taken up simultaneously in a number of doctoral theses. Since then, however, his influence has grown. At least two of America's greatest teachers, Merton and Parsons, acknowledge their debt to him and Parsons has made a brilliant analysis of the nature of the theoretical advance made in Durkheim's work. Moreover, the Americans, with their enormous financial resources, their scientistic ideology and their capacity for spelling out theoretical ideas in terms of statistical indices, have set about the systematic investigation of the correlates of varying degrees of social integration in terms of Durkheim's categories.

In all these ways, then, it can be seen that the work of Durkheim continues to play a large part in shaping the field of sociological investigation. Yet there are points in Durkheim's thought which remain extremely arguable and which may through overstatement be extremely misleading. Two deserve special mention.

One is his emphasis on social consensus and integration. It may well be true that the utilitarian conception of a society based solely on enlightened self interest is inadequate. But self-interest and class interest are none the less factors which must be taken into account in any interpretation of actual historical events. It is surely not sufficient to dismiss a society in which there is not a consensus but a conflict of norms as not really a society at all, but as a state of anomie. And if such a society is to be reintegrated we should say on the basis of which norms the integration is to take place.

The second point follows from the first. It is that, having said rightly that participation in a social and normative order is essential to human happiness, Durkheim seems to assume, wrongly, that any social and normative order, provided it is integrated, will guarantee this happiness. Here it is enlightening to compare Durkheim's philosophical standpoint with that of the early Marx. Marx too saw that, in his own words, 'the human essence is the ensemble of social relations.' But he also saw that while the system of social relations might liberate man and make him capable of 'self activity', they might also become a thing alien to man, confronting him and constraining him from outside. We may say that Marx failed to describe exactly the kind of pattern of social relations in which self activity would be possible. But he did at least see that there was a choice to be made, and that the mere fact of the involvement of man in an integrated system of social relations would not necessarily guarantee his self-fulfilment and happiness. It is his failure to see this which seems to make Durkheim, among the great sociologists, the arch apostle of the status quo.

Yet every sociologist's perspective is limited by the particular attitude which, for other reasons, he has towards social change. What we can say about Durkheim is that, given his standpoint, he was not afraid to pose the most important questions about the relation between the individual and society and that when he turned to empirical studies, they were never sterile and meaningless, but helped to advance our understanding of the human condition. When more sociologists approach their chosen empirical fields in this way, the subject will become far more fruitful than at present.

FURTHER READING

WORKS IN ENGLISH TRANSLATION

*The Division of Labour in Society*, tr. and introduced by G. Simpson (Macmillan, New York, 1947; Free Press, 1960).

*Education and Sociology*, tr. and introduced by S. D. Fox, foreword by Talcott Parsons (Free Press, 1956).

*The Elementary Forms of Religious Life*, tr. Joseph W. Swain (Free Press, 1948).

*Montesquieu and Rousseau: Forerunners of Sociology* (University of Michigan Press, 1960).

*Primitive Classification*, with M. Mauss, tr. R. Needham (Cohen and West, 1963).

*Professional Ethics and Civil Morals*, tr. C. Brookfield, preface by H. Nail Kubali, introduced by G. Davy (Routledge, 1957).

*The Rules of Sociological Method*, tr. A. S. Solovay and J. H. Mueller, ed. E. G. Catlin (Chicago, 1950; Free Press, 1962).

*Socialism and Saint-Simon*, tr. C. Sattler, ed. and introduced by A. W. Gouldner (Antioch, Yellow Springs, Ohio, 1958).

*Sociology and Philosophy*, tr. D. F. Pocock, introduced by J. G. Peristiany (Free Press, 1953).

*Suicide. A Study in Sociology*, tr. J. A. Spaulding and G. Simpson, ed. G. Simpson (Free Press, 1951; Routledge, 1952).

*Émile Durkheim. Selections from His Works*, introduced and commentaries by G. Simpson (Crowell, 1963).

'On the Relations of Sociology to the Social Sciences and to Philosophy'; and (with M. E. Fauconnet) 'Sociology and the Social Sciences' (*Sociological Papers*, vol. 1, Macmillan, 1904).

CRITICAL STUDIES

Jack Douglas: *The Social Meanings of Suicide* (Princeton, 1967).

Anthony Giddens: *Capitalism and Modern Social Theory* (Cambridge 1971).

Steven Lukes: *Émile Durkheim: His Life and Work* (Allen Lane, 1973; Peregrine, 1975).

Robert A. Nisbet: *Émile Durkheim* (Prentice-Hall, 1965).

Robert A. Nisbet: *The Sociology of Émile Durkheim* (Heinemann Educational, 1975).

Talcott Parsons: *The Structure of Social Action* (McGraw, 1937).

Kurt H. Wolff (ed.): *Émile Durkheim 1858–1917* (Ohio State University Press, 1960).

# GEORG SIMMEL

## (1858–1917)

### Anthony Giddens

GEORG SIMMEL was born in Berlin on 1 March 1858. His parents were of Jewish origin, but had been converted to Protestantism, and Simmel himself was baptized as a Protestant. When his father died, while Simmel was still a young boy, a wealthy friend of the family was appointed his guardian. The latter on his death left Simmel a sufficient sum of money for him to be able to live comfortably off the income.

Simmel received his higher education and spent the greater part of his academic career at the University of Berlin, which he entered as an undergraduate in 1876. At the university he first registered to study history, but subsequently changed to philosophy. He received his doctorate from Berlin in 1881, for a dissertation on Kant's philosophy of nature. Although Simmel was made *Privatdozent* (lecturer) in 1885, academic advancement came only very slowly for him. In 1900 he was promoted to the rank of *ausserordentlicher Professor* (honorary professor); but neither this position nor his previous one carried a regular salary, and for the whole period during which he taught at Berlin Simmel supported himself and his family mainly on the basis of the private income which had been bequeathed to him. In 1914, he finally obtained a full professorship, at Strasbourg. He died only four years later.

A number of factors combined to retard Simmel's academic career. One was his Jewish background; anti-Semitic elements were becoming increasingly powerful inside German universities, and particularly in Berlin, at the turn of the century. Another reason lay in the very encyclopedic character of Simmel's thought. Simmel lectured and wrote in an extraordinary variety of fields, including sociology, psychology, ethics, epistemology and aesthetics. His lectures were among the most popular in the university, and drew students from an even broader range of subjects than were embraced by his own work. In some quarters he thus acquired a reputation as an academic showman. Moreover, he frequently addressed himself to a popular audience, publishing widely in non-academic periodicals.

Simmel was a prolific writer. During his lifetime he published some 200 articles, and 22 books, although the latter included revisions of essays which had previously appeared in article form. Further works were published posthumously. His first works were primarily in the field of philosophy, as were his last. These include critical works on moral philosophy and the philosophy of history, and his culminating work in philosophy, *Lebensanschauung* (1918), as well as books on Kant, and Schopenhauer and Nietzsche. Unlike almost every other outstanding sociological theorist of the late nineteenth or early twentieth century, Simmel displayed little active interest in politics. He was, however, very much *au courant* with contemporary trends in literature and art, and wrote critical essays on prominent literary figures of his day. He also published biographical works on Goethe and Rembrandt, the latter of which was appropriately subtitled *An Essay in the Philosophy of Art*.

Simmel's sociology, like that of Max Weber, can be adequately understood only in terms of the broad intellectual traditions which both were deeply influenced by, but nevertheless reacted against. The two leading branches of German social thought during the nineteenth century were those of the philosophy of history (represented above all by Hegel and Marx), and the historical school of jurisprudence and political economy, with its central conception of the *Volksgeist*. There existed no positivist tradition of the sort which flourished in France even before Comte. Sociology emerged in Germany when scholars starting out from diverse standpoints in philosophy, economics and history found themselves increasingly compelled to recognize the relevance of social variables to problems in these various disciplines. But the resulting conception of sociology was quite different from that developed by the positivist writers in France and England. Simmel himself received his training mainly in philosophy, and his writings in both sociology and philosophy show how heavily he was influenced by Kant. Although Simmel was convinced that sociology could be founded as an autonomous discipline, he reacted against 'holistic' models of society, whether those of Hegel, or those of Comte and Spencer. In the conception of sociology advanced by Comte and Spencer, as Simmel saw it, society was endowed with an existence of its own over and above that of the individuals composing it. Society, it seemed to him, was thus conceived as a reality 'external' to individuals, and moulding every aspect of individual behaviour and consciousness. Simmel attempted to establish sociology on a new basis which would meet these objections.

It is difficult to separate Simmel's sociology from the broader ethical and epistemological problems in which he interested himself. The attempt to found a 'philosophy of life' was never far from the centre of Simmel's attention, even in his writings which are explicitly sociological in character. On the other hand, many of his essays concerned with subjects apparently lying outside sociology, those in the field of aesthetics, for example, are not without sociological significance: his writing is often rich with sociological insights and hypotheses. However, his most important contributions to sociology are contained in two major works, his *Philosophie des Geldes* (Philosophy of Money) (1900) and *Soziologie* (1908).

The earlier work must rank as one of the neglected classics of sociology. The title of the book is misleading. Simmel does deal at some length with problems which are mainly philosophical in character – such as the concept of 'freedom'; and with problems which perhaps strictly speaking belong primarily to economics – such as the theory of value: but much of the book is directly sociological in connotation. Marx had shown the development of a rudimentary money economy to be one necessary stage in the development of modern capitalism. Simmel argues that the transition to monetary exchange, replacing an economy based on exchange in kind, has much more far-reaching consequences than this. Money certainly facilitates trade and commerce. But Simmel attempts to show that the types of social relationships entailed by the predominance of a money economy are integrally connected with other dominant characteristics of the structure of modern society. Money is a particularly fluid form of property, subject to precise division, assessment and manipulation. The increasing use of money as a form of exchange promotes rational calculation in social relationships. In Simmel's view, the transition to a money economy is causally interrelated with the increasing 'rationality' characterizing modern society. The prevalence of a money economy and a 'rationalistic world outlook' are inextricably connected with one another. Money exchange tends increasingly in commerce to replace personal ties between employer and employee with impersonal, anonymous relationships. This process of rationalization, based on the possibility of abstract calculation, extends itself to all spheres of social life, but is manifest particularly in the development of the sciences, which depend upon precise measurement and quantification.

The basic proposition developed in the *Philosophie des Geldes* is that economic exchange can be studied as social interaction; and that the characteristics of an object (money) can only be defined in terms of its function within an interactive system. The notion of social interaction (*Wechselwirkung*: literally translated as 'reciprocal effect') occupies a focal position in Simmel's sociology. For Simmel, the 'social' exists when two or more individuals enter into interaction with one another: when we cannot explain the behaviour of one individual except as a response to the behaviour of another. Sociology studies *forms* of social interaction. The process whereby this is accomplished can be illuminated by analogy. A triangle can be drawn on paper, or made in metal or wood. The same geometrical properties pertain to the figure regardless of the substance in which it is constructed, in spite of the fact that, in one sense, there *is* nothing apart from the substance in which it is made. The geometrical properties of the triangle as a form cannot be deduced from a knowledge of the properties of the *content* or substance it is made of.

The separation of 'form' from 'content' here is an analytic one. The mathematician considers the triangle as an abstract form, and establishes generalizations about its properties which hold regardless of its content. An analogous procedure is involved when the sociologist studies forms of social interaction; as Simmel put it:

Any social phenomenon or process is composed of two elements which in reality are inseparable: on the one hand, an interest, a purpose, or a motive; on the other, a form or mode of interaction among individuals through which, or in the shape of which, that content attains social reality.

It is the task of psychology to isolate and study the content of behaviour (drives, desires, goals): sociology abstracts out and analyses forms of social interaction through which these are obtained or striven for. Any given item of social behaviour can be studied both in terms of its content, and in terms of its form. In the first case, we abstract out and analyse psychological needs and purposes (personality); in the second case, we regard the individual as a 'depersonalized' unit in a pattern of interaction. Forms of social interaction have properties of their own which cannot be deduced from studying the needs and purposes of individuals. The object of 'pure' or formal sociology is thus to isolate and study the conditions under which different forms of social interaction come into being, maintain themselves, and disappear.

Simmel conceived formal sociology as a discipline on an equal footing with, but separate from, the already developed social sciences like history or economics. He also envisaged, however, two other types of sociological endeavour closely related to the main discipline, formal sociology. Every science depends upon certain basic concepts and methods which cannot be analysed in terms of its own research – because this research is based on them. It is the task of 'philosophical' sociology to deal with these problems in relation to formal sociology, as well as with ethical problems arising from the findings of formal sociology. Secondly, Simmel recognized that sociological generalizations established in formal sociology would have to be used as part of the explanatory framework of the other social sciences. Economics necessarily involves the consideration of sociological principles, besides others, as does history.

In his *Soziologie*, Simmel attempts to illustrate the potential fruitfulness of formal sociology as he conceived it. He deliberately sets out to examine social phenomena which sociologists had previously ignored. Sociology, he points out, has been mainly concerned with those social forms which are mostly obviously 'super-individual', such as states, religious organizations or systems of stratification. But besides such relatively permanent and circumscribed forms of social organization, there are many more transient, directly interpersonal, relationships which can be studied sociologically. In *Soziologie* Simmel provides a socio-logical analysis of some of these apparently 'trivial' forms of social interaction – such as relationships in groups of two and three, leadership and subordination, the social significance of the strange, rivalry and secrecy. Relationships like these are con-stantly coming into being and being broken off: thus Simmel usually speaks of *Vergesellschaftung* (literally, 'societalization'; perhaps best translated as 'sociation'), rather than *Gesellschaft* (society). Sociation 'ranges all the way from the momentary getting together for a walk to the founding of a family, from relations maintained "until further notice" to membership in a state...'

It is possible here to give only a brief description of a few of the topics Simmel analyses; it is impossible to convey in so short a space the incisive character of Simmel's writing, his graphic use of analogy and his skill in using argument from paradox. *Soziologie* contains a long discussion of the significance of number in social life. Simmel points out, firstly, that as a group increases in size it has to develop mechanisms which a small group does not need. A very large number of people can be a unit only if there is a complex division of labour: as a social organization increases in size it has to develop defined mechanisms of communication and a hierarchical distribution of authority. But we can often establish more direct connexions between numbers and social life. For example, we can ask the question: why are aristocracies always so small? One reason, obviously, is that as an elite group an aristo-cracy would not rank as such unless it was exclusive, and set off against the mass of the population. But, according to Simmel, there is also an *absolute* limitation in number, beyond which the aristocratic form of the group cannot be maintained. A stable aristocracy must be 'surveyable' by every member of it: each family must be personally acquainted with every other. Relations by blood and marriage must be traceable throughout the whole group. Thus most aristocracies which have survived for long periods have had defined rules, such as unconditional primogeniture, leading to numerical limitation.

In another chapter of *Soziologie*, Simmel analyses conflict and antagonism. Conflict, he shows, can be regarded as a form of sociation in itself. Conflict is always conflict *with* someone: if two parties are indifferent to each other, there is no social relation between them. Sociologists like Comte and Spencer, Simmel points out, tended to see conflict as 'pathological'. This is based on that misconception that social order and social conflict are polar opposites. Simmel emphasizes that conflict is 'built in' to many social relationships, and may in fact be an essential element in their stability. There are few types of conflict which do not entail some defined and continuing relationship with the antagonistic party. Simmel goes on to hypothesize various ways in which conflict may function to maintain or even further integrate an existing form of social interaction. One of these, for example, is that groups tend to become more cohesive in the face of external conflict. This occurs in two ways: (1) through increased awareness of group unity, developed through the projection of common feelings of hostility against the outgroup; (2) through the development of a clearer articulation of authority in the group. Whatever the validity of the specific hypotheses that Simmel sets up, he undoubtedly substantiates his thesis: that the absence of conflict cannot necessarily be taken as an index of the stability of a social relationship.

Simmel's analysis of interaction in some ways strikingly parallels that later developed by G. H. Mead. Interaction, Simmel shows, presupposes *communication*. One of the first preliminaries on meeting someone, for example, is to be introduced: this is one indication of the 'mutual knowledge presupposed by every relationship'. We can investigate the clues people use to identify and categorize others, as well as the behaviour they employ to present a particular image of themselves to others. Simmel highlights this by examining cases of the deliberate distortion or restriction of communication: lying and secrecy. Lying, he indicates, is fundamentally an interactive phenomenon: what matters is not simply that the truth regarding a particular object is distorted, but that the person who is lied *to* is deceived about the private attitude of the liar. In the context of this discussion, Simmel constantly underlines interrelations between personality and social interaction. Self-esteem and self-identity, he shows, are intimately bound up with the individual's attachments to others. Personality is never a rigidly bounded system: the 'internal' organization of personality cannot be understood apart from the individual's 'external' relationships with others.

The very virtues of great breadth and variety in Simmel's work are at the same time the source of its limitations. Simmel's writings do not have the power and cumulative force of those of Durkheim, which attack fundamental theoretical problems through the careful marshalling of empirical data. Simmel's use of empirical method is cavalier: he quotes examples without documentation as if truth were self-evident – although this is bound up with what he repeatedly stressed as the provisional and exploratory character of his work. Simmel's terminology often tends to be loose to the point of carelessness.

Simmel's writings have perhaps been more influential in American than in German sociology. In Germany Simmel's work was rapidly overshadowed by that of Max Weber, in spite of the fact that some of Weber's central ideas were based directly on those developed earlier by Simmel. Several of Simmel's essays, however, appeared in translation in the *American Journal of Sociology* between 1893 and 1910. Park and Burgess's *Introduction to the Science of Society*, which exerted enormous influence for a considerable period in American sociology, borrowed heavily from Simmel. Many American sociologists were thus, perhaps unwittingly, indebted to Simmel.

### FURTHER READING

WORKS IN ENGLISH TRANSLATION

*Conflict and the Web of Group-Affiliations*, tr. K. H. Wolff and R. Bendix (Free Press, 1955).

*The Sociology of Georg Simmel*, tr. and introduced by K. H. Wolff (Free Press, 1950).

'The Sociology of Sociability', tr. Everett C. Hughes, *American Journal of Sociology*, vol. lv, no. 3, November 1949 (University of Chicago Press, 1949).

CRITICAL STUDIES

Theodore Abel: *Systematic Sociology in Germany* (Columbia University, Octagon Books, 1965).

Raymond C. F. Aron: *German Sociology* (Heinemann, 1957).

L. A. Coser: *The Functions of Social Conflict* (Routledge and Kegan Paul, 1956).

L. A. Coser (ed.): *Georg Simmel* (Prentice-Hall, 1965).

P. A. Lawrence: *Georg Simmel: Sociologist and European* (Nelson, 1976).

Nicholas J. Spykman: *The Social Theory of Georg Simmel* (Chicago University Press, 1925; Atherton, 1966).

Kurt H. Wolff (ed.): *Georg Simmel, 1858–1918* (Ohio State University Press, 1959).

# THE WEBBS
## BEATRICE (1858–1943)
## SIDNEY (1859–1947)

### Malcolm Warner

BRITISH sociology is to a large degree the offspring of a couple who by their writings and public activities made this country a very different place from what it was when they married in 1892. Beveridge points out that 'Britain today would have been very different from what it is if there had been no Sidney and Beatrice Webb. For more than 50 years, they were a ferment in society...'

Sidney Webb, described by Shaw as 'the ablest man in England', was born in 1859, the son of a Radical London accountant. Educated in Switzerland and Germany, he scaled the scholarship ladder to a post in the Colonial Office and later an LL.B. at London University. Like Henry Adams, his education never ceased.

Beatrice Potter was born of upper-middle-class parentage in 1858. She travelled extensively, accompanying her father on business trips for the railroad concerns from which the family derived its wealth. Yet 'there was no consciousness of superior riches' she has said, and the Potter family brought up their girls poor, but powerful. She acquired the habit of giving orders. However she was influenced by Spencer and Booth, the Great Depression and politics around her, enough for her social conscience to be aroused. She ended up investigating the social conditions of labour in the eighties; and, probing the Cooperatives, met the Fabian Webb. On the rebound from Joseph Chamberlain, she became engaged to Sidney in 1891. After her father's death in the following year, marriage quickly followed. Her private income gave them economic independence.

They worked as a partnership from the nineties until Beatrice died in 1943. They left, shaped by their hands in a significant way, the Fabian Society, the Labour Party, London education and government, the London School of Economics, the *New States-man*, a mountain of social and political studies and much social legislation via their work on several Royal Commissions. Sidney Webb was from 1922–28 an MP for Seaham, was a Cabinet Minister in two Labour Governments, and was created Baron Passfield in 1929. They are both buried in Westminster Abbey. 'We are all Fabians now' – it might be said – thanks to the Webbs. Both political parties believe in the 'inevitability of gradualness'; even if one party stresses the gradualness and the other, the inevitability. Via the Webbs it is commonly believed we have 'Social Science' and the Welfare State.

How did this all come about? To separate the means and the ends is not easy. Thought and action, method and manipulation are united. However, the work of the Webbs can be divided into two slices. One, organizational; the other, intellectual. The former depended very much on the latter. Although empirical in method in both activities, they had a firm notion of what they were about. This idea was collectivism – a socialist creature in Fabian cloth-ing: or so it seemed.

They were more than intellectuals of a mere scribbling kind. They institutionalized their thoughts. For example, the positivistic idea of the expert, well-equipped with facts to deal with social reform, became the LSE (1895). The idea of the national minimum became the Welfare State in so far as Britain eventually turned into the post-1945 legislation the suggestions they made in the Minority Report (of the Royal Commission on the Poor Law) published in 1909. Even if Lloyd George dished them by his Act of 1911, they managed to organize a campaign against the Poor Law. If the political mood favoured *contributory* social insurance and they were beaten, at least on that immediate issue, the Poor Law finally went in 1928.

They helped to organize the Fabian Society. Sidney found it as a set of cranks known as the Fellowship of the New Life in the early 1880s. He steered it past Marxism with the help of Shaw and by 1900 it was a well-organized pressure group largely due to his efforts. Its tracts laid vast arrays of facts before public opinion. It presented the case for socialism in language everybody could understand. There was method in his 'permeating' zeal which wanted to concentrate on measures rather than men (largely because the Liberals were not collectivist enough for his taste), and work through all parties. More and more of the intellectual middle class were persuaded that the 'inevitability of gradualness' was the right way to alleviate the sad condition of the people. But permeation as a policy ended in 1906. And eventually they moved to the left and set the tone of the Labour Party programme in 1918, with the virtual adoption of Sidney's *Labour, and the New Social Order.*

They also furthered their social reformist ends by being instrumental (with Shaw) in setting up the *New Statesman* in 1913. It was originally intended to be more like the present *New Society*, with a central interest in analysing social and political developments in a 'scientific' way, rather than fulfilling the polemical and literary role it so excellently performs today.

The educational system of this country, too, owes a good deal to the ideas and efforts of Sidney Webb. His work in organizing the reform of London local government, while chairman of many of its committees in the nineties, was outstanding. He set up the 'scholarship ladder', established technical education on a sound footing and collaborated with Balfour and Morant to produce the Education Act of 1902. This institutionalized the idea of secondary education for those with ability but not the means to pay, which the Butler Act of 1944 was to extend.

Their intellectual achievements were extravagant. Overnight they became the authorities on trade unions and cooperatives. They produced in the early nineties a torrent of facts. *The History of Trade Unionism* (1894), *Industrial Democracy* (1897), and a second edition of Beatrice Webb's *The Cooperative Movement in Great Britain*, as well as many additions in later years to the study of industrial relations. Their view of unions can be now considered a little old fashioned, in so far as they did not see unions as dynamic forces in a pluralist society. The Webbs never believed that conflict was a good thing. They wanted the unions to become respectable and to be absorbed into the body of society. Sidney opposed the repeal of the Taff Vale judgement of 1901 making unions liable for damages or losses arising out of industrial disputes. They later approved of the state domination of trade unions under Stalin. Yet their work still stands, in spite of criticism, as the standard reading on the subject. They above all had the good sense to point out that there were vocational bodies other than trade unions. They were sure the final end of society was the citizen, as consumer and producer.

Another facet of their intellectual work dealt with local government. Here was the same theory at work. The facts were again sacred. All had to be recorded – an anatomy of the body social had to be constructed. It was the application of the German 'scientific' historical school of writing to the study of society, past and present. Their ten volumes on English Local Government, written between 1906 and 1929, remain indispensable and have recently been republished.

In economics, they were doing work similar to that which Ely and Commons of the Wisconsin School were doing in America, and which Barbara Wootton has continued to do, for example in *The Social Foundations of Wage Policy*. De Tocqueville complained earlier last century to Nassau Senior that the question of wages could not be discussed without looking at the institutional background. The Webbs were to rectify this and to complement Marshall's economics by their writings on trade unions. They developed the concept of 'collective bargaining'. Generally their mentor was Jevons, not Marx. They became the exponents of the idea of 'national efficiency' and the 'economy of high wages' which Sidney had seen on his visit to America in 1888. Mrs Webb laid down her position in the appendix ('The Nature of Economic Science') at the end of her autobiography *My Apprenticeship*. There, she gave priority to the analysis of social institutions as the key to understanding economic processes.

Their dislike of abstract economics, however, kept them from fully assimilating and promoting Keynes's new ideas, although they were in close contact with him in the twenties. Keynes, however, according to Professor Robson, is supposed to have joked at a party given for Soviet Ambassador Solnikoff in the thirties, that he deserved little credit for the new economics and that Sidney Webb had thought up the possibility of contra-cyclical policies in the Minority Report in 1909. Sidney, however, voted for the cuts in unemployment relief in the 1931 crisis. When it came to political action, their economics were as orthodox as Snowden's.

They hammered their socialism home. Sidney started with *Socialism in England* (1890) but their main work was *A Constitution for the Socialist Commonwealth of Britain* (1920), which wanted one house of parliament to discuss political matters and, more important, the other to discuss social and economic questions.

Their other critique of society was *The Decay of Capitalist Civilization* (1923) which, on rereading, seems to show the start of the Marxist leanings which ended them up in their pro-Stalinist *Soviet Communism* (1935) phase. But Beatrice's early move towards socialism was basically a moral one. As she had exclaimed in 1884, 'My aim in life is to make life pleasanter for this great majority: I do not care if it becomes in the process less pleasant for the well-to-do minority.' She had to fall back on the altruistic experts because she thought (at least in 1900) that 'the middle class are materialistic, and the working class stupid, and in large sections, sottish, with no interest except in racing odds. . . .'

The Webbs have described their technique of social investigation in *Methods of Social Study* (1932). It is in the English empirical tradition: Simon, Booth (whom Mrs Webb had assisted, before her marriage, in his surveys), Rowntree, are in the same genre as the Webbs.

Beveridge reckons they wrote, in all, over 5,000,000 words in terms of their major work. Their minor writings, correspondence and diaries must give a similar total. Perhaps it was because of the influence of German scholarship or maybe it was because they escaped going to Oxbridge (actually Sidney had a Whewell Research Scholarship in Law at Trinity but turned it down because the Colonial Office would not give him leave of absence). Still it may have been a good thing that they were more like continental intellectuals from the point of view of their insistence on methodology and intellectual application.

Why did they produce so much detail? To read the ten volumes on local government is many weeks' work. Was it the urge to add to scholarship? Or did they want to create *authority* for their reformist advice? No one knows. The Webbs were obsessive and compulsive. They believed that the collection of facts via the sheer weight of historical evidence and contemporary statistics could overwhelm the opposition to reform and persuade it that something should be done. The Minority Report (1909) is a classic example of this approach. They went even further and suggested in a memorandum that there should be a permanent Royal Commission Office and staff – another attempt to institutionalize an idea.

Yet theirs was not a radical approach. The Webbs thought of a reform and then invented a tradition for it, for example, as they did with labour exchanges. In his contribution to the *Fabian Essay* (1889), the inevitability based on the precedents of collectivism justifies its extension. Their output was seen as an exercise in sociology and political science based not on *a priori* theory, but on description and analysis of institutions. And, as with all institutionalists, there was a conservative streak somewhere. They ended up authoritarian and pro-Stalinist. Bureaucratic collectivism was only benevolent despotism writ large. As Leonard Woolf has noted 'they mistrusted ideals and still more the idealists'. This is a perceptive observation, and is corroborated by Bertrand Russell who thought both of them fundamentally undemocratic 'and regarded the function of a statesman to bamboozle or terrorize the populace'.

By far the best work on the Webbs is by Beatrice. Her autobiography *My Apprenticeship* (1926) and *Our Partnership* (1948) are indispensable historical documents as well as being of literary importance. This is not to denigrate those who have written at length about them and the Fabians. But it seems true that most observers approach the subject from what might be called a *sinistra-centric* point of view. Most of them are too deeply committed to the same philosophy as the Webbs to give a sound historical assessment. They achieved much, but their success must be qualified. They did not completely mould the Labour Party. There were many, many others involved. Nor did they *found* the Welfare State. More credit is due to the Rowntree/Beveridge/Lloyd George connexion. Yet they were indispensable in its development.

Together they were a formidable and complementary pair. Beatrice Webb went a long way towards supplementing Sidney's stronger socialist streak with her social methodology. She followed Booth in trying 'to combine the qualitative with the quantitative examination of social statistics'. And as she concludes in *Methods of Social Study*, 'It is out of the vast array of social institutions of the fourth class – those deliberately devised with a view to increasing social efficiency – that an applied science of sociology might be expected to be (and indubitably is being) constructed.'

Their 'scientific' method, however, was partly systematized impressionism. This was due to their emphasis on the interview, as well as the document and personal observation. But it was an advance on the high speculation of Spencer and the extensive quantification of Booth, even Rowntree. It gave their work a certain depth others lacked: the Webb touch. What they say on the interview is still good advice to the young social researcher:

> The expert interviewer, like the bedside physician, agrees straight away with all the assumptions and generalizations of his patient, and uses his detective skill to sift, by tactful cross-examination of the grains of fact from the bushels of sentiment, self-interest or theory. Hence, though it is of the utmost importance to make friends with the head of any organization, we have generally got much more actual information from his subordinates who are personally occupied with the facts in detail. But in no case can any interview be taken as conclusive evidence, even in matters of fact. . . . It must never be forgotten that every man is biased by his creed or his self-interest, his class or his views on what is socially expedient. If the investigator fails to detect this bias, it may be assumed that it coincides with his own! Consequently the fullest advantage of the interview can be obtained only at the later stages of an enquiry, when the student has so far progressed in his analysis that he knows exactly what to look for.

Sociology in this country may be seen as a religion of facts. To a very large extent this is due to the work of the Webbs. But, according to some, they were unscientific in the sense that they did not prepare themselves to see a hypothesis refuted by the facts. Yet paradoxically the role of the hypothesis in the Webbs was not large enough. This was a strong intellectual limitation. Of course they had a point of view. This made them great as reformers, less so as sociologists.

The British empirical school, such as the Webbs, never had much time for the 'grand theory' of the continental masters. This had led to much sound work, but a distrust of ideas. Moreover, the Webbs present ambiguities of theory as well as of action: each acting on the other. Sometimes they are pluralists, sometimes elitists. While abjuring power, they seemed to be pursuing it: another paradox. Perhaps the Webbs really had no clearly defined theory of society.

Their theory of permeation seems to posit a power elite. Their socialism seems to envisage a new class of experts. Yet they devoted their lives to the study of voluntary associations and local government. Even if they did not always view the paternal state as the main organ of progress, it gradually in fact became dominant in their approach. This elitist streak is not divorced from their method. The Tories have often claimed the monopoly of British empiricism. They have not failed to absorb the contribution of the Webbs. This very gifted couple were more English and conservative than they seemed. In the end, duty triumphed over rights, empirical elitism over rationalistic pluralism.

Yet, however great their achievements, the Webbs were both very modest about their abilities. According to her own story, it was environment rather than a natural bent that made Beatrice a social scientist:

> I had neither aptitude nor liking for much of the technique of sociology; some would say for the vital parts of it. I had, for instance, no gifts for that rapid reading and judgement of original documents, which is indispensable to the historian; though by sheer persistency and long practice I acquired this faculty. And whilst I could plan out an admirable system of note-taking, the actual execution of the plan was, owing to an inveterate tendency to paraphrase extracts I intended to copy, not to mention an irredeemably illegible handwriting, a wearisome irritation to me. As for the use of figures, whether mathematical or statistical, I might as well have attempted to turn water into wine!

Sidney told little of himself, but, in terms of achievement, is probably, I suspect, the more important member of the Webb partnership. It was the task of his friends to outline the extraordinary talents he possessed. Shaw left several pithy descriptions and anecdotes. Even when Webb was barely twenty, G.B.S. saw his sheer ability:

> He knew all about the subject of the debate; knew more than the lecturer; knew more than anybody present; had read everything that had ever been written on the subject; and remembered all the facts that bore upon it. He used notes, read them, ticked them off one by one and threw them away, and finished with a coolness and clearness that to me, in my then trembling state, seemed miraculous.

Webb had a fantastic memory for detail. Shaw used to tell of a trip to a French post office. Sidney wanted to send home a bunch of official papers for what he insisted was a halfpenny rate. The clerk said he could not. Webb cited the French postal regulations, volume x, page x, paragraph x. A superior was consulted. Webb was absolutely right. After that Shaw boasted they could have sent home all their laundry for that halfpenny.

Today it is rather fashionable to criticize them, not merely as thinkers and public figures, but also as people. In the face of this, therefore, it is hoped that their intellectual achievements have been adequately praised above, and their organizational work reasonably evaluated. Even more necessary it seems a counter-balance to the personal criticism ought to appear as a coda. Again Shaw, Sidney's best friend, provides an illuminating tribute to his humanity. Once, when travelling in Holland, they sat in a train near a convict being moved from one town to the next. The man was chained, guarded and generally treated as a pariah. As he was led out, the man's attitude changed from shame to self-respect. Why had this transformation taken place? Earlier, Webb and Shaw had been eating marzipan. They had finished most of it, but Sidney had stuffed the remaining lump into the hand of the prisoner!

In spite of all the gossip to the contrary – the spartan hospitality, Beatrice's acidic intellectual honesty and the rest – it is surely inconceivable that the Webbs should have devoted their lives to the cause of social reform if they had been without humanitarian inspiration in the first place. As for their work specifically as social scientists, it must not be thought that they were dry, distant academics. They were always *involved*. Neither should a pseudo-Freudian explanation be accepted. They did not devote themselves to the cause of making Britain a better place to live in for the many, simply in order to satisfy their guilt feelings about their place in late Victorian society.

Finally, if the social philosophy of the Webbs has to be summed up, 'social service plus science' might be the answer. As they wrote in 1920:

There is good ground for expecting discovery in physical science to go forward by leaps and bounds, in a way that may presently transform all our dealing with forms of force and kinds of substance. But what is no less needed than this greater knowledge of things is greater knowledge of men: of the conditions of the successful workings of social institutions. That on which the world today most needs light is how to render more effective every form of social organization: how to make more socially fertile the relationships between men. . . .

Their sociology did not merely try to describe the world, but to change it.

### FURTHER READING

WORKS

Beatrice Webb: *My Apprenticeship* (Longmans Green, 1926).

Beatrice Webb: *Our Partnership* (Longmans Green, 1948).

Sidney and Beatrice Webb: *Industrial Democracy* (Longmans, 1897).

Sidney and Beatrice Webb: *History of Trade Unionism* (Longmans, 1894).

Sidney and Beatrice Webb: *Methods of Social Study* (Kelley, 1932).

Sidney and Beatrice Webb: *Soviet Communism: A New Civilisation?* (Longmans Green, 1935).

CRITICAL STUDIES

William H. Beveridge: *Power and Influence* (Hodder and Stoughton, 1953).

Margaret Cole: *Beatrice Webb* (Longmans, 1945).

Margaret Cole (ed.): *The Webbs and their Work* (Muller, 1949).

Margaret Cole: 'The Webbs and Social Theory' (*British Journal of Sociology*, vol. 12, 1961, pages 93–105).

Mary A. Hamilton: *Sidney and Beatrice Webb. A Study in contemporary biography* (Sampson Low, 1933).

Norman Mackenzie: 'A New View of the Webb Partnership', *Times Higher Educational Supplement*, 19 May 1978, pages 9–10.

Norman and Jean Mackenzie: *The First Fabians* (Weidenfeld and Nicolson, 1977).

Kitty Muggeridge and Ruth Adam: *Beatrice Webb* (Secker and Warburg, 1967).

Bertrand Russell: *Portraits from Memory, and other essays* (Allen and Unwin, 1956).

T. S. Simey: 'The Contribution of Sidney and Beatrice Webb to Sociology' (*British Journal of Sociology*, vol. 12, 1961, pages 106–123).

H. G. Wells: *The New Machiavelli* (John Lane, 1911; Penguin, 1946).

# G. H. MEAD
## (*1863–1931*)

### Alan Ryan

I T is the fate of all founding fathers to be more often referred to than read. G. H. Mead has, perhaps, suffered such a fate in a more extreme form than most. Almost any introduction to sociology makes its obligatory nod in his direction; no discussion of the concept of a social role would be complete, if it lacked an acknowledgment of Mead's distinction between the 'I' and the 'Me'; or failed to mention his notion of 'the generalized other'; or omitted all reference to the importance of our ability to 'take the standpoint of the other'.

But there is something slightly odd about these acknow-ledgments. They express a general conceptual debt, not the recognition of a body of substantial empirical truth. To many people they must appear to be nothing more than the recital of truisms. Who ever doubted that the concept of a role was central to sociological theory? Who ever denied that self-conscious human beings can talk about what 'I *did*' and what happened '*to me*'?

Mead was by profession a philosopher, not a sociologist, for all that it is sociologists rather than philosophers who take an interest in him now. He didn't do any empirical work of his own, and his legacy is certainly conceptual. It is equally true that many of his ideas have become what you might call the common-sense of sociology. But they were not the commonsense either of those of his predecessors who tried to reduce sociology to zoo-logy, and so neglected just what was peculiar about human societies; or of those of his predecessors who regarded society as a contractual scheme set up by fully-fledged rational adults in some unhistorical state of nature.

Mead did not bring about this shift in what sociologists take for granted as the subject matter of their science single-handed. He was part of a movement of thought, which in some respects was very distinctively American, and which in others was simply typical of turn-of-the-century thinking.

He was, in an important sense, an *exemplary* figure in the history of sociology. He belonged to the pragmatist movement in philosophy and to the 'Chicago school' in sociology, and was thus a founder member of what was most American in social theory. He was not in the same philosophical league as Pierce and William James (less acute than the one, more inhibited than the other), and his admiration for John Dewey would always have led him to play second fiddle in the movement for democratic education which Dewey led. But to the usual pragmatist emphasis on the active and creative aspects of knowledge, Mead brought a concern for the social conditions and social origins of learning and understanding, which turned pragmatism in a direction which sociologists could find fruitful.

There is surprisingly little direct evidence of his impact on the sociologists who were his contemporaries at Chicago, but there is no doubt that he acquired a concern with socialisation in the early 1890s, and took that concern from Michigan to Chicago, when he began to teach there in 1894. W. I. Thomas was a pupil at Chicago; his notion of 'the definition of the situation' could as easily have been Mead's, and there was obviously some mutual influence there. Mead would also have been an unlikely Chicagoan as well as an unlikely pragmatist if he had not shared the interest of Small, Park and Znaniecki in how the social mores of European migrants affected their adaptation to the environment of this new city.

George Herbert Mead was born in February 1863 at South Hadley, Massachusetts, and died in April 1931 in Chicago. His career was, in a strange way, an exemplary one. His father was a Congregationalist minister, and his mother a decidedly distinguished lady who was for some years president of Mount Holyoke College. Highminded puritanism was a diet which Mead did not much like. In later years, he said that it had taken him his second twenty years of life to unlearn the falsehoods taught him during the first twenty. From the age of sixteen he studied literature and philosophy at Oberlin, and there got his first glimpse of intellectual freedom from a friend, Henry Castle, whose sister he was later to marry.

Castle was already a good deal further emancipated from Nonconformism than Mead, and encouraged him in his conviction that the supernatural elements in religion were literally false. But like Durkheim and most other sociologists of the age, Mead was always preoccupied thereafter by how society could preserve sufficient moral unity to restrain the anti-social impulses of its members and to give their lives some more than merely selfish meaning, without relying on an exploded faith. And like Durkheim, he thought that the feelings which religion satisfied were important ones, and that the way in which religion satisfied them owed a lot to our desire to belong to an idealized community in which our desires and society's norms would be at one with each other.

Mead graduated in 1883. He had a variety of jobs in the next four years; an early venture into teaching miscarried when he used his power to dismiss unruly or ineducable pupils so enthusiastically that after four months he was sacked for lack of students. Later, he and Henry Castle seem to have been rather more successful. He also worked as a railroad surveyor. His son's suggestion that this led to a lifelong interest in the impact of technology on science looks like a romantic afterthought, although it certainly was something of an *idée fixe* with Mead that what was distinctive about the post-Renaissance world was the growth of scientific knowledge. No pure philosophy that was not a philosophy of science was worth the paper it was written on, and no philosophy of history that placed the rise of science anywhere but in the forefront was remotely adequate. Though he greatly admired the evolutionary aspects of the philosophy of Hegel, for instance, he nevertheless thought that his grasp of the achievements and nature of science was pathetically inadequate.

Yet it was through Hegelianism that he made his way to the views for which he is remembered. In 1887 he went back to school to Harvard. His studies were still mainly literary and philosophical. Though William James was the obvious figure to whom he ought to have become attached, it did not happen. And this is all the odder, not merely because Mead did become a pragmatist in due course, and not merely because James's concern with the elusiveness of the self and its differences in different settings reflected Mead's later interests so exactly, but also because Mead lived in James's house and acted as tutor to James's children.

It was Josiah Royce who held Mead's interest. Mead later said that he found in Royce's teaching 'clear ideas and luminous vistas, subtle athleticism of thought and inexhaustible universe of explication and illustration'. James's characterization of Hegelianism as offering a 'moral holiday' may also have had much to do with it. The Hegelian promise was that all would in some fashion come right with the world, and that it wasn't our fault if the world seemed from time to time to be imperfect. At any rate, Mead himself wrote of his relief at finding that 'philosophy was no longer the handmaid of theology and the textbook for a formal logic and a puritan ethics'.

His extended apprenticeship next took in German and psychology at the University of Berlin. He never finished this PhD. Indeed, he was never able in his life to write a finished piece of work longer than an article, and the books by which he is best known mostly derive from transcripts of his lectures, which devoted students had the wit to make when it became clear that he never would get out the books he hoped.

Even in Germany, his studies were as much philosophical as psychological, and he worked under Dilthey and Paulsen as well as with Ebbinghaus. Although the psychology of Wundt, with its emphasis on gesture and communication might have served as the starting point for Mead's own work, it seems that it was only on his return to America that Mead really became a social psychologist as well as a philosopher.

In 1891, Mead returned from Germany to start work as an instructor in philosophy at the University of Michigan. And it was here that he came under the influence of John Dewey. In 1894 Dewey was appointed to the chairmanship of the combined departments of philosophy, psychology and pedagogy at Chicago, and took Mead with him.

It was an ideal setting for Mead. The absence of departmental barriers suited him perfectly, and the University of Chicago was an extraordinary and stimulating place to be. The university was founded with $5 million of John D. Rockefeller's money (between 1892 and 1910 his benefactions extended to $35 million altogether) and it was founded on the grand scale by wholesale piratical raids on the departments of older universities. The town, too, which had taken off with a rush after the fire of 1871 grew in the same self-confident and expansive frame of mind. It is sometimes said that pragmatism was the ideology of the reformist stage of American capitalism. Chicago was a good place to breathe that atmosphere.

As I noted earlier, Mead's published work consisted during his own lifetime of a string of articles and reviews. But he was also known as a considerable conversationalist, and the lectures which eventually got published as *Mind, Self and Society, Movements of Thought in the Nineteenth Century, The Philosophy of the Act* and *The Philosophy of the Present* are extremely readable. *Mind, Self and Society* is the best-known of them, and quite rightly. It sets out Mead's views on social psychology as they developed through a period of a quarter of a century. Mead says of the doctrines he develops that they are an account of social psychology 'from the standpoint of the social behaviourist'. Perhaps the first step towards understanding the peculiarities of Mead's analysis is to understand what that means.

One of Mead's pupils at Chicago was J. B. Watson, who founded the behaviourist school of psychology. Watson only began to publish his views after he had left Chicago, but he and Mead were very good friends while he was there. Watson remarked somewhat wrily that he'd never understood what on earth Dewey and Mead were on about in their lectures, but that Mead was a splendid man to wander round the animal lab with.

Mead meant his kind of behaviourism to be clearly distinguished from that of Watson. He did not think that linguistic behaviour, for example, was to be understood either as a conditioned reflex (Watson's view) nor in terms of the minute muscular reactions which might or might not accompany our thinking of what to say. Mead seems to have had no particular interest in Watson's reductionist programme, whereby all appeals to 'consciousness' or to terms implying consciousness – such as 'intending' or 'meaning' – were to be dispensed with. The sense in which Mead was a behaviourist lay in his claim that the way to understand language and analogous forms of communication was in terms of the behaviour which they stimulated.

To cut a lot of corners, one might summarize Mead's behaviourism by saying that he analyzed our understanding of a word or a gesture in terms of our having the disposition to respond appropriately. If I see someone take off his hat to me, I can be said to know what the gesture means, if I have the disposition to (say) nod or remove my own hat, or, as Mead recognizes, if I decide to cut him dead and keep my hat firmly on my head as I walk past with eyes averted. The behaviourism is social in that Mead thought that the starting point for explaining human communication lay in our membership of a social group within which a gesture had a meaning, not in the supposedly innate ability of human beings to use *language*. He thought that the characteristic vice of previous writers had been to see society as a construction of individual selves, fully equipped with the human ability to speak, to monitor their own behaviour and so on. Social behaviourism maintained that having an individual self was the result of social processes rather than a presupposition of them.

The psychological unit of inquiry, claimed Mead, was the act. That is, the basic unit is a completed action, not the components of such an action. This position was extremely apposite for a pragmatist, for the pragmatist view of the world emphasized that the world was meaningful only because it contained organisms with a point of view to give it meaning. The most famous exposition of the view was James's claim that eggs were 'things-not-to-be-too-much-sat-on' to the creatures that laid them.

Mead saw all organisms as ready to respond to stimuli in the outside world in a fashion which was *appropriate*, rather than merely random. Things were picked out from a background in terms of their ability to satisfy the needs of the organism. This was Mead's integrating principle, which covered the behaviour of simple organisms at one end of the evolutionary scale, and the activities of the research scientist at the other.

It provided a principle of what can be termed 'objective relativism' – the world is taken for granted as an objective entity existing in its own right, but there are any number of accounts of it to be given, according to the standpoint of those who give them. A faintly scandalous implication which Mead thought he saw in this doctrine was that the past exists only in the present – or, more soberly, that history is always an account of the past from some present (and therefore itself transitory) perspective.

The crucial steps in Mead's account of the self's place in society can be simply spelled out. Though language is built up from the animal's gestures, which served it to arouse appropriate responses in fellow animals, human language operates at a level of greater university than that. For words and other symbols to have meanings, they have to be understood from no particular standpoint – that is, they have to be seen from the viewpoint of 'the generalized other', or society at large. The individual human being learns through social interaction that he wears an appearance to others, just as they wear an appearance to him; and he learns to take account of this double aspect of social relationships.

Two nice touches in Mead's account of this are worth noticing. The first is his emphasis on the role of play in education. He distinguished quite neatly between *play* and *games*; a child who plays at hospitals on his own will play the various roles of doctor, patient or nurse in succession – as if the social drama is a matter of learning its cast list. But later, when he takes part in games, the child plays one role for the duration of the game, integrating his performance with that of the other actors. The moral, of course, which is drawn by Mead, is that this integration is only possible because at this stage the child can take on the role of the generalized other, too.

The second is his famous distinction between the 'I' and the 'Me'. In essence, the distinction is not between two parts of the personality so much as between two parts of the process of interaction. The 'Me', as its grammatical role suggests, is the object of other people's perceptions, and, indeed, the object of the 'I's perceptions. The 'I' is an elusive creature, something like Kant's transcendental ego, but open to empirical investigation as that was not. Crucially, the I introduces freedom into the world. I feel insulted, and the feeling is a state of the Me. But the reflective I might commit the Me to turning the other cheek *or* raising the other fist.

Mead regarded sociological determinism as almost a joke in view of the existence of the I. Having grown up in an environment in which any concern for the organic and biological basis of society was thought to commit the theorist to a determinist philosophy of history, Mead carefully denied that science's search for uniform laws in nature posed any threat to human freedom. Rather, it offered more human control of the world, and therefore made the range of freedom so much greater.

Pragmatism equipped Mead with an ethical theory which straddled the gap between utilitarianism and Hegelianism. Mead denied that our impulses were satisfied for the sake of pleasure, as the utilitarians had held. For him, the sequence – impulse, perception, manipulation, consummation – was self-explanatory. But actions were rational insofar as they allowed the satisfaction of impulse on the largest scale; irrational insofar as the satisfaction of one impulse blocked that of another. A genuinely ethical standard, as opposed to the standard of individual prudence, had however to be universal, as Kant and Hegel had held. Just as we have to adopt the standpoint of the generalized other to share a society's understanding of the meanings of its sentences and gestures, so we must adopt the desires of the generalized other to share the moral ambitions of the society. Religion expresses this attachment of individuals to the demands of society in an ideal form.

The importance of Mead's work is a matter of debate. In some ways, it is hard to dispute the view that what he succeeded in doing was creating a new 'common sense' for sociologists; and this is an achievement which in the nature of the case looks more impressive against the background of rigid behaviourism or rigid biological determinism than it does to a later generation. His analysis of language and of the nature of symbols is unattractive to philosophers today. It is clear, for example, that analysing meaning in terms of our disposition to respond in certain ways is to put the cart before the horse. It is only if I already understand the *meaning* of the gesture of raising the hat that I can be disposed to react to the gesture, either politely or impolitely. This is, however, not to deny that Mead's analysis offers the beginnings of an account of *learning* the meaning of a gesture, and, indeed, in ways reminiscent of the Wittgenstein of *Philosophical Investigations*.

Again, much understanding simply defies dispositional analysis in anything but question-begging terms. What disposition explains my knowing that the battle of Actium was fought in 32 BC other than the disposition to say '31 BC' if asked the date of the battle? Sociologists are more sceptical than was Mead about the existence of *a* or *the* generalized other. The meaning of behaviour varies from one subculture to another in ways which Mead's analysis hardly takes account of – though, of course, Mead's framework for analysis tends to push us in the direction of asking the appropriate questions.

Mead is likely to seem naive to readers of Erving Goffman or the ethnomethodologists. His distinction between the I and the Me certainly allows room for reflection and manipulation in our behaviour. But social life appears altogether less of a patched-up affair in Mead than in his successors. And the politically sceptical will think that Mead leaves out too much of the power that lies behind the imposition of meanings on the world. The notion that society *makes* events and behaviour wear a given meaning is one way in to a theory of ideology. But Mead doesn't begin to wonder whether there are systematic biases behind those meanings.

Still, there is a sense in which all such criticisms are also a form of praise. They all amount to saying that Mead's approach to sociology ought to have been pressed harder or along slightly different lines. It is his own weapons which have been turned against him. To be the victim of one's own success in this fashion is rather more of an achievement than to have constructed some elaborate system of ideas which, fifty years later, lies decaying in a corner, an object of merely antiquarian curiosity.

## FURTHER READING

WORKS

*George Herbert Mead on Social Psychology*, ed. A. Strauss (University of Chicago Press, 1956).

*Mind, Self and Society*, ed. C. W. Morris (University of Chicago Press, 1934).

*The Philosophy of the Act* (University of Chicago Press, 1938).

CRITICAL STUDIES

P. L. Berger and T. Luckman: *The Social Construction of Reality* (1966; Allen Lane, 1967; Penguin, 1971).

W. R. Corti (ed.): *The Philosophy of George Herbert Mead* (Winterthur: Amriswiler Bücherei, 1973).

Fred H. Mathews: *The Quest for an American Sociology* (McGill, 1977).

B. M. N. Meltzer, J. W. Petras and L. T. Reynolds: *Symbolic Interactionism* (Routledge and Kegan Paul, 1975).

Israel Scheffler: *Four Pragmatists* (Routledge and Kegan Paul, 1974).

# L. T. HOBHOUSE
## (*1864–1929*)

### Morris Ginsberg

LEONARD TRELAWNY HOBHOUSE was born on 8 September 1864 at St Ives, Cornwall. In 1883 he entered Corpus Christi, Oxford, with a classical scholarship and there he had a career of great distinction. He was appointed Assistant Tutor in 1890 and elected a Fellow in 1894. His teaching work was mainly in philosophy, but already in these early years he formed a fairly clear idea of the principal trends which his inquiries were to take and which involved an empirical study of the evolution of mind in the animal and human worlds. He acquired an ever-widening grasp of social realities by wide historical and comparative studies and by active participation in the social movements of his time – the extension of trade unionism among unskilled workers and agricultural labourers, the economic education of co-operators and the development of Toynbee Hall and other university settlements.

The prevailing philosophic thought in Oxford, dominated by the British Idealists, as well as its political tone, proved uncongenial to Hobhouse and in 1897 he decided to throw himself into active journalism and political movements. He was persuaded by C. P. Scott to join the staff of the *Manchester Guardian* and he lived in Manchester until 1902. The great value of Hobhouse's contributions to the *Manchester Guardian*, their acuteness, grasp and power, has been warmly attested by its then editor, C. P. Scott. Their range is very wide, covering the areas of domestic and foreign and colonial policy. Thus we find numerous articles dealing with the new social issues of trade unionism and governmental control of industry, but also with China, India, Russia and with the dangers of the new imperialism, more particularly with the Boer War, in relation to which he powerfully supported the unpopular line adopted by the *Manchester Guardian*.

Though written *ad hoc* and with great speed these articles have a permanent value, revealing, as they do, a social philosophy which was steadily forming in Hobhouse's mind and which we may here briefly outline in the form which it was to take later in his *Elements of Social Justice* (1922). This is based on principles differing fundamentally alike from *laissez-faire* liberalism and the bureaucratic or, as Hobhouse called it, 'official' socialism of the Fabians. It is perhaps best described as Liberal Socialism or what is now called Democratic Socialism. He provides the most cogent analysis known to me of the relations between personal liberty and state control. On the economic side, he envisaged a type of organization in which there was to be no functionless wealth and in which income was the reward of social service and, cases of charity apart, of social service alone. The final ownership of capital had to be dealt with by the control of inheritance and he thought that the gradation of death duties should be supplemented by adopting some such scheme as that proposed by Rignano, imposing extra taxation on each passage of property at death. The effect would be that inherited wealth would be a diminishing asset and the balance would go to the community.

As to industrial organization he looked forward to an extension of public ownership or management, but warned against the dangers of concentration of power in the hands of the state. The state was indeed to be responsible for the ultimate direction of industry, but this did not mean that everything had to be nationalized or that it had in all cases to assume managerial functions. The general conditions of work and remuneration were to be laid down by law, but adjusted in detail by appropriate boards, such as the trade boards, in many of which Hobhouse acted as chairman. The actual management would be in the hands of joint boards of consumers and producers, municipalities, co-operative associations, or left to private enterprise according to the requirements of particular industries.

Readers of current restatements of socialism in European countries and in Britain cannot fail to recognize the relevance of Hobhouse's analysis to the problems confronting Socialists in our own day and I can see no excuse for their failure to profit from his acute handling of the relations between social ownership and governmental control.

While still in Manchester, Hobhouse carried out experimental investigations in animal psychology, the results of which were published in *Mind in Evolution* (1901). This was the first in a series of studies in which he sought to trace the growth of mind in the animal world and in the collective achievements of mankind.

The pressure of this work, as well as his desire to re-examine the social implications of his philosophical theories, were the chief reasons for his decision to leave Manchester. Fortunately, this decision coincided with the beginnings of a movement for the formation of a sociological society. In this Hobhouse played a very important part and it is clear from his contributions to the early meetings of the society that he had already formed a conception of sociology as a unifying science which was to guide him in all his later work. For a time, however, his philosophic and scientific work was interrupted by fresh political and journalistic preoccupations. For some years he acted as the Secretary of the Free Trade Union and for a year and a half he was the political editor of the newly formed daily paper, *The Tribune*. His leaders showed the same depth and vigour as his contributions to the *Manchester Guardian* and were inspired by the same tendency to move from individualist liberalism to what he was later to describe as liberal socialism.

The divergence between his views and those of the management eventually led to his resignation in 1907 and in the same year he was appointed as the first holder of the newly created Martin White Professorship in Sociology in the London School of Economics. He continued to contribute articles and reviews to the *Manchester Guardian* and in 1911 he became a director of the company. For a time also he acted as editor of the *Sociological Review* but this he gave up after three years.

For the remainder of his life till his death in 1929 Hobhouse devoted himself mainly to his philosophical and scientific pursuits, but he never abandoned his earlier passionate interest in the deeper issues of politics, internal and foreign. In all his activities he combined the empirical and rationalist approaches and I think that J. A. Hobson was fully justified in his verdict that: 'no man of our time has more fully vindicated the unity that underlies theory and practice.'

Although already in his earlier writings Hobhouse noted with foreboding the anti-humanitarian movement which set in after 1870, he was profoundly shaken by the war of 1914. Despite the massive evidence with which he supported his belief in the reality of progress in his *Morals in Evolution*, he felt compelled to raise the question whether the partial successes of the humanitarian spirit in the eighteenth and nineteenth centuries were merely temporary in character and not in the main line of future development. These pessimistic doubts, however, did not prevent him from contributing to the *Manchester Guardian* a series of powerful articles in which he explored the possibilities of salvaging what could be salvaged of the fundamental decencies of civilization. At the same time he continued his interest in labour problems and after the war he acted as chairman of several of the newly instituted trade boards, while, on the theoretical side, he tried to lay the foundations of an ethically justifiable order of industrial relations.

His contributions to sociology were on an encyclopedic scale. *Morals in Evolution* (first edition 1906, seventh edition, with an introduction by the present writer, 1951) was described as a study in comparative ethics, but its scope is, in fact, much wider. It is indeed a synthesis of data derived from comparative religion, history and anthropology, in the light of Hobhouse's own work in comparative psychology, the theory of knowledge and moral philosophy. To this day it remains the most comprehensive and balanced comparative study of social institutions known to me. It is safe to say that the book marked an epoch in the development of sociology. It was followed in the twenties by three volumes under the general title *Principles of Sociology* (*The Rational Good*, 1921; *The Elements of Social Justice*, 1922; *Social Development*, 1924) in which Hobhouse gave a systematic exposition of his lifelong studies in sociology and social philosophy.

Hobhouse will be remembered not only as a sociologist but as a philosopher and psychologist of great distinction. He did pioneering work in experimental animal psychology and he made enduring contributions to social psychology, ethics and social philosophy, logic and the theory of knowledge and to metaphysics. Among his major works may be mentioned: *The Theory of Knowledge*, first edition 1896, third edition 1921; *The Metaphysical Theory of the State*, 1918; *Development and Purpose*, first edition 1913, second edition, revised 1927. The work last mentioned gives the fullest exposition of his philosophical outlook.

The link between sociology and social philosophy he finds in the notion of development, which may be studied both as a question of historical fact and from the point of view of ethical valuation. The scientific problem is to correlate the several aspects of social change and to estimate the kind and amount of growth, in the light of criteria not necessarily ethical, but analogous to those that might be employed by a biologist in dealing with organic evolution. Hobhouse finds four such criteria: growing efficiency in control and direction, extension in the scale of social organization, increasing cooperation in the satisfaction of mutual needs, and greater freedom or scope for personal fulfilment. The ethical problem is to determine whether the development thus established, if it be established, satisfies ethical standards. These, he deduces from his theory of the rational good, as consisting in the harmonious fulfilment of human potentialities. He shows that although ethical and social development have a common end, they do not in fact concide. For in actual fact social development proceeds by a union of partial developments; these may not be and often are not in conformity with ethical requirements, and indeed may conflict and frustrate each other. What he claims is that on·the whole a substantive advance has been made as judged by ethical criteria.

In the extension of organic harmony Hobhouse finds the reality of progress. Progress is not automatic or unilinear but depends upon human thought and will. Humanity has not in his view reached the stage of self-direction, but reviewing the state of the world in the twenties he felt justified in concluding, despite serious misgivings, that it contained many essentials of such self-direction and that these were sufficient to define the direction in which social development proceeds.

From the practical point of view, hope is on the whole a better counsellor than fear, but we are looking at the matter as it bears on social theory and theoretically we are compelled simply to register a *non liquet*. We can only say that the alternative appears to be not merely the cessation of progress, but the break up of our distinctive civilization. Humanity would have to go back upon its traces and find some other way, as it has done before. All that has been said of modern achievement must be held subject to this overhanging doubt. (*Development and Purpose*, p. 232.)

To explain development, Hobhouse put forward a hypothesis that there is a broad correlation between social development as estimated by the criteria of scale, efficiency, mutuality and freedom and the growth of mind, as seen in the advance of science, in the increasing control man gains over nature, in the ethico-religious sphere and in art. The hypothesis is supported by a very wide survey of the history of institutions as seen in custom and law and of the main phases of mental advance.

It is further strengthened by an examination of the conditions affecting social change – environmental, biological, psychological and distinctively sociological. The correlation alleged is far from complete. There is in particular a lag in the accommodation of social to ethical development. Yet in the modern period certain ideas have emerged which may make it possible to bring the two into line. The distinctive achievement of modern ethical and political thought is that it has deepened the notion of freedom and has shown its importance, not only for social cooperation but also for efficiency in large-scale organization. Hobhouse claims that the principles of freedom and mutual service have shown themselves capable of reconciliation with good order, high industrial efficiency and a considerable extension of scale. We cannot be sure, in view of many retrogressions and the gross inequalities in the level of development attained by the different communities of the world, that these gains can be generalized. Yet we may find some elements of hope in the fact that the problem of furthering human development by conscious direction is at last beginning to be faced on a worldwide scale.

We must judge the possibilities of a solution not from the failures that have occurred, when it has never been properly posed, but from the successes of human effort in solving partial problems of the same nature, e.g. in the establishment of national unity. (*Social Development*, p. 335.)

Hobhouse's contributions to sociology were extensive and profound and they do not lend themselves to a rapid summary. Something must be said, however, of the relevance of his teaching to the situation today. First, then, his view of sociology as a unifying science, not independent of the social sciences, but working through them and with them, is worth reasserting today. Sociology still suffers from claiming either too much or too little. It claims too much when it sets itself up as a kind of *scientia scientiarum* purporting to give a complete explanation of human life and even to supply a whole philosophy. This is true of some Marxists and of other writers who write as though sociology could take the place of epistemology, ethics and even metaphysics. It claims too little when it gives up the attempt to discover the central conceptions needed to bring the specialisms into relation with each other and if it merely lumps together under sociology all investigations having any sort of social reference. Hobhouse's procedure avoids both these dangers.

Secondly, Hobhouse's careful analysis of the relations between judgements of fact and judgements of value retains its importance. There are still those who conclude that certain changes or developments are good because they 'have history on their side' or because 'they have the future with them'. It is essential in all social investigation to distinguish clearly between questions of what is desirable or what ought to be, and questions of what has been or probably will be: and to keep the issues distinct throughout the inquiry. On the other hand, it is equally important at some point to consider them in relation with each other. Hobhouse's work shows, I think, that such a synthesis is possible.

Thirdly, Hobhouse was decidedly right in the emphasis he laid on development as the central conception of a comparative sociology. He saw clearly that the problem facing mankind is, essentially, how to reconcile extension in scale of economic and political organization and growing efficiency in the utilization of the forces of nature with freedom and mutuality. His treatment avoids alike the mistakes inherent in a crude evolutionism which have brought the theory of development into disrepute, and those that result from the one-sided emphasis on economic factors implicit in many forms of historical materialism. His method is to examine the connexions between advances in scientific knowledge and the changes in law and morals and in the social structure. These movements have a partial independence and in following their own courses may not only fail to advance evenly at every stage but may impede and obstruct one another.

The task of sociology is to obtain a deeper knowledge of the conditions making for one sidedness and discrepancies in development and those making for correlated growth or overall development. For such a study there now exists much richer material relating to both pre-industrial and industrial societies than was available when Hobhouse was at work.

At the same time the increasing pace of social change, the unevenness of development in different parts of the world and the failure of changes in ethico-religious thought and in social organization to keep in step with changes in science and technology make the study of the condition of development at once more urgent and more difficult. It is not the least of Hobhouse's merits that he has marked out the paths which such a study might profitably follow.

FURTHER READING

WORKS

*Development and Purpose* (Macmillan, 1913).
*The Elements of Social Justice* (Allen and Unwin, 1922).
*The Labour Movement* (Fisher Unwin, 1893).
*Liberalism* (Williams and Norgate, 1911).
*The Material Culture and Social Institutions of the Simpler Peoples*, with G. C. Wheeler and M. Ginsberg (London, 1915).
*Mind in Evolution* (Macmillan, 1915).
*Morals in Evolution* (Chapman and Hall, 1951).
*The Rational Good* (London, 1921).
*Social Development* (Allen and Unwin, 1924).
*Sociology and Philosophy: A Centenary Collection of Essays*, introduced by M. Ginsberg (L. S. E. and George Bell, 1966).
*The World in Conflict* (Fisher Unwin, 1915).

CRITICAL STUDIES

Ernest Barker: 'Leonard Trelawny Hobhouse' (*Proceedings of the British Academy*, vol. xv, 1929).

John A. Hobson and Morris Ginsberg: *L. T. Hobhouse: his life and work* (Allen and Unwin, 1931).

John E. Owen: *L. T. Hobhouse: Sociologist* (Nelson, 1974).

# ROBERT E. PARK

## (*1864–1944*)

### Everett C. Hughes

SOCIOLOGY was a social movement before it was part of the academic establishment. In the joining of movement and establishment, which took place earlier at the University of Chicago than in most universities, Robert E. Park was a central figure although not one of the founders. The road by which he got a place in the University of Chicago was unusual even in those days when few people who called themselves sociologists had any academic licence to do so.

In 1912 William I. Thomas, professor of sociology at the University of Chicago, was invited to a conference on race relations to be held at the Tuskegee Institute in Alabama. Tuskegee was the 'industrial school' for Negroes of which Booker T. Washington was the single-minded and popular head. Thomas himself had left the teaching of English at Oberlin College to study sociology, a new subject, at Chicago, a new university. He took a doctorate there in 1896 and stayed on. Thomas accepted the invitation to Tuskegee, expecting to remain for a couple of days. He stayed two weeks, walking the red clay roads in company with the brooding, infinitely curious and widely read Park, of whom he had never heard.

A little later, in 1914, Park – aged fifty – went to the University of Chicago as professorial lecturer for a year with little salary and an understanding that under no circumstances would his appointment be renewed. He remained, became the central figure of the department and, for a time, of American sociology.

Born in Pennsylvania, but reared in Minnesota – then 'the West' – Park had gone to the University of Minnesota against the will of his father, builder of a successful business. After gaining a bachelor's degree in philosophy with John Dewey, 'back East' at the University of Michigan, he became a newspaper reporter and in that capacity in the next few years walked the streets of New York, Chicago, Denver and Detroit. But he did more than report; he ruminated on the nature of man and society; he came to believe, with Dewey and others, that the key lay in communication (without an s) and public opinion. If only the reporting of events, large and small, were complete and the circulation of the news equally so, human progress would proceed apace.

Eventually his interest in public opinion and news brought him back to the university. He took an MA in psychology and philosophy at Harvard with Hugo Munsterberg, William James and Josiah Royce. It is said that James told him he was not bright enough to study philosophy. Park, indeed, always thought of himself as a slow man; the truth is that he was not easily satisfied with solutions to problems he thought fundamental. In 1899, at the age of thirty-five, he went to Berlin, where he listened to Georg Simmel. It was his only formal instruction in sociology – instruction that influenced him and the course of American sociology deeply.

He went on to study at Strasbourg, with Windelband; there he met L. J. Henderson, a fellow American student, who became a noted biochemist, and who turned the attention of his Harvard colleagues to the sociological treatise of the Italian engineer and economist, Alfredo Pareto. In the late 1930s, I spent a lively day with Park and Henderson in northern Vermont. Henderson, a tremendous talker, allowed that his old friend Park was a good sociologist mainly because he had learned it for himself rather than from professionals, but maintained that all future good sociology would be done by scholars trained in the physical and biological sciences. Park, as usual, talked in his quiet, speculative – sometimes profane – way about ideas, ignoring Henderson's outrageous condescension. It was clear they liked and respected each other. The strands of the sociological movement have not been so separate as we often believe.

Park followed Windelband to Heidelberg and there took a doctorate with a thesis described thus: *Masse und Publikum, eine methodologische und soziologische Untersuchung von Robert E. Park aus Watertown, South Dakota.* (The Crowd and the Public, a methodological and sociological investigation.) Park, then forty years old, husband of an attractive woman who was also an artist, the father of four children, was sick – he said later – of the academic world, ashamed of the little book which was the only tangible product of seven years of postgraduate study and generally convinced that he was a failure. He came back to Boston, built a handsome house on a hill in Quincy (on a site so well chosen that his son, a Boston lawyer, can still look out over the city as well as his parents could sixty years ago) and became for one year an assistant (not assistant professor, he made it clear) in philosophy at Harvard. Here he continued briefly his connexion with the Harvard pragmatists, William James and Josiah Royce.

The Harvard connexion did not last. He was soon engaged by the Congo Reform Association, an arm of the Baptist Missionary Society, as a secretary; that is, as a press agent or public-relations man. Again he was in the business of bringing about reform by telling the news. For *Everybody's Magazine*, foremost among the muck-raking organs, he wrote 'A King in Business: King Leopold of Belgium, Autocrat of the Congo and International Broker', 'The Terrible Story of the Congo' and 'The Blood-Money of the Congo' in 1906 and 1907.

In course of this work, in which he was quickly somewhat disillusioned by the bickerings of missionaries, he met Booker Washington, who suggested that he should acquaint himself with the oppressed Negroes in North America before going to Africa. Thus Park became for about seven years publicity man to Booker T. Washington, the leading American Negro of that generation. In a conversation years afterwards, he said:

I was disgusted with what I had done in the university, and had come to the conclusion that I couldn't do anything first rate on my own account. I decided the best thing I could do was to attach myself to someone who was doing something first rate. Washington was not a brilliant man or an intellectual, but he seemed to me to be doing something real. So I went. I guess maybe I neglected my family during this period.

After seven years of travelling with and ghost-writing for Mr Washington, Park organized the conference to which he invited William I. Thomas. Thomas was just then in the midst of his great study of *The Polish Peasant in Europe and America*, with the aid of a young Pole, Florian Znaniecki. Into the five volumes of that work the authors put a deal of fact and theory concerning American social problems and institutions. It was but natural, for in American cities the masses of immigrants from other lands seemed to aggravate every social problem.

When the social survey movement, best represented in England by Charles Booth's *The Life and Labour of the People of London*, came to America it became obvious that all that concerned poverty and slums also concerned recent immigrants and Negroes. American empirical sociology became study of immigrants, ethnic groups and what happens when several of them live in the same city, work in the same economy and are citizens of the same body politic. When Park joined Thomas, a man who knew the relations of Negroes with white Americans better than any social scientist in the country met the man who had done most to understand what happened to rural Europeans and their institutions in urban America. They met in a new lively university, not too proud to admit a new branch of study, and in a city whose terrain was so flat and uncomplicated that the forces that build cities could play themselves out in such a fashion that a map was also a systematic chart.

Perhaps it was Park's combination of German philosophical training with concern over the problems of American cities that led Albion W. Small, head professor of sociology at Chicago, to allow him to come even for a short time. For Small was two men: one of him wrote in a Germanic sort of way on the history of sociology and on its place among the disciplines; the other attacked the evils of capitalism and monopoly with such vigour that his style sometimes became almost lively. Indeed, he wrote a novel, so called, entitled *Between Eras from Capitalism to Democracy*, in which he told at boring length the horrendous stories of characters who can be identified only as Chicago tycoons and their coddled sons. At any rate the coming of Park gave new impetus to that combination of interest in social reform with earnest concern with theories of the nature of society which had characterized the department of sociology at the University of Chicago since its founding twenty years earlier.

Already at Chicago was Ernest W. Burgess, a long generation younger and I suppose one of the first sociologists not to have come in from some other occupation. Small, Thomas, Park, Burgess – these four men captured the energy and imagination of several generations of graduate students. Thomas was forced to leave the university not long after, and his place was taken by Ellsworth Faris, a man not always rated at his true value as social psychologist and teacher. Faris, as chairman, brought William F. Ogburn to the department in the 1920s just as Small was retired and as Park approached retirement. They were joined by several of their more brilliant students. Together they went through the years of the Great Depression, with many students at work on research financed by the New Deal.

As a sort of inaugural work, Park had written in 1915 'The City: Suggestions for the investigation of human behaviour in the urban environment' for the *American Journal of Sociology*. It contained, in the germ, most of the studies of cities made by his students and others in the years following. Not long after its publication Small called the faculty of the several departments of social science together and proposed that they all work on a common project – the city – and that they start their work at home. With support from a foundation, this became in fact a programme. Historians, political scientists, economists, anthropologists, geographers and sociologists joined in. Park was the natural, if never the official, leader of this very energetic movement.

The First World War had broken the careers of many young Americans of religious and reforming bent. For a number of them who turned up in the department of sociology at Chicago, Park made an object of study and a new career out of what had been a personal problem or a crusade. Two, Frederic Thrasher and Clifford Shaw, probation officers, wrote *The Gang* and *The Natural History of a Delinquent Career*, ground-breaking monographs. Wirth, a social worker, became a sociologist and wrote *The Ghetto*. For the many monographs about the city, race relations, news and collective behaviour, Park wrote introductions; sometimes, one must admit, to the book he had hoped the author would write, rather than to what he did write. If the incoming student did not bring a personal cause with him Park assigned him a problem about which he was to make his career. It mattered not to him whether the student was brilliant, so long as he would work on something of interest.

Thus the man who considered himself a failure at the age of fifty became the centre of a great movement of social investigation. His formal career at Chicago lasted fifteen years, starting during the world war and ending at the onset of the Great Depression. But he did not stop with formal retirement. He travelled about the world, visiting former students and observing multiracial societies. After that he settled down to teach at Fisk University, thus continuing his role as observer of and participant in Negro education until his death in 1944. He had only to come to the University of Chicago campus to bring a seminar into being for as long as he stayed. I do not remember that he ever, in that phase of his life, spoke of failure. Nor did he speak of any special achievement.

It was in the Chicago period, and following, that he did most of his sociological writing. With Ernest Burgess he prepared a set of readings to be used in teaching sociology; in 1921 they published them as *Introduction to the Science of Sociology*. It contained the readings, but it was also meant to be a treatise. It began with a long chapter on the relation of sociology to the other social sciences, and then developed, chapter by chapter, the concepts which Park considered necessary for the analysis of human social behaviour. He was also co-author of one and author of another of two books which grew out of the American concern over the loyalty of her immigrants: *Old World Traits Transplanted* (with W. I. Thomas and H. A. Miller) and *The Immigrant Press and its Control*.

He undertook, in the early 1920s, a study of the Asiatic immigrants, and their children, on the Pacific Coast. The only publication to issue from that undertaking was 'East by West', a special number of *The Survey Graphic* containing poetry, portraits and personal documents of Chinese Americans, as well as a few general articles, including one by Park himself. From then on, he wrote a great many articles, and inspired others to write both articles, and monographs, and to assemble articles into symposia. The most famous of the latter was *The City*, which contained Park's own paper, one by Burgess on the natural areas of the city, and a bibliography on cities gathered by Louis Wirth. That little book was the manual and guide to sociological research on cities for a number of years.

Park left no *magnum opus*. He regarded his writings as prolegomena to research which would result in a more systematic knowledge of human social life. If he was tempted to write a treatise, he was diverted from it by his interest in on-going social changes, in the events and problems of the day. If he was ever tempted to become an 'expert' on some particular social problem, he was held back by his conviction that every event had a place somewhere in the universal human processes, that no situation can be understood until one finds in it those universal qualities which allow one to compare it with other situations – however near or distant in time, place and appearance.

But if there is no *magnum opus*, there is a large body of writing, mainly articles and his introductions to monographs written by his students and protégés. Nearly all of it is available in three volumes published some years after Park's death. *Race and Culture* contains the little-known paper in which he introduced a concept – the marginal man – so well known that few think of its origin: 'Human Migration and the Marginal Man'. When that first volume of papers appeared I used it in a seminar of sociologists and anthropologists. A graduate student of anthropology, who had heard little of Park, reported that after reading a couple of the papers he wondered why that man Park had not footnoted his debts; then he noted the dates of original publication, and wondered why his favourite authors had not acknowledged *their* debt to Park.

The second volume, *Human Communities*, contains the paper on the city and Park's many papers on human ecology, a term and a branch of study he introduced into sociology. Park took from botanists the idea of a community of competing and mutually supporting organisms and applied it to human communities, making due allowance for the fact of human culture. Indeed, he tended to view cultures as in competition with one another or supporting one another in a kind of world-wide division of labour constantly altered by trade, migrations and conquests.

Into the third volume, *Society*, Professor J. Masuoka of Fisk University and I put the remaining papers. They turned out not to be a remnant, but a series of papers on the nature of society itself, on those lively forms of collective behaviour engaged in by enthusiastic or restless men either in last ditch defence of or determined attack upon an existing social order, and on the ways in which society may be studied. Posthumously collected and arranged papers are never quite 'books'; they never arrange the thoughts of a man as he would have arranged them. The way to read them is to dip in when one is interested in a problem. or an idea.

Park, man of wide experience, avid reader of poetry and fiction as well as of science and philosophy, recognized no academic line fences in his choice of problems and methods. His inclination was towards realism, towards the study of wholes. He was interested in current goings-on, but never content until he could put a news story into some universal theme of human inter-action. Thus came the apparent anomaly, that the man who wanted to make sociology deal with the news was also the one who based his scheme on the work of the most abstract of all sociologists, Georg Simmel. He had no desire to form a system, yet he was primarily a systematic sociologist. His sources were whatever came to hand – Gilbert Murray, Walter Bagehot, William James, Karl Marx, Charles Darwin, Walt Whitman.

The main thing to say about Park here is that he was part of a great social movement for the investigation of human societies, great and small. One of the last remarks I heard him make was that there was no Negro problem in the United States, but a white problem. Not long before that he had shocked a young liberal political scientist by asking why there should be racial peace before there was racial justice.

FURTHER READING

WORKS

Ralph H. Turner (ed.): *Robert E. Park on Social Control and Collective Behavior* (University of Chicago Press, 1967).

CRITICAL STUDIES

Robert E. L. Faris: *Chicago Sociology, 1920–1932* (San Francisco, 1967; University of Chicago Press, 1970).

Fred H. Mathews: *The Quest for an American Sociology: Park and the Chicago School* (McGill Queens Press, 1977).

Winifred Raushenbush: *A Biography of Robert E. Park* (Durham, N.C., Duke University Press, forthcoming).

# MAX WEBER

## (*1864–1920*)

### John Rex

MAX WEBER was born in 1864. He was the son of a wealthy merchant family and his father was prominent in the National Liberal Party in the time of Bismarck. His original studies were in law but he quickly turned his attention to economics and economic history. His first important academic appointment was as professor of economics in the university of Freiburg in 1893. Three years later he moved to Heidelberg.

At Heidelberg he suffered from a serious mental illness and was unable to continue his academic work for four years. After his recovery he did not return to his teaching duties, but devoted himself to research and writing while also assuming the joint editorship of the *Archiv für Sozialwissenschaft und Sozialpolitik*. During the period which followed, Weber embarked upon his methodological studies, his comparative studies of Chinese, Indian and Jewish civilizations. He continued to be concerned with political affairs and while remaining a German patriot was a critic of the Kaiser and those who surrounded him. In the Weimar Republic he served on the committee of experts which drafted the constitution and unsuccessfully sought nomination to the newly constituted assembly. In 1917 he was visiting professor in the University of Vienna. In 1919 he accepted a chair in Munich. He died at the age of fifty-six in June 1920.

The work of Max Weber has had very little influence in England and, in the age of the computer, shows little sign of having much influence in the future. This is not due to Weber's inadequacy: even those who show least understanding of his contribution to sociology usually pay him lip service. But of all the great teachers of sociology, Max Weber was the most sensitive to the philosophical, methodological and theoretical problems of the discipline. Moreover his empirical contributions to sociology were on a scale which has not been paralleled before or since his time and any one of them is worth more than thousands of the little articles which crowd our journals. Weber is ignored in England simply because we know that few of us are capable of making an effective contribution if the discipline is defined in his terms.

Many who have become acquainted with Weber through his slight work, *The Protestant Ethic and the Spirit of Capitalism*, his chapters on bureaucracy or through secondary discussion of his use of 'ideal types' will think these claims extravagant. But if they read some of the increasing number of translated chapters of Weber's *Wirtschaft und Gesellschaft* they will find there a comprehension of the problems of the subject and an illumination of their research problems which they will find nowhere else.

Perhaps the first thing to be said about Weber is that he was passionately engaged in the affairs of his nation and deeply concerned about the internal tensions of Western capitalist society. Thoughout his life as a scholar he remained a member of and participated actively in the work of the Association for Social Policy, which was concerned with practical social and political questions. And throughout his life he remained actively engaged in German politics, spending the last few years of his life trying to understand Germany's defeat and trying to see some basis in the future for a stable German society and lasting European peace.

But to have such concerns was by no means incompatible with a scholarly and detached approach to social questions, and Weber was always concerned to argue that the social scientist could make his own special contribution to the solution of social questions only if he was prepared for a time to suspend his value judgements and to study what actually occurred. To understand his work, therefore, we must begin by considering his methodological ideas.

The first of these ideas concerns the use of 'ideal types' in sociology. Many seem to imagine that this means a turning away from the facts to a contemplation of 'pure forms'. But what is the alternative? Durkheim, who advocated a radical empiricism in *The Rules of Sociological Method*, was sophisticated enough to see that sociologists could not talk about all social phenomena simultaneously and hence must have some conception of a species type. But he argued, without ever explaining what he meant, that this type could be based upon some sort of statistical average.

This idea turns out to be absurd. For what after all is an average frog? Or, what is more important, what relationship would this average frog have to all the particular frogs which the biologist observes? The problem of the scientist is to construct a type against which existing cases can be compared and their deviation from the pure type measured. For this purpose the statistically average type has nothing especially to commend it. Weber saw this and urged that our first task in the study of society and culture must be to clarify the elements united in a particular structure, and to set these out in an ideal type so that when we approached the particular case we should know what features were especially worthy of exact observation and measurement.

Weber, however, had a good historical training and he was aware how misleading abstract conceptions like that of 'economic man' could be. He therefore urged that the sociologist should go beyond saying 'This is how it would be other things being equal' to saying, 'This is how the thing works in this case, given its peculiar historical setting.' He wanted his types to be illuminating in unique and specific historical circumstances. In practice his resolution to do this broke down, and happily so. For, while it is true that there is a task to be done in illuminating the unique instance, it is also true that the unique instance is greatly illuminated by comparison. So Weber went on from a penetrating analysis of the uniqueness of Western capitalism to see that uniqueness as a particular value given to variables of social structure, whose other values could be seen in other civilizations.

But what are the special phenomena which the sociologist seeks to illuminate through ideal types? Durkheim had seen these as reified supra-individual entities and his empirical orientation ends up in the mysticism of some kind of group mind concept. In fact there are no such supra-individual entities. They are simply constructs which we all, sociologists and non-sociologists alike, make up to help us predict what other people are going to do. The concept of 'group' refers to nothing else but a set of expectations which individuals have of each other's behaviour and which they take into account when they plan their own action. Thus Weber concluded that the most elementary concept of all in sociology was that of 'action' and that all group concepts had to be built up from a starting point which posited a hypothetical actor planning his action and taking account of the action of others.

This seems laborious and it implies a lot of hard theoretical work. But such theoretical work clarifies the question, 'What data are relevant?' It is the empiricists, who pretend that there is a class of facts 'out there' labelled 'social' which simply have to be read off, who really mystify the process of social investigation. The greatness of Durkheim perhaps lay in the fact that he saw how difficult his own position was. But it was Weber who undertook the labour of deducing every important general sociological concept from the notion of 'action'.

One of his earliest investigations was concerned with the condition of agricultural workers in east Germany. Weber saw in the situation there the clash of two cultures and two kinds of social interaction. One was the residually feudal order presided over by the Junkers. The other was the new market economy. Weber had little respect for the Junkers, who in practice behaved like capitalists, yet still had the pretensions of a feudal nobility. Thus he came to ask the questions which perplexed him all his life. 'Is market behaviour natural, or is it itself the product of a particular ideological situation?' and 'Does market behaviour imply a collapse of social order into some sort of economic war of all against all or is a society based upon market relations necessarily dependent for its continued existence upon a particular type of social ethic?'

Weber naturally became associated at Heidelberg with Troeltsch who had already produced something of a sociology of Christian social teaching and who had shown very clearly the connexion between Calvinist theology and capitalist ethics. Weber gave this work a sounder sociological foundation by showing that there was a factual connexion between these two phenomena. He demonstrated that it was precisely in those areas where Calvinism had gained a hold that capitalism flourished, and he spelled out clearly the ideal types of the Calvinist social ethic and expected capitalist behaviour in the West.

The method which Weber uses in this and subsequent studies is of some importance. For Weber does not rest content with telling, as he says, 'a plausible story' about the congruence of Calvinism and capitalism. Such a proof, which would have been acceptable to many German historians, seemed to him to be 'adequate in the level of meaning' only. It needed supplementation by a proof which was 'causally adequate'. On the other hand, however, Weber would not have been content with a proof which was only causally adequate. It was the special feature of sociology that it was capable of showing and had a duty to show the meaningful relations between phenomena which were known to be empirically associated.

This sensitivity of Weber both to the need for 'understanding' in the human studies and to the need for scientific rigour of proof in accordance with the canons of science is what really makes his sociology distinctive. Historians and critics too often seek 'insight' without ever showing that their plausible interpretative models actually apply to the facts. Empirical sociologists on the other hand demonstrate correlations *ad nauseam* without ever showing why such connexions exist. Weber does justice to both traditions and is able to do so because the theoretical models in terms of which he interprets social phenomena are on the one hand set out as testable hypotheses and on the other stated in terms of the meaning of the situation as it appears to a hypothetical actor.

Weber's embarkation upon his comparative historical studies may have followed from his desire further to underpin the causal proof of the relation between Protestantism and capitalism, for he begins by showing that although there were many factors conducive to the development present in China a crucial difference lay in the totally different world outlook of Confucianism. But Weber was not naïve enough to suppose that European and Chinese civilizations differed only in a single factor. In any case he had already suggested in a study of the Western city that the dissociation of the city from kinship and village ties and its emergence as a confessional association was another factor peculiar to the West and one which, along with Protestantism, played an important part in the emergence of Western capitalism. What he now set about was a study of the particular institutional complexes of China, India and ancient Palestine.

It is not possible here to review all the contributions to general sociology which flowed from Weber's comparative studies. We shall discuss only two. These are his types of legitimate authority and administration and his systematic typology of religious doctrines and religious functionaries. It should be remembered, however, that, along with these went discussions of guilds, kinship, cities, social classes and status groups, types of law, and systems of what Marx called the 'social relations of production'.

No one can study China without being struck by the distinctiveness of its administrative system. To the Westerner it appears to have important bureaucratic elements and yet not to be a bureaucracy as we understand it. Weber described the situation in his *Religion in China* but returned to its analysis in his later systematic work where it is comprehended in a frame of reference which throws light upon European feudalism, religious leadership and modern European politics and administration and politics. Typically here Weber starts from a particular historical case but goes on to illuminate it by comparison.

The key notion which Weber starts with is 'authority'. There are many reasons why one man should be able to ensure the compliance of another. But the most important of these is a subjective feeling on the part of the other that the authority is legitimate. Once kinship and community collapse as bases of social organization, organizations based upon this feeling of legitimate authority are the most important in the analysis of social systems (apart perhaps from market structures).

Systems of authority are classified by the reasons which men give for thinking the authority legitimate. The first distinction is between traditional authority where the compulsion to obey a person in a certain position is justified on the ground that 'it has always been so' and charismatic authority where the leader or ruler is obeyed for an opposite reason that he has 'unusual qualities'. Both these forms of authority however are relatively arbitrary compared with the rational-legal form where the ruler is obeyed because he is thought to be acting in accordance with general principles or laws.

Each of these types has its own dynamics or tends to produce a characteristic type of struggle for power and each has its own type of 'administrative' staff. Charismatic leaders initially rule with the aid of a 'band of disciples', the leader interferes with the administration at all levels and there is considerable uncertainty about the succession. Traditional rule takes two forms, the patrimonial in which the administrators approximate to the position of palace servants under the total power of the ruler and the feudal in which authority is decentralized and the vassals are bound to their lord by a *voluntary* contract of obedience. Rational-legal authority rules through bureaucrats, whose spheres of competence are precisely laid down, who are responsible to their superiors in a hierarchy, whose official life is so clearly demarcated from their private life and who can never become indispensable.

Weber saw religious ideologies and organizations more clearly as a result of his Chinese studies. Confucianism represented a minimal type of religion for it preached a doctrine of acceptance of the world, and its officials became secular officials. The great interest of religion as an element in history, however, really arose only in those cases where there was some kind of religious rejection of the world and where religious leaders stood outside the administration. But there were a number of different cases of this kind. The religious rejection of the world as it was might lead to an attempt to master it (the ascetic alternative) or it might lead to an attempt to escape from it (the mystical alternative).

The above paragraphs sketch only the essentials of what Weber had to say even in the fields with which they deal. But it is now perhaps possible to consider their contemporary relevance.

The less insular our sociology becomes the more we may need to turn to Weber's comparative historical approach. This is more and more forced upon us as we recognize that our Western institutions are not readily transferable to the underdeveloped countries. We see the really problematic nature of rational-legal politics and bureaucratic administration when an attempt is made to fit them into a charismatic or traditional setting. And we see how important some functional equivalent to the Calvinist world outlook is for economic development when we witness the failure to achieve an economic take-off in those countries where cadillac capitalism flourishes.

But Weber's importance is by no means confined to extra-European contexts. It is of the greatest importance for the achievement of any sensitive understanding of the problems of administration and stratification in our own society. One of the most absurd criticisms of Weber is that his theory of bureaucracy is wrong because it does not exactly describe systems of political and industrial administration as they are to be observed in our society. For the greatness of Weber lies precisely in the fact that he never merely described what he saw but, in setting up a pure type, also indicated the principal directions in which actual cases might deviate from it. Thus his theory of bureaucracy taken together with his analysis of traditional and charismatic structures still provides the most illuminating framework for analysing administrative systems.

On the question of stratification Weber faced all the central questions which Marx did, but saw these as only a part of the problem. With Marx he sees that the existence of a labour market may give rise to class conflict. But when he equates a man's class situation with his market situation, Weber goes on to point out a whole range of possible market situations (for example the landlord – tenant situation) other than that in the labour market. He also distinguishes status situations sharply from market situations, seeing them as concerned with the differential distribution of prestige. But he does not, like other theorists of status, see status groups as passive. He sees them as developing a 'way of life' which they might preserve as against that of the wider society, or which they might seek to impose on that wider society. And perhaps most interestingly of all he sees the possibility that the incumbents of roles within a particular social sub-system (for example the administrators, the priests, the merchants, the artisans) might form a status group in this sense.

It was with these tools that Weber sought to understand the institutional roots of Western capitalist society. We still need them to achieve that understanding.

## FURTHER READING

WORKS IN ENGLISH TRANSLATION

*Ancient Judaism* (Free Press of Glencoe, 1952).

*The City* (Free Press of Glencoe, 1958).

*Economy and Society*, ed. G. Roth and C. Wittich, 3 vols., (Bedminster Press, New York, 1968).

*From Max Weber. Essays in Sociology*, tr. and ed. H. H. Gerth and C. Wright Mills (Routledge and Kegan Paul, 1948; Galaxy, 1958).

*General Economic History* (Free Press of Glencoe, 1950; Collier Books, paperback, 1961).

*Max Weber. Selections from His Work*, introduced by S. M. Miller (Crowell, 1963).

*The Methodology of the Social Sciences*, introduced by E. Shils (Free Press, 1949).

*The Protestant Ethic and the Spirit of Capitalism* (Allen and Unwin, 1930; Scribner, 1958).

*The Religion of China: Confucianism and Taoism* (Free Press of Glencoe, 1951).

*The Religion of India: The Sociology of Hinduism and Buddhism* (Free Press of Glencoe, 1958).

CRITICAL STUDIES

Raymond Aron: *Main Currents in Sociological Thought, 2* (Weidenfeld and Nicolson, 1968; Penguin, 1970).

Reinhard Bendix: *Max Weber: An Intellectual Portrait* (Methuen, 1960).

Reinhard Bendix and G. Roth: *Scholarship and Partisanship: Essays on Max Weber* (California University Press, 1971).

J. Freund: *The Sociology of Max Weber* (Allen Lane, 1968).

Anthony Giddens: *Politics and Sociology in the Thought of Max Weber* (Macmillan, 1972).

Donald G. Mackae: *Weber* (Fontana, 1974).

Talcott Parsons: introductory essays to Weber's *Theory of Social and Economic Organisation* (Hodge, 1947).

Talcott Parsons: *The Structure of Social Action* (McGraw-Hill, 1937).

Talcott Parsons, in Harry E. Barnes (ed.): *Introduction to the History of Sociology* (Chicago University Press, 1948).

# MARCEL MAUSS
## (1872–1950)

### Michael Wood

A T a moment when social science has begun to look like a rather fragile art form, Marcel Mauss is perhaps a dangerous figure to contemplate: fecund, but inconclusive. On the other hand, he may help us to see what ought to be 'hard' and what ought to be 'soft' in this shifting discipline.

Mauss was born into a pious Jewish family in Épinal, in the Vosges, in 1872. He read philosophy at Bordeaux under the watchful eye of his uncle, Émile Durkheim, and he was one of the first and most assiduous contributors to the *Année sociologique*, the journal that Durkheim started in 1896. He studied Sanskrit and the history of religion, and in 1901 became Maitre de Conférences at the École Pratique des Hautes Études in Paris.

He worked for a long time at, and finally abandoned, a thesis on prayer. In 1925 he helped to establish the Institute of Ethnology of the University of Paris, where he taught, and of which he was for a period the director. From 1930 to 1939 he was a Professor at the Collège de France, and since the death of Durkheim in 1917 had generally been regarded as the head of the French school of sociology. He was a lifelong socialist, in the style of Jaurès, whom he knew well, and he was a member of the group which founded the newspaper, *L'Humanité*.

He was a man of delicate intelligence and formidable learning, proficient in Greek, Latin, Sanskrit, Celtic and Hebrew studies, as well as being at home in several European languages, including Russian. He was much shaken by the German occupation of Paris in 1940, and seems not to have recovered the full use of his mind after the war. His last piece of writing was sent off to the printer in 1941. He died in 1950.

Very large claims have been made for Mauss's authority and influence. Claude Lévi-Strauss suggests that readers of Mauss's best-known work, *The Gift* (1925), are likely to feel much as Malebranche felt on first looking into Descartes – convinced that they are 'witnessing a decisive event in the evolution of science'. Louis Dumont, another anthropologist, the author of *Homo Hierarchicus*, says that 'faithfulness to Mauss's profound inspiration seems increasingly to be a condition of success in our studies'.

Now, *The Gift* is a very brilliant essay, full of interesting implications, but I would have thought it was rather too scattered and diffident to be seen as a decisive event. And Mauss's 'inspiration' seems impossible to assess, since good teachers always *become* their students in one sense. All their thoughts are modified in their students' minds, and the roll-call of distinguished Frenchmen who studied with Mauss (Michel Leiris, Maxime Rodinson, Jacques Soustelle, Roger Caillois, Jean-Pierre Vernant, and many others, as well as Dumont and Lévi-Strauss) compounds the problem. What do they have in common? Where is Mauss in all this?

A further difficulty lies in the nature of the group surrounding the *Année sociologique*. Durkheim thought scientists spent too much time ranking each other and not enough time ranking each other's work, and felt science could not progress 'except through collective labour'. And so Mauss worked on Durkheim's book on suicide; Durkheim and Mauss together wrote an essay on primitive classification; Mauss and Henri Hubert together wrote essays on sacrifice and magic; Mauss and Paul Fauconnet wrote an important early encyclopaedia article on sociology.

It is tempting to speculate, as Rodney Needham does, that Durkheim had a large hand in the work on primitive classification, since the argument is so full of Durkheim's besetting habit of calmly, even emphatically, assuming the truth of the very thing he's setting out to prove. But as Needham adds, this sort of curiosity is no doubt misdirected, because the group around Durkheim embodied a coherent collective consciousness of the very kind they were so busy studying in societies far and near.

One more difficulty, the most subtle and challenging of all. Mauss published enough essays and reviews to fill four volumes. (A selection of his work called *Sociologie et Anthropologie* was published in 1950, and a three-tome *Oeuvres* was published in 1968 and 1969.) But he did not, in his lifetime, publish a book. There is no *magnum opus*, not even the beginning of one. Even *The Gift*, as Mauss himself says, is 'all suggestions'.

There is no false modesty here, and there is no accident either. Mauss is not in a hurry, or sketching out work he himself is going to do. He is speculating for us, sorting out, proposing directions, *comparing* – 'for,' he once wrote, 'when it comes to social phenomena, one can arrive at some sort of explanation only by means of comparison.' The connections of his arguments often look like what Merleau-Ponty has nicely called 'affective cement', conceptual glue to hold disparate things together for a short, contemplative space of time. Mauss is looking for what he calls 'intelligible relations', and the more one reads him, the more varied and relaxed the possibilities of intelligibility seem.

But Mauss remains elusive. At this point, the invisible scholar is replaced by a number of visible, but rather miscellaneous figures. There is a Durkheimian Mauss, for example, faithful to the end to the teachings of his uncle, who indeed said he was '*un peu mon alter ego*'. There is a structuralist Mauss, who has read his Saussure, and who drops hints for Lévi-Strauss about language and the hidden depths of social systems. 'In magic, as in religion, as in linguistics, it is unconscious ideas which do the work.' Lévi-Strauss thinks that Mauss's message is that social life is a *system*; but for Dumont the message is that the system is *social*; and clearly Mauss is saying both of those things.

At times he sounds like some sort of phenomenologist, seeking 'the fleeting moment when the society and its members take emotional stock of themselves and their situation as regards others'. And in one dizzying passage he seems to stand all his own and Durkheim's arguments on their head. In his unfinished work on prayer he says, rather suddenly, that it is not his intention to 'explain the complex by means of the simple'. Which is odd, since that is just what he seems to be doing, and since that would seem to be the whole purpose of looking, with Durkheim and after Durkheim, for the 'elementary forms' of anything. 'For the most rudimentary forms', Mauss goes on, 'are not in any degree more simple than the most developed forms. Their complexity is only of a different nature.'

If I understand these sentences correctly, they abolish not only the notion of the 'primitive' and the 'elementary' but also Mauss's preferred term, the 'archaic', as well. Once we are dealing only with different sorts of complexity, we can scarcely think of *stages* in the history of culture at all. 'Rudimentary' is what literary critics these days call self-consuming: it becomes meaningless by the time Mauss gets to the end of his thought. There is a logical muddle here, to be sure, but there is also a provocative question. What is the difference between different complexities, between pre-literate cultures, say, and high civilization? Or if it comes to that, between anthropology and sociology?

Don't say there isn't any difference, and don't retreat to safe ground. Mauss's great talent is for sustaining such questions without resolving them; he has a rare tolerance for the useful ambiguity. It is for this reason, of course, that he says different things to different people.

Steven Lukes speaks of Mauss's 'somewhat refined Durkheimianism'. The remark is apt in two ways, since Mauss both tests Durkheim's thoughts in rather refined regions, and refines the thoughts as he goes. At times he refines the thoughts only into confusion. Writing togther, for example, Durkheim and Mauss suggest that men got their systems of classification not from their minds and not from nature but from the social orders they inhabited. 'The first logical categories were social categories; the first classes of things were classes of men.' It is this sort of thinking which Evans-Pritchard calls a 'sociologistic metaphysic', adding rather tartly: 'It was Durkheim and not the savage who made society into a god.'

On his own or writing with Hubert, Mauss tends to look for the social in the most secret, unlikely places – in prayer and magic – and to find it. But then he dissolves it back again into a sort of privacy. He says, for instance, that prayer is 'above all' and 'essentially' a 'social phenomenon'. He then worries over a couple of particular cases and says they show, anyway, that it's possible that prayer *can* be only a social phenomenon.

Over the page he proposes, even more modestly, that at least it's not 'an essentially individual phenomenon', and a little later he seems to have changed sides entirely. 'But when we say that prayer is a social phenomenon, we do not mean to say that it is in no way an individual phenomenon . . . We do not think that society, religion, or prayer are extraordinary things that can be conceived without the individuals who realize them . . .' But no, he hasn't changed sides, he is still insisting on the social after all. 'In reality we are simply reversing the order in which the two terms [i.e. society and the individual] are usually studied, we don't deny either of them.'

This seems to me genuinely muddled, and not only logically, and the conclusion is lame and feebly conciliatory. I'm not holding this writing up for admiration. But I think it shows the movement of Mauss's mind, and we are on important and treacherous ground here. It is the ground of Marx's famous remark about social being determining consciousness. To say that society is everywhere, even in the most unlikely recesses of the heart, can mean anything from a truism (the social dimensions of your life have something to do with who you are) to a horrible prescription for despair (you have no life that has not already been settled for you by the system), with many stations in between.

Mauss and Durkheim (and Marx) stood somewhere in between, of course, but Mauss, even more than Durkheim, seems to have been uncertain about just where he stood. Steven Lukes, in his biography of Durkheim, quotes a remarkably honest and distressing letter from Mauss, which regrets the failure of French sociologists to foresee that their notion of society could lead even more easily to Hitler than it could to a generous, socialist world. They were right, but right about the wrong people. 'We should have expected this verification through evil rather than a verification through goodness.'

What I have called Mauss's tolerances for ambiguity, then, can be a dangerous thing, a means of blurring what ought to be clear. But it can also be a virtue, a means of saying contradictory things without sacrifice of complexity, and it is *the* virtue of *The Gift*. The essay explores the implications of the patterns of exchange found in many 'archaic' communities, where 'everything' ('food, women, children, goods, talismans, ground, work, services, priestly offices and ranks') can be offered and received as a gift. Mauss is interested in the nature of the obligation to give, and to receive, and to give in return, and also in the properties in the gift itself which attach it forever to its original owner, however many hands it may pass through.

To develop two analogies Mauss merely hints at, it is as if every gift bore the same relation to its giver as a book bears to its author – it's still his in some sense even when he's sold it – or as if we gave away *only* those things which had sentimental value for us. The world of *The Gift* is a mythological land, pieced together from ethnological reports on Melanesia and Australia and north-west America, very much influenced by Malinowski's *Argonauts of the Western Pacific*, and very much reflecting Mauss's expert knowledge of ancient Rome and ancient India. It is a place where all transactions are both intense and formal, where people are deeply involved in social ritual.

It is in one way a utopia, and both Lévi-Strauss (in *The Elementary Structures of Kinship*) and Richard Titmuss (in *The Gift Relationship*) insist on the contrast between this 'non-economic' (Titmuss) or 'supra-economic' (Lévi-Strauss) kingdom and the crass cash universe we have constructed for ourselves.

Mauss certainly seems to suggest something like this when he talks scornfully about 'utilitarianism' and bemoans the fact that man has become a 'calculating machine'. Mauss is undoubtedly saying that we might learn how to live with each other again by observing those societies where people are fully engaged in relatively unmediated social encounters. He wonders, rather wistfully, whether social welfare in the twentieth century may not mark the beginning of a return to an older mode of community.

It should be clear, though Mauss nowhere says so, that we are dealing with a likeable but dreamy, above all non-marxist, alternative to contemporary capitalism. I think of Dickens wanting to sort out industrial unrest without recourse to trade unions; and Mauss is at his flattest when he is most explicit. Communism and individualism are both harmful, he says. And so are abstinence and greed. 'The life of the monk and the life of Shylock are equally to be avoided. This new morality will surely consist of a good, moderate mixture of ideal and reality.'

But Mauss's principal argument is more complicated, and more interesting. He is not really opposing a non-economic paradise of commitment to our grubby alienated scrabblings for money, but asking us to contrast one economy with another – just as he had earlier suggested that we should compare complexities. More precisely, he is saying that exchange in the communities he describes is a 'total social fact' – that is, a fact which is economic, legal, moral, sentimental, magical, religious and much else, all at once. Or to put that yet another way, these exchanges belong to an economy which has not seceded from the rest of social life, and one can read Mauss as saying just the opposite of what Titmuss and Lévi-Strauss find in him.

He may be saying that economics is even more central to these communities than it is to ours – only it is a *different* economics. Certainly there is money in their 'archaic' societies, Mauss thinks. There are 'economic markets'; there are surpluses; there are contracts. Following Malinowski, Mauss speaks of economic and legal relations between husbands and wives in the Trobriand Islands, and the 'salary /gift' the husband pays/ gives his wife when she sleeps with him.

By this time the anti-capitalist, non-utilitarian utopia seems rather a long way off. Mauss gets into the same swampy water when he tries to suggest, in a lecture this time, that exchange in 'archaic' societies is both voluntary and obligatory, 'It is conceived as a present,' he says, 'not as barter and not as a payment; and yet it is a payment.'

Having set up the vital social involvement of these alien communities, Mauss begins to find them oppressive, discovers that nothing is free and nothing is disinterested – the Indians of North America knew all about competitive, conspicuous consumption without having read a word of Veblen. There is a similar wobble in Mauss on the subject of violence in these communities. They are exchanging goods and wives and courtesies so they won't have to murder each other. As Lévi-Strauss says, paraphrasing Mauss and raising the stake, 'Exchanges are peacefully resolved wars, and wars are the result of unsuccessful transactions.'

At this point we may hanker for our calculating machines, and the world of Malinowski begins to look not only more economic than it did, but more aggressive and dangerous. What we really see in Mauss's essay, I think, is one of the last appearances of the noble savage, that curious child of our guilt and our condescension. The work is an eloquent, decent, confused and ultimately defeated quest for people in the world who are simpler and better than we are. 'Their complexity is only of a different nature.' And yet of course these communities *are* different, and their modes of exchange are *not* ours, and we *can* learn from them.

Rodney Needham says Mauss 'established the sociological significance of exchange', and Evans-Pritchard suggests that social anthropology is still living on the 'theoretical capital' accumulated by Mauss and his colleagues in France – nice metaphor, in the light of the anti-marxist polemic. Mauss himself saw the special subject of French sociology (in which he included anthropology as we understand it) as 'the social history of the categories of the human mind', and he has a fine bit of rhetoric on this theme which everyone (Needham, Lévi-Strauss, Merleau-Ponty) quotes:

We must first of all draw up as large as possible a catalogue of categories, beginning with all those which it can be discovered that mankind has ever employed. It will then be seen that there have been, and that there still are, many dead moons, and others pale or obscure, in the firmament of reason.

I would add only that this all sounds a little more orderly than Mauss ever seems to me. His work is full of theoretical and practical possibilities, and they are so alive because he preferred those possibilities to his own arguments. 'A single social institution,' Mauss says, 'can have the most varied functions, produce the most opposed effects . . . It is by no means the case that a simple logical contradiction is the sign of a real incompatibility between the facts.'

This slight regard for logic strikes me as impressive, even

heroic, in a Frenchman. Mauss was an alert, graceful, many-minded scholar whose best thoughts quarrelled fruitfully with each other.

### FURTHER READING

WORKS IN ENGLISH TRANSLATION

*The Gift*, tr. Ian Cunnison (Cohen and West, 1966).

CRITICAL STUDIES

Jean Càzeneuve: *Sociologie de Marcel Mauss* (Presses Universitaires de France, 1968).

Victor Karady: 'Présentation' in *Oeuvres de Marcel Mauss* (Éditions de Minuit, 1968, 1969).

Seth Leacock: 'The ethnological theory of Marcel Mauss' (*American Anthropologist*, vol. 56, 1954).

Claude Lévi-Strauss: 'Introduction à l'oeuvre de Marcel Mauss' in Mauss: *Sociologie et Anthropologie* (Presses Universitaires de France, 1950).

Steven Lukes: 'Marcel Mauss' (*International Encyclopaedia of the Social Sciences*, vol. 10, Macmillan, 1968).

Maurice Merleau-Ponty: 'De Mauss à Claude Lévi-Strauss' in *Signes* (Gallimard, 1960).

Rodney Needham: Introduction to É. Durkheim and M. Mauss: *Primitive Classification* (Paris, 1903: tr. Cohen and West, 1963).

# A. R. RADCLIFFE-BROWN
## (*1881–1955*)

### John Beattie

MODERN social anthropologists frequently refer to Radcliffe-Brown, but as often as not they do so only to point out how wrong he was. For a scholar who spent a lifetime as a professional social anthropologist his written output was small, and many of his ideas were second hand. Such fieldwork as he did was mostly of the old-fashioned, 'questionnaire' type; he worked through interpreters and not through the vernacular languages, and his writings about the peoples he studied quite lack the detailed immediacy and vividness of his contemporary Malinowski's. Nevertheless, with Malinowski, he is rightly regarded as one of the founding fathers of modern social anthropology. Why?

Alfred Reginald Brown (the 'Radcliffe', his mother's maiden name, was added later) was born in Birmingham in 1881. He read mental and moral science at Cambridge, and also studied anthropology there under Rivers and Haddon. From 1906 to 1908 he engaged in anthropological fieldwork in the Andaman Islands, and in 1909–10 he lectured both in Cambridge and at the London School of Economics. In the latter year he went to Western Australia, where he carried out what would nowadays be called an ethnographic survey among some of the aboriginal peoples of the area. After the First World War, which he spent mostly in Australia and Tonga, Radcliffe-Brown went to South Africa, where in 1920 he was appointed to the new chair of social anthropology at Cape Town. His most celebrated book, *The Andaman Islanders*, was published in 1922. Four years later he returned to Australia to occupy the new chair at Sydney, and in 1930 he published his second important work, *The Social Organization of Australian Tribes*. In the following year he left Australia to become professor of anthropology at Chicago, where he remained until 1937, except for a brief visit to China in 1935. In 1939 he came as professor of social anthropology to Oxford, and there he stayed, with an intermission of two years at São Paulo, Brazil, until he reached retiring age nine years later.

Even after that he kept moving, teaching at Alexandria, London, Manchester and Grahamstown, South Africa. He came back to England in 1954, and died in London the following year, aged seventy-four. As well as the two books mentioned above, Radcliffe-Brown produced a number of lectures and articles, some of the more important of which were republished during his lifetime as *Structure and Function in Primitive Society* (1952); others in two posthumous volumes. He married in 1910 and had one daughter.

Radcliffe-Brown's peripatetic career gives the first clue to his importance and influence: he really put social anthropology, as a university subject, on the world map. As a young man he was a forceful and unconventional personality (at Cambridge he was known as 'Anarchy Brown') and a vivid if sometimes didactic conversationalist. In his prime he was a stimulating and exciting teacher, as I can myself well remember, having attended a course of his lectures at Oxford in the autumn of 1939. He was also said to have been a good listener, at least until he was affected by illness and old age, and observers have spoken of his patience and sympathy with both informants and administrators in the field. So he was admirably qualified to act as both prophet and proponent of 'the newer anthropology' (or 'comparative sociology', as he wanted to call it), and he did so with remarkable success in all five continents.

But his reputation rests not only on his personal charm and his brilliance as a teacher; in fact he possessed a good deal less charisma than Malinowski, and he never founded or wished to found a 'school'. He sought students, not disciples. His chief contribution to social anthropology derives from his clear and systematic thinking (perhaps sometimes a bit too systematic) about the subject and its problems, and from his brilliantly lucid and incisive style of exposition. It owes little to his fieldwork, which in originality and depth was far inferior to Malinowski's. He never got to know an Andamanese or aboriginal community 'from the inside', but he gave a new clarity to his subject, and a new precision to the problems it studies, which have done much to establish it as a respectable and autonomous member of the social sciences. Radcliffe-Brown is often wrong, but at least we nearly always know what he is saying.

When Radcliffe-Brown started publishing in the early 1920s, social anthropology in England was in something of a muddle. The evolutionary theories of the Victorians had for the most part been replaced by diffusionist hypotheses. But the trouble with both of these approaches was that with preliterate societies there was usually no way of testing their conclusions, since they referred to past events for which there could be little or no valid evidence. Also, and more importantly, the increasing amount and higher quality of reports from the field were bringing home to anthropologists the fact that 'primitive' societies were not just ragbags of savage customs, each of which could be understood only by somehow tracing it back to an earlier form or to diffusion from elsewhere. It was now becoming apparent that such societies were real working systems, which demanded to be understood in their own right.

But how? Radcliffe-Brown had the answer. One of the most formative influences on his thinking had been the French sociological tradition which had begun with Montesquieu and had developed, through Saint-Simon and Comte, into the mature sociological system of Émile Durkheim. Like his French predecessors he believed that societies are systems. This means that they must be made up of parts, related systematically to one another and to the whole society, in accordance with general principles which, as soon as we know enough, we shall be able to discover. In other words, societies have 'structures' (Radcliffe-Brown defines 'structure' as 'the complex network of actually existing relationships in any society'). And their component parts, 'particular social usages', have (or may have – Radcliffe-Brown is less dogmatic on this point than his theory would seem to require) *functions*, a function being defined as 'the contribution which a partial activity makes to the total activity of which it is a part'. Thus societies are quite like the physical organisms studied by some natural scientists, even though they are not altogether like them; Radcliffe-Brown himself points out some of the more obvious differences. So what social anthropologists should aim at is a 'natural science of society'. By systematically comparing societies of diverse types, we shall eventually achieve a body of scientific knowledge about all human societies everywhere, expressed in unexceptionable general laws.

Nowadays all this looks pretty naïve to most of us, and few modern social anthropologists regard their discipline with such simple optimism, or even as being quite this kind of enterprise. To begin with, in spite of his philosophical training (or because of it?) Radcliffe-Brown did not really understand what science is about, or what might be the nature of the 'general laws' which he supposed it to be seeking. He wrote as though he thought that scientists simply aimed at recording 'regularities' of the form 'all As are Bs'. He quite failed to see that what is essential to a scientific law is not that it states a regularity but that it explains one, by means of some new synthesis.

Again, we now see more clearly that human societies differ from the mindless systems which most natural scientists study in that their component members are, or appear to be, influenced by shared concepts, beliefs and values. And the understanding of these requires methods quite different from those used by natural scientists, methods which are interpretative as well as analytical, and which are in this respect much more like those used by historians and philosophers than they are like those of physicists or zoologists. This was plain enough to Durkheim and his school, but although Radcliffe-Brown himself used such interpretative methods, as any good social anthropologist must, he was so obsessed with his view of social anthropology as a natural science that he failed to develop their methodological implications. It has taken years of protest by Evans-Pritchard and others to make the study of such 'ideal' or conceptual phenomena, sometimes dismissed by rigid structuralists as 'culture', respectable again.

Finally, it has been pointed out often enough that the static (or homeostatic) view of society which is implicit in the Radcliffe-Brown approach affords no adequate – or indeed any – model for understanding social change, for if a system is really 'functional' *any* change must disrupt it. Radcliffe-Brown was not as oblivious of these difficulties as has sometimes been asserted, but his somewhat doctrinaire approach to the question of what the social sciences are about effectively prevented him from facing up to them. But here, as elsewhere, the crucial thing is that his clear if mistaken theoretical statements have enabled others to see some of the problems more clearly and so deal with them more effectively.

It remains true, however, that very often social and cultural institutions *are* functionally interconnected, and the discovery of these not always obvious causal links provides a highly important means of understanding them. The recognition of this was the real 'revolution' in anthropology, and despite their differences Malinowski and Radcliffe-Brown were equally its authors. It formed the basis for Radcliffe-Brown's clear and still valid distinction between ethnology, the branch of anthropology which is concerned with how things came to be as they are, and social anthropology, which is concerned with how they work and what they mean at the present time.

This distinction is still often blurred, with consequent confusion. As Radcliffe-Brown conceived it, social anthropology was 'ahistorical' rather than anti-historical; where historical evidence was available he quite explicitly admitted it, but in most of the societies studied by anthropologists up to that time there just wasn't any. In such cases historical conjecture was usually profitless, but this did not mean that they could not be profitably studied as going concerns. Both historical and functional methods were legitimate, but they were *different*; this was Radcliffe-Brown's central point. It is above all the recognition of this, with its corollary that the field anthropologist should live in the society he studies and observe what actually happens, instead of just asking people what they think happens or ought to happen, that has made possible the modern social anthropological monograph, based on the writer's own intensive fieldwork.

Hardly anybody now accepts Radcliffe-Brown's ideas about theory and method, though his clear statements of them have helped others to think up better ones. But his work in some of the more specialized fields of social anthropology has been more positively influential, in the sense that further progress has been along the lines he laid down, rather than in opposition to them.

Three fields in which his contribution has seemed to me to be particularly significant are those of ritual, of social control, and of kinship.

Radcliffe-Brown's first and most celebrated book, *The Andaman Islanders*, is in effect an attempt to test in the field the Durkheimian hypothesis that the primary function of ritual is, by giving expression to the collective 'sentiments' of a society, to contribute to social cohesion, and so to the maintenance of a social system through time. But in later writings he went further; he claimed that ritual might express more than merely man's dependence on society; even more basically it expresses his dependence on his whole environment, physical as well as social. Nowadays most students of ritual would go even further still, and would say that ritual may express any notion which is of shared value and 'concern' in a society. But what is of major importance in Radcliffe-Brown's statement is his emphasis of the fact that ritual is essentially *expressive*; it is a way of saying something as well as of doing something. Once this is recognized, it becomes possible to see (as Evans-Pritchard pointed out more clearly later) that magic and religion are not, as Tylor and Frazer had thought they were, just misguided and ineffective attempts to be scientific.

For Radcliffe-Brown, there are two important things to be found out about any ritual procedure; first, what it means to the people who have it, and second, what its social consequences are. Even though he did not see as clearly as he might have done that the first of these kinds of inquiry calls for methods not allowed for by his brand of functionalism, his clear statement that there *are* these two kinds of questions to be answered opened the way for the deeper studies of magical and religious behaviour later carried out by Evans-Pritchard, Nadel and others.

Though Radcliffe-Brown did no fieldwork explicitly devoted to the problem of social control, he provided a characteristically clear and precise framework for its investigation in smaller-scale societies. Taking, first, its political aspect, he adapted the classical formulations of Weber and others, and defined political organization as being concerned with 'the maintenance or establishment of social order, within a territorial framework, by the organized exercise of coercive authority through the use, or the possibility of use, of physical force'.

Though there is little that is original about this formulation (and in any case a little reflection shows it to be inapplicable to those many societies in which some sort of order seems to be maintained without 'the organized exercise of coercive authority') it does at least provide social anthropologists with clear criteria for determining what they should regard as political, and for distinguishing different types of political control.

In the study of what used to be called 'primitive law', Radcliffe-Brown's contribution has been both more original and more important. He saw, as some of his contemporaries, including Malinowski (whose *Crime and Custom in Savage Society*, brilliant though it is, simply adds to the confusion), failed to do, that terms like 'law', properly applicable to the complex judicial institutions of Western society, are a good deal less appropriate if they are applied to the varied means whereby social order may be maintained in 'primitive' societies. Durkheim thought that 'primitive' societies were dominated by a kind of prototypical 'criminal law'; 'civil law' being characteristic of more advanced societies. Malinowski reacted against this one-sided view with the equally one-sided claim that simpler societies (by which he meant the Trobriand Islanders) were on the contrary just as concerned with 'civil law', that is, with relationships of economic and other kinds of reciprocity. (In fact his own evidence showed that they weren't.) But the trouble with both of these approaches was that they attempted to comprehend the unfamiliar mechanisms of small-scale, preliterate societies in Western terms. Radcliffe-Brown saw this clearly, and he offers a concise and very much less culture-bound method of classifying and understanding these institutions.

This is his theory of social sanctions. A sanction is 'a reaction on the part of a society or of a considerable number of its members to a mode of behaviour which is thereby approved or disapproved'. Sanctions can be classified as positive and negative (rewards and punishments), as organized and diffuse, and as primary and secondary (depending on whether action is taken in case of a breach of rule by the whole community or its recognized representatives, or by the injured party, with popular approval). In this schema the sanctions of the criminal law of Western society are neatly subsumed under the rubric of 'organized negative sanctions'. But they are only one kind of sanctions, and some societies manage very well without them. This schema enables field workers to take adequate and coherent account of such factors of social control as the blood feud, ritual beliefs and procedures, and public opinion, factors which can be referred to as 'law' only at the cost of clarity and common sense.

In the study of kinship, finally, for many students Radcliffe-Brown introduced clarity and order into what had hitherto been something of a jumble of ethnographic *minutiae*. His first important work in this field was his comparative analysis of Australian kinship usages and terminology in *The Social Organization of Australian Tribes*. But he went on to review the kinship systems of the peoples of other continents, especially Africa, and the results of this review are admirably summed up in his long introduction to the symposium *African Systems of Kinship and Marriage*, which is still indispensable reading for students.

Here again his great merit was that he discerned very clearly the essential elements in the welter of kinship material which was pouring in from the field in increasing quantities. Like an expert jigsaw-puzzle solver, he saw quickly and clearly what went with what, and which were the essential features of the pattern. It can be and has been argued that phrases like 'the unity of the sibling group', 'the unity of the lineage', and 'the equivalence of siblings' add little or nothing analytically to our understanding of kinship relations. But in fact they do sum up in a phrase essential elements in certain broad types of relationship which had not hitherto been so explicitly, or at least so succinctly, stated.

It was known, for example, before Radcliffe-Brown wrote that in some societies membership in particular descent groups was more important, and important in more contexts, than the particular kinship links which join two individuals, though the implications of this were not always fully appreciated. But by picking out this essential 'group' element in many relationships and giving it a name, Radcliffe-Brown highlighted its importance, and so helped to provide a firm base for the great advances in kinship and lineage theory later made by Evans-Pritchard, Fortes and others.

It has often been said, and with some justice, that Radcliffe-Brown's chief contributions were made at the beginning of his career, and that most of his later writing did little more than reiterate, sometimes modify, themes already stated. It is therefore worth noting that in the field of kinship studies at least he made a significant advance on an earlier position of his own, though he is not always credited with it. In his celebrated early essay, 'The Mother's Brother in South Africa' (Chapter I in *Structure and Function*) he argued that the intimate, privileged relationship often found between men and their mother's brothers in societies where membership in patrilineally organized groups is important, is due to an extension of the warm, friendly feeling that a man has for his mother, to her male siblings. In accordance with the principle of the equivalence of siblings these men are in some sense and in some contexts thought of as 'interchangeable' with her, as being the same *kind* of relative.

Later anthropologists have rightly criticized this view, pointing out that there is little if any evidence for such affective transference, and that in any case it does not seem to apply in matrilineal societies, where although no doubt children love their mothers just as much, the mother's brother and not the father is the figure of authority. They have advocated a more 'structural' interpretation of this usage, based on the recognition of the differential group membership of the persons concerned. But they have not always mentioned that Radcliffe-Brown himself, in a later essay (reprinted as Chapter V in *Structure and Function*) made exactly the same point, that the essential thing about the relationship is that although men and their mothers' brothers in patrilineal and exogamous societies are closely related, they belong to different and distinct lineages. Thus their relationship involves both separation and attachment, and the joking relationship is admirably adapted to cope with this ambivalence.

Social anthropology has turned into something very different from what Radcliffe-Brown expected, even, probably, from what he would have wished. We are really hardly any nearer to the formulation of empirically based 'general laws', applicable to all human societies everywhere, than we were when he first formulated this as the chief aim of social anthropology, in the 1920s. On the other hand, our understanding of the cultural and social institutions of simpler, smaller-scale societies has advanced enormously in the decades since then. It has done so both on the contextual, 'functional' level, and in the interpretative study of symbols and meanings.

Much of this advance we owe to scholars who have either been pupils of Radcliffe-Brown (as many of the present senior generation of social anthropologists have), or have been influenced by his writings. He is still important, not because of his originality as a theoretical social scientist (his ideas about what society is show little advance on Durkheim's), but rather because of his capacity to formulate concisely and clearly some of the issues in the major fields of anthropological inquiry which are as important in our day as they were in his. His genius was for seeing the essential aspects of things, the provision of 'guiding formulations', in Redfield's phrase, rather than for the discovery of new and hitherto unsuspected syntheses, the 'laws' which he was so anxious to find. Although he quite failed to do what he set out to do, the conceptual tools which his clear thinking provided in many fields of social anthropology have been indispensable in the later development of the subject to which he devoted his life.

FURTHER READING

WORKS

*The Andaman Islanders* (Cambridge University Press, 1922).

*Method in Social Anthropology*, ed. M. N. Srinivas (Chicago University Press, 1958).

*A Natural Science of Society* (Free Press, 1964).

*The Social Anthropology of Radcliffe-Brown*, ed. A. Kuper (Routledge and Kegan Paul, 1977).

*Structure and Function in Primitive Society* (Cohen and West, 1952).

CRITICAL STUDIES

John Beattie: *Other Cultures: Aims, Methods and Achievements in Social Anthropology* (Cohen and West, 1964; Free Press, 1964; Routledge and Kegan Paul, 1966).

Fred Eggan (ed.): *Social Anthropology of North American Tribes*, second edition (Chicago University Press, 1955).

Meyer Fortes: 'Radcliffe-Brown's Contribution to the Study of Social Organisation' (*British Journal of Sociology*, vol. 6, no. 1, March 1955). Also as chapter 9 of Meyer Fortes: *Times and Social Structure* (Athlone Press, 1970).

Meyer Fortes (ed.): *Social Structure: Studies Presented to A. R. Radcliffe-Brown* (Oxford University Press, 1949).

Adam Kuper: *Anthropologists and Anthropology: The British School, 1922–72* (Allen Lane, 1973; Penguin, 1975).

Robert H. Lowie: *The History of Ethnological Theory* (Holt, 1937).

# BRONISLAW MALINOWSKI
## (*1884–1942*)

### Audrey Richards

MALINOWSKI'S famous monographs on the Trobriand islands were certainly the most formative influence on the work of British social anthropologists from 1922, when he published his first field study, until his death in 1942. Most of the leading British anthropologists since the 1930s were partly or wholly trained by him and these include Evans-Pritchard, Firth, Fortes, Leach, Mair, Nadel, Read, Schapera, Godfrey Wilson as well as a number working out of Britain such as Hogbin, Kuper, Oberg, Powdermaker and Wagner. Those who later reacted most strongly against him were as much influenced in the nature of their work as those who remained his supporters.

Bronislaw Malinowski was a Pole, born in Cracow in 1884, the son of a Professor of Slavic Philology. He was awarded a doctorate in physics and mathematics in 1908, but illness and bad eyesight interrupted his work. He claims that he first became interested in anthropology through the reading of Frazer's *Golden Bough*. He worked for two years at Leipzig University under William Wundt and Karl Buecher, and came to London in 1910, attracted to England by the presence of Westermarck, Hobhouse, Seligman, Haddon and Rivers. He spent four years at London University where he produced his first book *The Family among the Australian Aborigines* in 1913.

Seligman became his friend and adviser and helped him to get funds for his first field expedition in 1914, when he visited Motu in Papua, and the Mailu of New Guinea, and spent from 1914–15, and 1915–18 in the Trobriand islands. He joined the staff of the London School of Economics in 1910 and was appointed to its first Chair of Social Anthropology in 1927. He later became interested in applied anthropology, especially in relation to the then British colonies in Africa. He trained a group of young anthropologists who were to take part in an International African

Institute scheme for comparative research on the effects of European contact on different African tribes. The scheme was the first attempt made in this country at large-scale comparative research of this kind, instituted largely on the initiative of J. H. Oldham of the International Missionary Council. The anthropologists included names famous today such as those of Fortes, Hofstra, Nadel, Oberg, Margaret Read, Wagner and Godfrey and Monica Wilson.

This work attracted Malinowski's interests to the African field. He later visited a number of his students at work there and wrote articles on what was then known as 'culture contact'. Anthropological thinking was a considerable influence on the development of African administration at the time, more so probably than at later periods.

Malinowski made several trips to America where he found stimulus and friendship. There he visited the Hopi of Arizona in 1926, and he was engaged in a study of marketing among the Zapotec of Mexico in the last years of his life. He was appointed visiting Professor of Yale University in 1939 and died there suddenly in 1942.

Malinowski's field monographs, *Argonauts of the Western Pacific* (1922), *Sexual Life of Savages* (1929), and *Coral Gardens and their Magic* (1935), produced a revolution in the aims and field techniques of the younger anthropologists. They are still quoted in text-books on the history of method in the social sciences. Anthropologists were then mainly interested in studies of the distribution of customs and artefacts which would show the contact of one people with another, and hence make it possible to reconstruct the movements of peoples from one region or continent to another. It was still generally taken for granted that the anthropologist was the theorist, who sat at home while others, such as missionaries, travellers or administrators collected facts for him in the field.

Pioneer work had been done in the form of general surveys of the peoples in particular regions such as the Cambridge expedition to the Torres Straits (1899), Boas' Jesup expedition to the north Pacific coast (1883), as well as Seligman's work on British New Guinea (1910), later to be followed by his survey of Nilotic tribes (1909–22) and the field studies of Rivers (1901, 1908, 1914), Thurnwald (1906–9) and Lindblom (1910). A few good outline monographs had been written by missionaries and administrators such as Codrington, Casalis, Junod, Roscoe and Rattray. Professional ethnographers could, however, be counted on the fingers of one hand.

In these circumstances, Malinowski's first monograph struck a new fresh note. It was an intensive study produced by an anthropologist who lived closely with a people for two or more years, spoke their language and acted as what is now known as a 'participant observer'. It is in fact the method now normally used by anthropologists in the field. Malinowski became absorbed in his tiny community. He was interested from the first in each custom, belief or artefact in relation to the working of the total society, which was for him a system. Each custom, he claimed, had a 'function' to play in this system. It was never a mere survival from the past. Hence his use, almost *ad nauseam*, of the term 'functional anthropology', to distinguish his work from that of the evolutionists and the diffusionists of his day. Radcliffe-Brown originally used the term 'function' in much the same way and both these anthropologists protested loudly against the type of fanciful historical reconstruction then current.

The characteristics of Malinowski's field studies were, first of all, the very detailed first-hand observations he made of the major activities of the Trobriand islanders – such as their *kula* overseas trading expeditions or their agriculture. This work was on an entirely different scale to anything produced before. The chosen activity was viewed as part of a whole 'institution', a group of people organized under a leader to use their simple tools in a particular environment. The chosen activity was shown to be coordinated with sets of other activities, ritual or instrumental, governed by a set of rules and facilitated by linguistic usages.

The nature of these basic activities was documented by charts, land tenure maps, seasonal calendars and the like and they were described in vivid eyewitness style. The people's attitudes and values stand revealed in the way they swaggered, boasted and displayed their food crops and dressed up in festal rig for the accompanying dances. Both the descriptive detail and his method of correlating activities, beliefs and norms behaviour were then new.

Secondly, Malinowski was interested from the first in social grouping, which he called 'personnel' or, rather eccentrically, 'social organization'. This interest probably sprang from his activities approach, and the automatic linking of what was done with 'Who did it?' The ethnographic survey can say little more than that the Xs or the Ys are yam cultivators. Malinowski described the Trobriand yams as dug by one set of kinsmen, carried in presentation to their relatives-in-law or exchanged with other sets of kinsmen for baskets of cooked food. A funeral crowd was no longer a mass of people wailing their heads off, but a group of matrilineal kin of the dead sitting aloof and silent, while the widow, her kinsfolk and the dead man's sons, who are not his heirs in a matrilineal society, together wailed, handled the corpse, exhumed and reburied it. Malinowski also realized, on the basis of empirical evidence, that groups and social roles may be in conflict, as for instance in the case of the traditional rivalry between a man's son and his sister's son. He thus anticipated the work on social tensions and social conflicts which has dominated so much recent anthropological theory, particularly in the case of the work of Gluckman and his pupils.

It is often said that he was only interested in individuals and not in social groups. This position can possibly be maintained by those who read only his more superficial works on theoretical issues, but not by those who study his major field monographs. A recent rereading of these after many years confirms my views on this point. Certainly at the time it was the material on social relationships and social tensions which seemed to his students to be so striking. 'The Zulu do . . . or think' turned into 'Members of the sub-clan or the relatives-in-law' do this or that. Such work on social structure was in its infancy, but the interest is un-mistakable and this combination of detailed observation of activities together with the recording of the personnel, the social groups involved, was new at the time.

The individual appears in the Trobriand field material of course. The emotions of particular men and women are described and particularly perhaps emotions in the face of death. There was also a stress on the function of magico-religious rites and beliefs as a solace to the distressed and worried individual as well as to the group to which he belonged. This emphasis on individual needs was subsequently rejected by a number of British anthropologists, notably Evans-Pritchard, Fortes, Leach and Gluckman, all writers who consider ritual as an expression of the values underlying social structure and social roles. The function of ritual both for the individual and for the group are of course indissolubly connected and Malinowski, both by empirical evidence and the subjective analysis of his own emotions, showed it to be so.

Individuals also appeared in the Trobriand monographs as people involved in dramatic incidents which seemed to Malinowski to illustrate some special feature of social structure, a quarrel, a suicide or a case of adultery. This was an early form of what would now be called 'the case history method' although his cases were never subjected to statistical analysis. We do not know how many cross-cousins quarrelled, or how many young people really settled down to happy, stable unions after the period of casual love affairs which Malinwoski described as a good preparation for marriage. Nor did he make any village surveys such as are now an almost invariable part of anthropological work. He counted the baskets of food exchanged at marriage and harvest but he did not collect quantitative data on the kinship and clan structure of particular villages, on marriage or property. H. Powell's subsequent work on the Trobriands shows how valuable this would have been in his case (1960).

Lastly, Malinowski's linguistic texts were superb, probably fuller than any collected at the time except those of Boas from the north-west Pacific reaa. But Malinowski's texts and his examination of the words which composed them were presented in the context of the actual situation in which they were used, as organizing an activity like gardening, expressing kinship relationships, and forming magic imperatives. Thus *Coral Gardens and their Magic* (vol. ii, 1935), one of Malinowski's most original but least read books, gives his whole theory of the part played by language in culture.

Malinowski wrote in a vivid personal style often describing

his own adventures in field work. The crude comparisons he made between Trobriand, Polish and British society stimulated, not only missionaries and administrators in the then colonial territories, but social scientists and social reformers. The Trobrianders, some 1,200 strong, living in their minute and inaccessible islands became familiar figures in the literature of psycho-analysis and education. Social anthropology became a popular subject.

This is hardly the case today, for descriptive work is now rather despised, and anthropological observations are largely expressed in kinship diagrams and paradigms. This is a curious phase in the history of anthropology. Medieval or other historians seize avidly on any eyewitness account of a royal court, a battle or a village scene but many young anthropologists, who have the most enviable opportunities to record such scenes in living societies, feel that it is somehow inferior to do so. The general public suffers, as will future historians.

Malinowski had a strong personality, and this no doubt attracted attention to his work. He was brilliant, witty, sensitive, touchy, egoistic, very dependent on the appreciation of his friends and students, and usually quite unfair to his opponents. He became a notable figure in academic circles in London in the 1930s. Wherever two or three anthropologists sat gossiping, Malinowski's latest theory, *bon mot*, swear word or eccentricity was certainly being discussed. It is difficult, in fact, to consider his fame apart from his personality, for not only did he raise strong emotions, positive and negative, at the time, but these attitudes survived after his death. In fact it is probably only the sociologists of today and tomorrow who will be able to give an objective analysis of his work.

He was a brilliant, informal teacher using what he called the Socratic method. His seminars at the London School of Economics acquired an international reputation and Malinowski would often flash retorts in several languages. His directness forced the student to face the problem and express its essentials simply. Students were attracted or repelled according to their temperament, but they were always stimulated. His disciples tended in the first days of his teaching, in the early 1930s for example, to view themselves as a team attacking the forces of reaction, then seen in terms of evolutionism, diffusionism and the hunt for 'survivals' in present-day societies.

Malinowski asserted his claims in extravagant fashion. His students were enthusiastic, intolerant and no doubt aggressive, but it must be admitted that the violence of his attacks certainly hastened the birth of social anthropology as a science. It is also true, regrettable as it is, that such movements of intolerant attack have a great attraction for students and often coincide with periods of productive activity.

Did Malinowski manage to teach his field methods? The answer depends of course on what you consider a good field worker to be. Is he a man with a theory specially adapted to stimulate empirical observations, or a person with a flair for personal contacts and observation, and a gift for vivid and evocative description of the scenes he has witnessed? Is he a man with the physical strength required to talk all day in a foreign language and to copy notes all night, or one who is immune from malaria or, alternatively, able to work with malaria?

Malinowski certainly had a flair for this exciting work. His linguistic gifts were phenomenal. He made quick contacts. More important, he had an intuitive grasp of the relevant facts and saw the connexions between them. He was indefatigable in the collection and analysis of data once his theoretical interests had been aroused. He wrote three large volumes on the Trobriands. The books on kinship and on mortuary ritual which he planned, but did not publish, would probably have been as full. Critics say that he stayed so long in the Trobriands only because he was interned there in the war, as an enemy alien. I do not think this is true. Field work simply fascinated him although, as a recently published diary (*A Diary in the Strict Sense of the Term*, 1967) shows, he had violent moods of revulsion and irritation with his informants. He continued doing field work till he died for he was engaged at the time on a study of Mexican markets. When he visited me in northern Zambia in 1934 he refused to be a mere spectator, but immediately started to work on a project. I published some of his observations on house building after his death (*Man* Vol. 1. 1950).

These temperamental and intellectual gifts of course cannot be taught, although he gives a very full account of what he did in the field and of the success or failure of his methods: an instructive practice, but not one often followed now since anthropological interests have shifted from empirical observation to the analysis of cognitive systems. What students learnt from him was his enthusiasm, his standards and the example of his persistence. He also helped them immensely to enlarge the field of their observations by the use of a series of synoptic charts by which each institution was examined methodically from a number of aspects – environmental, technological, structural, normative, from the point of view of the native theory of knowledge, his magico-religious beliefs and his values and his linguistic usages. The family, kinship groups, chieftainship, agriculture or marketing, or whatever the problem was, were all analysed according to this type of scheme, and the relationship between each column was systematically examined. I personally found such schemes invaluable, in stimulating both the collection and the analysis of data. The method produced material on a much wider front than is common nowadays. It is probably of special value in the study of peoples not yet described.

What will remain of the work of his unusual and creative personality? It is difficult to say. His polemics against evolution, diffusion and historical reconstructions date badly and seem tedious to students. Historical 'just-so stories', as he called them, are out of fashion, although serious historical reconstructions based on documentary evidence or the analysis of tribal devices for preserving history are definitely to the fore. Such work Malinowski would have supported. In fact his later charts had a column on the historical facts available on each particular institution.

Malinowski tackled many problems – family organization, kinship terminology, conflicts in matrilineal society, primitive law, economic incentives, magic, religion, myth and linguistics – and had something original to say on each. In fact the fertility of his imagination left his path littered with unfinished projects, and ideas not pursued to their conclusions. His pragmatic approach to the study of magic and religion is now a part of anthropological thinking. His book on law (1926) now seems slight but he analysed the sum total of sanctions, positive and negative, which induce conformity to rules even in societies without law courts, and this proved a seminal work at the time. His work on matrilineal kinship is still constantly quoted. I am inclined to think that his concept of myth as a charter for the legitimate exercise of group rights and magic acts will prove to be one of the most fruitful of his ideas since it leads to the whole question of the legitimacy of institutions in traditional societies, and methods of transferring rights.

Malinowski's general theory of culture and his use of the term 'institution' for a group, activity, norm, dogma, knowledge, language, tie-up seem to me unlikely to survive, though it produced so much fruitful analysis in field workers of his day. There was some confusion and much repetition in his last statements of his 'functional' theory, especially in his posthumously published book *The Scientific Theory of Culture* (1944). New schemes of culture and society are in the market.

Malinowski's work in fact fell into disrepute after the war. His exhaustive study of a particular community was useless for the development of political and kinship typologies which became the current interest. 'Culture' was out, and 'structure' became the only reputable subject of study. But fashions change quickly. Rigid distinctions between 'culture' and 'structure' were already breaking down as I wrote my contribution to the first edition of this book. Of recent years the attention of many anthropologists has been centred on the structure of different peoples' ideas rather than on the structure of their social groups and the typologies which can be based on these. To Lévi-Strauss in fact 'structure' means the structure of ideas. He and those who think on similar lines in Britain such as Leach, Needham, Douglas and many of the younger generation of anthropologists declare their interest to be in the universal patterns of thought and symbolism rather than in those of the Trobriand islanders or any such particular group. To these Malinowski's careful analysis of the symbolic use of words and actions in magic spells seems tedious and useless. They do not give the required answers to questions on the dichotomies believed to be universal as between, say, left and right, male and female, the realm of nature and that of society. But those who study in detail the symbols used in the myths and rites of a particular society stumble across the multiple meanings attached to one symbol, whether a word, a gesture or an art form, and they find the crude universal dichotomies limiting and ultimately stultifying. So the whirligig of anthropological fashion may take another turn! But what I think is certain is that the *corpus* of Malinowski's field material will remain a treasure-house for sociologists, psychologists and linguists and compulsory reading for students intending to go into the field. There is a creative touch in Malinowski's finest descriptive work which still sets the young field-worker rearing to go.

### FURTHER READING

WORKS

*Argonauts of the Western Pacific* (1922; Dutton, 1961).

*Magic, Science and Religion and other essays* (1925; Doubleday, 1954).

*Crime and Custom in Savage Society* (1926; Littlefield, 1976).

*Coral Gardens and their Magu* (2 vols., Allen and Unwin, 1935).

*Sex and Repression in Savage Society* (1927; New America Library, 1955).

*The Sexual Life of Savages in North-Western Melanesia* (1929; Harcourt Brace, 1962).

CRITICAL STUDIES

Raymond W. Firth (ed.): *Man and Culture. An evaluation of the work of Bronislaw Malinowski* (Routledge and Kegan Paul, 1957).

M. Gluckman: 'Malinowski's Contribution to Social Anthropology' (*The Rhodes-Livingstone Papers*, no. 16, Oxford, 1949).

Adam Kuper: *Anthropologists and Anthropology: The British School, 1922–72* (Allen Lane, 1973; Penguin, 1975). Ch. 1.

Rhoda Metraux: 'Malinowski' in *Encyclopedia of the Social Sciences*, 1962.

Michael Panoff: *Bronislaw Malinowski* (Payot, 1972).

H. A. Powell: 'Competitive Leadership in Trobriand Political Organisation' (*Journal of the Royal Anthropological Institute*, vol. 90, 1960).

J. P. Singh Uberoi: *Politics and the Kula Ring* (Manchester University Press, second edition, 1971).

# PITIRIM SOROKIN
## (1889–1968)

### F. R. Cowell

'STARTING my life as a son of a poor itinerant artisan and peasant mother,' Sorokin writes in his autobiography, 'I have subsequently been a farmhand, itinerant artisan, factory worker, clerk, teacher, conductor of a choir, revolutionary, political prisoner, journalist, student, editor of a metropolitan paper, member of Kerensky's cabinet, an exile, professor at Russian, Czech and American universities, and a scholar with an international reputation.' No other sociologist, not even Saint-Simon, has had so varied a background. Sorokin was therefore a very unusual recruit to American academic life when, after arriving to give a few lectures in 1924, he was offered a chair in sociology at the University of Minnesota. There he spent six happy and fruitful years until, in 1930, he was asked to create the department of sociology at Harvard University. He retired, at the age of seventy, in 1959.

During the course of that long academic career his output of lectures, books and articles was prodigious. A man of volcanic energy – 'that violent man', as Professor R. K. Merton, one of his students and collaborators, has described him – he has to his credit some 30 volumes and over 200 contributions to learned journals.

More completely than any living sociologist, Sorokin sought to provide a complete account of sociology, psychologically based and philosophically orientated. His approach, he agreed, is a vast 'macroscopic' conspectus rather than a detailed survey of limited, particular problems. Not that he neglected such 'microscopic' studies. His early works on social mobility, rural–urban sociology and 'time-budgets' (how people spend their day) show the attention to specific problems also evident in his later studies of the whole of history and of sociology.

Evidence of his range appeared within two years of his arrival in

America – in his *Contemporary Sociological Theories* (1928). Still one of the best among the few histories of the subject, it then came as a revelation. Most American academic instructors in sociology had been slow to equip themselves with an adequate historical background and few of them showed much interest in European contributions to their subject. Sorokin's book was a powerful stimulant. His index listed over 1,000 writers. Still more valuable was his classification of sociological theories by schools of thought and prevailing tendencies.

He maintained his keen watch upon the spate of sociological production. In 1966, already well past seventy, he produced a sequel to his earlier history with *Sociological Theories of Today*, a critical account of contemporary work which few could rival. The critical note of the book was strong, for the reform of sociology had long been among his tasks. In 1956 he had delivered some resounding blows in *Fads and Foibles in Modern Sociology and Related Sciences* which, curiously, were re-echoed three years later by Wright Mills in a volume in which Sorokin's prior, more comprehensive onslaught had no mention.

But Sorokin's main contribution to sociology is his theory of social and cultural reality and the manner in which it changes over time. He worked unceasingly on this for some ten years between the wars, with teams of helpers. The result was a three-volume study, *Social and Cultural Dynamics* (1937–40). It was an encyclopedic survey classified under fluctuations of forms of art, of systems of truth, of ethics, of law, of social relations, war and revolution. It related to the whole of recorded history, from ancient Egypt to the present. In 1941 a fourth volume appeared. Here, in the light of many comments and criticisms, Sorokin gave a fuller account of his principles and methods, and re-examined the basic problems he had handled. The furore is not yet stilled.

The leading American journals were in no doubt about the commanding character of Sorokin's achievement. The slight interest aroused by large American treatises on sociology in England in the 1930s and the outbreak of the Second World War, are the main reasons for the scanty interest in *Social and Cultural Dynamics* over here. The mass of detailed information (much of it in tables and graphs), the highly individual presentation, the use of one or two unusual words in a technical sense – all these combined to deter. The 'statistics' liberally provided were Sorokin's effort towards clearer estimations of influences by using a numerical scale of importance (from 1 to 12) instead of vague expressions like 'slight', 'more', 'considerable', 'very great'. He was unjustifiably accused of trying to quantify qualities.

His vast survey reported long periods of time over which certain patterns of human activity, behaviour, thought and creativity in the arts, philosophy and sciences were predominant. Individual lives, and the quality of the civilization throughout which such patterns endured, were characterized by coherent relationships that were beyond the range of chance. But such patterns did not last. When they broke up, there was often 'a time of trouble', in Arnold Toynbee's phrase. Then, after an uneasy readjustment, the old ways were replaced by new values which also fell into a coherent pattern. Not *all* the old values disappeared. The change in civilization is rarely an all-or-none affair, but sociology is concerned with the prevalent dominant type at any one time – if there is one.

There was, Sorokin holds, a clearly dominant influence of the Christian religion from roughly the sixth to the twelfth century A.D. All branches of knowledge, science and philosophy were aspects of religion and theology. Architecture, sculpture, painting, music, literature and drama were, Sorokin estimated, between 85 and 97 per cent religious and Christian. Ethical values and rules of conduct were derived from the Bible's revelation of divine commandments. Secular law had to accommodate canon law. The ethics of hedonism and of utilitarianism were unknown, and economic ideas in our sense had no place.

To describe such a period, Sorokin revived a seventeenth-century adjective, 'ideational', which the Oxford English Dictionary says relates to 'the formation of ideas of things not present to the senses'. When almost all the leading ideas and strivings in different fields combine into a comprehensive pattern, Sorokin calls it – rather offputtingly – a 'logico-meaningful sociocultural supersystem'. This is, in fact, a very succinct description.

First, *logico-meaningful*: Sorokin claims to have gone beyond the earlier search for 'causal-meaningful' relationships by which philosophers of history from Buckle to Ellsworth Huntington hoped to explain the development of civilization and culture in terms of geography, climate, race or economic resources. Such factors become merely influences on human beings who are ruled by the ideas or values seen in language, science, religion, the fine arts and ethics (which collectively compose the *sociocultural supersystem*). And *logico-meaningful supersystems* are complex wholes in which there is a threefold logical compatibility and specific dependence or inter-dependence of each of the elements upon other elements: of the elements upon the whole system: of the system upon the elements. This tightly knit concept of organic unity – which has evident wide applications elsewhere, in biology, for example – was adapted by Sorokin from St Thomas Aquinas.

The medieval, 'ideational' way of life – being a matter of ruling cultural values – was discernible only in the leaders of medieval society. It is hard to know how genuinely it was shared by the silent masses, although the fact that it endured for so many centuries makes it difficult to doubt that the religious outlook was real and general.

The 'modern' way of life, which has now all but swept the 'ideational' way into limbo, stands in complete contrast. Knowledge and truth are derived not from the holy scriptures or the works of the fathers of the church, but from the evidence of the senses and the reasoning based upon them. Science and philosophy consequently change completely in character with the rise of empiricism, materialism, positivism and pragmatism. Religious topics cease to provide the staple of art or literature. All other departments of human activity change. The everyday world of human passions, strivings and enjoyments supply the only themes that matter. The old, other-worldly didactic literature and art are found boring. Abstract ideas are suspect or dismissed as meaningless. A great amusement industry arises based upon its success in ministering to as many of the five senses as possible. The insistent demand for bodily comfort, wealth and ease creates economic science and changes the character of employment, industry, the law and the penal code. Science and technology develop to produce miracles revolutionizing the life of man and prolonging it through the progress of medical science. The modern hospital is one of the finest achievements of the new way of life. All these activities and interests are congruent, complementary and cohesive. Each serves the others and fortifies the whole pattern of life, just as in the earlier period all activities cooperated in the service of religious beliefs. The 'ideational' pattern has been replaced by a 'sensate' pattern – one, as the Oxford dictionary defines it, 'perceived by the senses'.

'What is there new in all this?' it may be asked. The sacred-secular dichotomy is not, of course, Sorokin's invention, but one of hoary antiquity. Sorokin's achievement is to fashion a logically organized, coherent system of interpretation upon the basis not of the hunches on which his predecessor's ideas mostly rested, but on a patient and thorough collection of facts, so stupendous in their sheer bulk that, as Toynbee has observed, no one before him had dared to attempt to put together anything on the same scale. In so doing, Sorokin discerned much that the crude sacred-secular contrast missed. There is, for example, the fruitful combination of a religious period as it wanes with the dawning of a new sensate age. Then, as 'the Word takes flesh', an extraordinary creative energy blossoms briefly but gloriously. Such was the Greece of the fifth century B.C. and twelfth- and seventeenth-century western Europe.

Here is a new insight into the subject matter of sociology, the way of life and the achievements of mankind in societies. The only way to order, arrange and classify the multitudinous facts about the science, religion, fine arts, and ethics of any people at any time must be through the discovery of the meanings, values and norms latent in them. Sociological phenomena can only be understood in the light of the cultural system upon which they rest.

While Sorokin was at work on his great investigation, the 'cultural interpretation' of history was in the air, particularly in Germany, through the work of philosophers and historians following Dilthey. Spengler dramatized it for millions, but on too slender a philosophical basis, which Sorokin has criticized. If Sorokin is to be remembered by one word, as Darwin is by 'evolution', then that word is 'value'.

To emphasize values as the key to sociology courted a bad reception in the analytical mid twentieth century, but there was no help for it: values were the facts thrown up in endless profusion by Sorokin's empirical quest for sociological reality from the historical record. In writing about 'ideational' or 'sensate' supersystems, Sorokin has been charged with inflating these abstractions so that humans are lost sight of or reduced to mere pawns. He is innocent of this – it is just that presentation demands a kind of shorthand.

Subject to this caution to look beyond the 'system' to the science, art and ethics which are its substance, Sorokin would say that all cultural systems change, as do all living human creations, by developing according to their innate potentialities until, worn out by constant repetition, they collapse through boredom or exhaustion. Their 'imminent development' proceeds to its limits in accordance with the psychological principle that every activity ultimately makes its recurrence more difficult. Religious devotees tend to lapse into accidie: sensate indulgence exhausts the power to respond, despite ever-stronger stimuli.

With the completion of his ten years' toil over the mountain of sociological facts to be found in history, Sorokin had reached a watershed in his own development as a sociologist and it is likely to be seen as a watershed in sociology also. In 1947, with his *Society, Culture, and Personality* (the best source for a general presentation of his views as a whole), Sorokin returned to the staple topics of much sociological writing: those 'structural' problems of 'groups', 'classes', 'roles', 'social structure' and 'social mobility' upon which so many unfortunate students are forced to break their teeth for singularly little intellectual nourishment. Sorokin's value theory infuses these notions with meaning.

Sorokin was not content to regard either the human fate as inexorably conditioned, or sociology as impotent to suggest any practical remedies. This was shown in a startling manner in 1946 when he established the Harvard Research Centre in Creative Altruism. He set to work upon a pioneering sociological investigation of the power of love as a dynamic in human society. Not love, meaning sexual attraction, but in the sense summarized by Leibniz, *voluptas ex felicitate alieni*, joy through another's bliss. At about the same time in England, Lady Wootton reached the same conclusion in her *Testament for Social Science* – that a developed altruism, or love, was the motive power that society lacked.

Sorokin died in February 1968. He lived to see his ideas win through to a growing influence and authority. His major works are reprinted. After too long a delay he was given a spectacular election to the presidency of the American Sociological Association. Honoured in very many countries – for he is probably the most translated twentieth-century sociologist – this former Russian peasant boy achieved a fame and a distinction in the United States which is rare for a prophet in his own life-time, in his adopted country.

FURTHER READING

WORKS

*Social Mobility* (Harper, 1927).

*Contemporary Sociological Theories* (Harper, 1928).

*Fads and Foibles in Sociology and Related Sciences* (H. Regnery, 1956).

*Social and Cultural Dynamics* (Porter Sargent, 1957).

*Society, Culture and Personality* (Harper, 1947).

CRITICAL STUDIES

Philip J. Allen (ed.): *Pitirim A. Sorokin in Review* (Duke University Press, Durham, N.C., 1963).

Edward A. Tiryakian (ed.): *Sociological Theory, Values and Socio-cultural Change: Essays in Honor of Pitirim A. Sorokin* (Free Press of Glencoe, Collier-Macmillan, 1963).

F. R. Cowell: *History, Civilisation and Culture: An introduction to the historical and social philosophy of Pitirim A. Sorokin* (London, 1952); revised and expanded in *Values in Human Society* (Porter Sargent, 1970).

# ANTONIO GRAMSCI
## (*1891–1937*)

### Gwyn A. Williams

'THE so-called laws of sociology have no causal value: they are almost always tautologies ... a baroque form of Platonic idealism,' wrote a sleepless Antonio Gramsci in his prison cell as, under Mussolini's personal supervision, his teeth fell out, he spat blood and succumbed to Pott's disease and arteriosclerosis. He was commenting on Robert Michels's analysis of party and on a celebrated manual of historical materialism by Comrade Bukharin which, Gramsci considered, had shrivelled marxism into a 'sociology'.

Antonio Gramsci, a Sardinian from the impoverished household of a disgraced petty official, won a scholarship to Turin university and made his home in the militant workers' movement of that classic industrial monolith of a city. He lived forty-six years of almost unremitting work and struggle between 1891 and 1937. Many of them were years of disillusionment, isolation and misery. During ten of them, from 1916, he produced critical and creative journalism of a brilliance and subtlety which are probably without equal in the history of the socialist movement.

The last ten years of his life were spent in prison where, in appalling conditions, he filled dozens of notebooks (which take up some 2,350 printed pages) in an intellectual enterprise which has come to be regarded as an unfinished classic of marxist thought. He was one of the creators of the Italian Communist Party in 1921; and from 1923, in the shadow of victorious fascism, served for three years as its leader.

Gramsci was no more a founding father of social science than he was of Eurocommunism. That his 'noonday devil' of History should have disinterred him to so serve would probably have brought out in him that dark and caustic 'delight' in defeat, which occasionally comforted this maimed and brilliant spirit.

For he was as alert to the absurd as a motor force, and to the ironies of history, as one of the many mentors he subjected to his unrivalled historical imagination, the Vico of the eighteenth-century *La Scienza Nuova*.

'Nobody wished to be the "manure" of history,' he wrote towards the end of his life, but 'now, something has changed, since there are those who adapt themselves "philosophically" to being "manure".' There are worse roles for an organic intellectual of the first, aborted, European communism. One key to the multiple Gramscis whom 'History' has created, however, is surely the fact that the historical Gramsci was essentially a marginal figure, as man and marxist.

The first two years of a person's life, Gramsci thought, did not count; in the fourth year of his own, he was permanently crippled. A dwarf hunchback, subject to periodical attacks of illness, irascibility and withdrawal, makes an unusual leader for a workers' movement. How can I love a collectivity, he asked himself once, when I have never personally loved or been loved? In his biography, Alastair Davidson has noted perceptively that it was after his totally unexpected love affair with the beautiful, talented but unstable Giulia Schucht in Moscow in 1922 that the 'monster' Gramsci (become a priest, his fascist brother Mario had told him: you'll never know a woman) first moved purposefully to displace Amadeo Bordiga and to create a new communist leadership against the Italian grain. There is no call to succumb to the psychologism he despised. But his personal predicament – viewed as he would have wished it viewed, in social context – without doubt charged his intellectual convictions with a highly distinctive *tone*, rare among marxists.

There is his overpowering obsession with the human will as an operative historical force – that will which ensured his survival as a thinker even in the atrocious conditions of his imprisonment. It ran into confluence with his intellectual formation in an Italy dominated by the Idealist philosopher, Benedetto Croce, who made the 'ethico-political' into a driving force of the *history* which possessed him. This was the Italy of Georges Sorel, he of the Myth and of Violence, who saw marxism as 'social poetry'; of Labriola who made marxism a 'philosophy of praxis'; of theorists of 'the act' and the élite.

Characteristically, Gramsci's first essay in socialist journalism was almost his last. It was a disastrous article in October 1914 which demonstrated considerable sympathy for the leader of Italian socialism and an early hero of his – the Benito Mussolini who had just advocated Italian intervention in the first world war in the interests of 'revolution'. The hostile socialist response plunged Gramsci into one of those crises of confusion, withdrawal and breakdown which periodically assailed him; it haunted him for the rest of his life. 'Bergsonian! Voluntarist! Mussolinian! . . .' they shouted at him in congresses.

It was this instinct, however, which powered his striking reassertion of the primacy of human action, of ideas, of the 'ethico-political', of *politics* itself, conceived as a science and as an art, within the marxist schema. Gramsci belonged to a generation in revolt against the determinism, the positivism, the 'economism' of what passed for marxism in the Second International.

He was revolted, in particular, by its crude and mechanical interpretation of the classic distinction which marxism had originally made (but in terms which both Marx and Engels came to regret) between a 'structure' and a 'superstructure'. *Structure* signified a mode of production, with all its complex 'relations of production', which was the ultimately determinant force in social life; Second International orthodoxy reduced this to a simple and determinist 'economic base'. *Superstructure* signified the world of ideologies, culture, religion, politics, which existed in subtle and complex dependency on this 'structure' (and to which Marx, in his political and historical writings, had accorded a considerable degree of 'autonomy'); orthodoxy reduced this to a simple, one-to-one 'reflection' or by-product.

Though several commentators have argued to the contrary, I do not think Gramsci ever lost his grip (once he had found it) on the notion of the mode of production as the ultimate determining force in a society (indeed, many of his most 'unorthodox' theories are incomprehensible without it). But, more consistently than any other marxist thinker, he shifted the focus of marxist practice bodily into the realm of the 'superstructure'. His assimilation of marxism was piecemeal and progressive; as late as 1917, he could hail Lenin's revolution as a revolution 'against' Marx's *Capital*. But it was Gramsci's sustained exploration of the interaction between the two spheres which has added a dimension to marxist analysis.

What emerged from that analysis was a vivid conception of the Communist Party as *The Modern Prince*, a title he gave one of his prison texts. Machiavelli, Gramsci thought, had been a 'precocious Jacobin' of the Renaissance. In trying (and failing) to create an Italian 'national-popular will', he had elaborated the first autonomous *politics*, as a theoretical practice, a *praxis*. The Communist Party was to be a collective Machiavelli, to apply a marxist political science or art to a complex society, shape a 'national-popular' revolutionary will and, by means of the liberating dictatorship of the proletariat, effect a revolution which would be as total a transformation of civilization as the Christian revolution had been.

For this presentation of the party and the revolution – which was, to say the least, unusual in marxist writing – Gramsci found a warrant (or manufactured one) in the Lenin whom he saw as an activist state-building revolutionary and in the Marx of the essentially political writings.

Central to this pattern of thinking and feeling was a commitment to discipline, hard work, precision and production, which gives an authoritarian tone to Gramsci's most libertarian writing and which can stun a reader. He reacted no less violently against the empty rhetoric of political Italy and its Socialist Party – the Barnum's Circus of the Land of Pulcinella, as he called it, in the most savage and vicious onslaught on socialism and parliamentary democracy ever penned by a communist. It is visible, above all, in his analyses of those critical areas of social intercourse in which a subject class is conditioned into a 'voluntary' acceptance of its subjection.

Bourgeois society established what he was to call a 'hegemony' over the mind and spirit, so total that it was never perceived as such at all. It registered on the mind as 'normality'; serfs were no more aware of their serfdom than they were of the force of gravity. Yet those were precisely the points where a new communist consciousness, a new morality, a new civilization, could effect an entry.

There was education, where society reproduced itself and its hegemony, generation after generation, but where marxism, working through the 'folklore' of popular 'commonsense' (itself an embryonic 'philosophy', suppressed and distorted by the omnipresent hegemony of the exploiters) could transform that 'commonsense' into world-renovating power; consciousness become a material force.

There was the factory. Technology and a trained working class had made capitalists and managers as irrelevant as monopoly and imperialism had made parliaments. The crisis in the mode of production would first register here, at the point of production. Workers, moving beyond and shedding the defensive institutions they had created in the parliamentary age of classical competitive capitalism, the trade unions and the Socialist Party, would, in their developing system of councils, conquer a 'historical autonomy' for themselves.

Through a communist consciousness which would begin to grow, at first as 'folklore' out of this very crisis, they would begin to think like a ruling class capable of building a state. They would produce their own 'organic' intellectuals who, mobilized in their Modern Prince of a party, would lead other classes and groups, driven into revolt by the crisis in the mode of production, to create a new mode with its new hegemony.

Thinking of this order, presented at first in a highly dramatic and Utopian form, governed Gramsci's editorship of the remarkable journal *L'Ordine Nuovo* ('The New Order'), when he assumed a leading role in the factory council movement of the Turin car workers during 1919–20, the most original of the council communisms of Europe after 1917. Its isolation within the socialist movement, and its defeat, left Gramsci himself isolated during the angry summer of 1920.

He took his stance alongside but independent of the intransigent communist faction of Bordiga. He fully shared Bordiga's conviction that communism in Italy had to define itself historically in total rejection of socialism, of bourgeois society and its democracy. But his experience of the council movement deeply influenced his conception of the Communist Party and of the way it had to operate in a complex and 'polyglot' society, shaped by a plurality of modes of production. After he had displaced Bordiga with the support of Comintern, this challenging and difficult concept of the party found expression in his *Lyons Theses*, one of the classic documents of communism.

Gramsci's 'historical will' was thus a will increasingly disciplined by marxism. In some striking passages on Freud in the *Prison Notebooks* and *Letters*, he used the language of repression and the unconscious, but located individual crises firmly in the historical, and asserted that every man could be his own doctor by bringing his will and the ends he could achieve into equilibrium. But he could do this only if he thought 'historically and dialectically' and identified his own 'task' dispassionately.

For Gramsci took Marx's *Theses on Feuerbach* with total seriousness. Man was the 'ensemble of social relations', but 'men create their own personality' in the same dialectical manner as they 'make history'. This was the fulcrum of much of Gramsci's thinking.

It is difficult not to feel that his own personal marginality made it easier for him to see himself as history and, as a marxist but in a manner which disconcerts many marxists, to locate marxism itself in history. Only a truly profound historical relativism could compare the marxism of his own day to the Reformation in its cruder ideological formation, and to look to a re-translation (one of his favourite words) of Croce's Idealism to transform it into a culture of the classic stature of Greece or the Renaissance.

This kind of writing – perhaps inevitably – was characterized by a 'detachment' rarely found among marxists, by a constant shift in perspective as he 'played' with an idea. In the *Prison Notebooks*, this style becomes very insistent and very difficult; at times, it is impenetrable. The curiously 'third-person' quality of much of his writing surely owes something to the fact that Gramsci as an individual was doubly marginal. He was not only a cripple but a Sardinian cripple.

The Sardism of Gramsci, like his command of marxist

political economy, seems to have been under-estimated. He was twenty before he left the island and was very much a Sard in Turin. The integration of the country people of the Italian south ('I am a southerner,' he rasped at one of Mussolini's gorillas in the Chamber of Deputies) with northern workers in a communist movement was central to his life and a seedbed of his marxist originality.

He became more Sard towards the end. In one of his last illnesses, he raved for days in the Sard dialect – about the immortality of the soul (in a 'realistic and historical sense', of course). During his final isolation, he was almost totally immersed in Sardinia. In one of his letters, he described himself abruptly as 'a Sard without psychological complications'; a characteristically Gramscian statement in its creative ambiguity.

He hated the place, of course: the backwardness, superstition, primitivism, every decade named after a bandit. He greeted Turin, modernism, the sheer revolutionizing drive of *production*, with a kind of disciplined rapture which no doubt made it easier for him to respond to the Futurists (as he was among the first to appreciate Pirandello). He painted his Sardinian childhood in terms unutterably bleak. Yet he was obsessed with the island; a close reading of his work (and one which 'listens to the silences') would suggest rather different emotions.

Some debts to his origins are obvious. There is his projected fusion of workers and peasants in a single movement (in his early writings they form a single class). The Risorgimento he interpreted as an unfinished revolution. He minutely explored the near-colonial southern predicament and asserted its centrality to the Italian revolution. There is his probing of folklore and popular culture. These were the analyses which have proved such a happy hunting ground to the sociologists he feared.

There are subtler debts to Sardinia. His concentration on language, linguistics and philology, on language as an *organizational* factor is one that comes naturally to thinkers from a minority and marginal people – particularly if they try, as Gramsci did, to 'nationalize' themselves and escape from provincialism. He perceived human communities as *plastic*, a marxist corollary which flows from his concept of the making and self-making of a 'national-popular will'. Above all, of course, there is Gramsci's focus on 'intellectuals', and his enormous extension of that notion.

This was to become a major organising principle of his thought, but it stemmed in part from an initially tactical pre-occupation with the southern petty bourgeoisie and bureaucrats – the 'intellectuals' as they were called, into whose world Gramsci, the village registrar's son, had been born.

There was, further, a subtly marginal quality in the very process by which Gramsci made himself a communist and exercised leadership. It is singularly difficult and in fact un-rewarding, to try to fit Gramsci (or Bordiga, or several other spokesmen of the first communism) into the familiar patterns of communist history which centre on the struggles in Russia and in the Comintern. Even to assimilate him to the Bukharin of the late 1920s would be mistaken. Political leadership was twice thrust on Gramsci by historical 'accident' (which, as he would be the first to point out, was not historically accidental): first, when the decimation of the Turin militants after the rising of 1917 left him a survivor; secondly, when the fascists eliminated the first communist leadership in 1923 at a point of maximum tension between an intransigent Bordiga and a Comintern committed to the 'united front'.

Gramsci had served the Comintern in Moscow in 1922–3, and his assumption and exercise of leadership in Italy in 1924–6 was conducted in terms of complete loyalty to leninism and 'bolshevization' – but, to use his own term, in translation into Italian. His practice was, in fact, increasingly autonomous. In 1926 he sent his famous letter to the Russian party, protesting against the factional struggle within the communist movement. Sent on the eve of his arrest by the fascists, it precipitated the breach with the younger Togliatti, who had already left him once in 1920, and who was to succeed him as party leader. In prison, of course, his thinking diverged radically from Comintern practice during a period of communist sectarianism. His last recorded message to the party in the days of the 'popular front' is as obscure as most of his writing at that stage, but it clearly had a distancing intention.

Gramsci was, pre-eminently, a revolutionary leader in a non-revolutionary situation. His own distinction between an 'epoch' (which was revolutionary) and a 'situation' (which was not); his elaboration of the notion of a 'historic bloc' to bridge this gap between the structural and the conjunctural, were attempts to get to grips with this predicament. His most creative periods were in truth those of relative isolation: prison, the summer of 1920 after the defeat of the council movement when his basic attitudes assumed some permanence, and his year as a communist leader in 1926, when the parallel with the summer of 1920 was often in his mind. It was then that he began to develop the themes germinated in 1920 and pursued much further in the *Prison Notebooks*.

At least initially, those *Notebooks* were an effort to think this situation through. (After all, what 'hegemony' was more ubiquitous than that of the triumphant fascists around 1930?) It is customary and correct to single out Croce and Lenin as the twin polarities of this thinking. But Gramsci's project in the *Notebooks* also bears strong affinities to the Marx of the *Theses on Feuerbach*, *The Holy Family* and the *18 Brumaire of Louis Bonaparte*. Even Gramsci's Hegelianism – certainly present in his style – often turns out to be the 'Hegelianism' of *that* Marx.

In their original intention and in their concentration on the shift from 'war of manoeuvre' to 'war of position', the *Notebooks* strongly recall the shift in perspective in Marx during 1850 (as he abandoned 'permanent revolution') between the third chapter of the *Class Struggles in France* and its anti-climactic fourth chapter, followed by the brilliant *18 Brumaire*. Though his explorations carried him into a different world, the *Notebooks* in some important senses were Gramsci's '18 Brumaire of Benito Mussolini'.

This response to ineluctable circumstance ran in accord with a crucial feature of his thinking: a concentration on the strategic and the long-term, on the revolution as a total transformation of civilization. At no point in his writing, not even when he was consciously working for armed insurrection, is it easy to detect in Gramsci that preoccupation with 'revolution' in the more immediate sense which tends to engage many communists.

'The revolution is not a thaumaturgical act. It is a dialectical process of historical development.' It is never very easy to see just how Gramscians, in vulgar reality, actually 'take power'.

The relative ease with which Gramsci was absorbed into non-marxist thinking – and particularly into that social science which the historical Gramsci denied – probably derives from this pattern of characteristic absences and presences. The central focus of that pattern are those monuments to the human intellect and to sheer human courage, the *Prison Notebooks* and the *Letters*.

The *Notebooks* present difficulties which are probably insuperable. They were written, in dreadful conditions, and in a necessary code, with the essentials of marxism 'taken as read'. They were constantly reworked in at least three major revisions, before fascist brutality bludgeoned him into silence and Sardinia. They are episodic, unfinished, sometimes contradictory. They expand from an examination of the 'creative popular mind' into an exploration (both global and molecular) of almost every aspect of human experience.

The result is breathtaking. But only since 1975 has a critical and uncensored edition of those *Notebooks* enabled the necessary filigree work to be set in train. A coherent Gramsci of the *Notebooks* will have to be reconstructed. The job may prove to be impossible. The hungry reader is condemned to a permanent diet of *hors-d'oeuvres*.

In the *Notebooks*, Gramsci's is an exciting, and frustrating, world in which the crudities of 'structure' and 'superstructure' are transcended in an endless wrestling match with the neo-Hegelian Croce which paralleled Marx's with Hegel himself (a parallel of which Gramsci became too conscious). In bridging that divide, he vastly extended the concept of 'intellectuals' to embrace any who exercised an organizing function in society. He evolved the idea of 'organic intellectuals' to describe those who expressed and defined the self-consciousness of a class or group entering into historical existence (the Communist Party was itself to be a collective organic intellectual). These he confronted with 'traditional' intellectuals who were, presumably, once organic themselves (the clerics of feudalism, for example).

This seminal argument Gramsci buttressed with minute and imaginative explorations of Italian and European history. Catholicism itself he interpreted as a 'historic bloc', in a natural obsession (partly influenced by Sorel), which more northerly thinkers, even in the marxist tradition, find some difficulty in appreciating. His analysis remains partial, bubbling with apparent contradictions. It is difficult to assimilate to general marxist practice in the virtual 'absence' of a marxist political economy (sometimes more apparent than real, since such a political economy is central to the argument). It constitutes, nevertheless, a major extension of marxism, and it has certainly added a dimension to social analysis, whether marxist or no.

The role of the Gramscian 'intellectual' is at the heart of one of his presentations of the concept of hegemony; a regime's achievement of the historical *moment of consent*. The exploited and the subaltern (to use his term) internalize their status and accept it as 'voluntarily' as workers 'normally' do in a capitalist economy and a bourgeois state. The objectively intolerable is made tolerable in a complicated dialectical process.

Gramsci's exploration of this concept, with its wealth of historical 'verification', is enormously rich and stimulating, but it remains a shifting and sometimes contradictory idea. He links it to a discrimination between 'state' and 'civil society' and to a comparison between eastern and western Europe, which was evidently influenced by the conflict between Stalin and Trotsky. This, too, shifts in focus and perspective, and is multiple in its overlapping meanings.

Through this extraordinarily stimulating and extraordinarily frustrating discussion of hegemony runs his thematic of an independent marxist political art: the New Machiavel. For Gramsci, the Communist Party never seems to be a 'mass party' in the customary usage; yet he never sees it in isolation from 'the masses'. Once again, a directive idea is elaborated in a specific detail and in a loose-end incompleteness which stretch the mind.

All this thinking is swathed in that relativism – that earth-satellite perspective – which has given birth to a no less epic (and confusing) debate on his 'historicism'. And always, there is his engaging but infuriating tendency to break away from his original purpose to play with ideas; the play is no less purposive.

After the Liberation and, more particularly, after the marxist emancipation of the mid-1950s, it was this Gramsci who became the hero and the instrument of an Italian Communist Party which was committed to the democracy that the historical Gramsci despised, to the mass party he distrusted, and to the 'historic compromise' with Christian Democracy he never made.

It was this Gramsci who served as a liberator for those dissidents hungry for a marxism which seemed humanist or libertarian or merely intelligent. The Gramsci of the *Notebooks* was painlessly housed among the many mansions of that bourgeois hegemony which became the major object of his concern. He would have been wryly amused as his letters were awarded a prestigious literary prize and were translated by poets, and as some of his ideas were debated among comrades with a scholastic sophistication and intensity worthy of traditional intellectuals at their most traditional.

In being re-translated into a 'social scientist', however, Gramsci has disintegrated as totally as Marx did. I have the awful suspicion that all the dialectic's men may not be able to put him together again.

To the end of his political discourse, Antonio Gramsci, the man, remained a revolutionary communist, committed to the dictatorship of the proletariat. He consciously set out to be 'a Lenin of the west'. In some important respects he was successful enough for us to perceive that such a Lenin would bear little resemblance to the Lenin we all know and whom most of the left seem obliged to love.

His work indirectly calls into question the very existence of that heraldic beast, marxism-leninism. It certainly demonstrates yet again – if such a demonstration is needed – that the only serious infantilism which afflicted Europe's first communism was infanticide.

## FURTHER READING

WORKS IN ENGLISH TRANSLATION

Quintin Hoare and Geoffrey Nowell Smith (eds): *Selections from the Prison Notebooks; Selections from the Political Writings 1910–20 and 1921–26* (Lawrence and Wishart, 1971–78; paperback versions available or in train).

Lynne Lawner (ed.): *Letters from Prison*; selections from critical 1965 edition of the prison letters.

C. K. Maisels (ed.): *New Edinburgh Review* (Edinburgh, 1974); three special Gramsci numbers bound as one volume: full translation of 1947 edition of prison letters by Hamish Henderson and other texts; individual numbers in paperback.


CRITICAL STUDIES

Perry Anderson: 'The Antinomies of Antonio Gramsci', *New Left Review*, no. 100, 1977.

Carl Boggs: *Gramsci's Marxism* (Pluto Press, 1976).

John M. Cammett: *Antonio Gramsci and the Origins of Italian Communism* (Stanford University Press, 1967).

Phil Cozens: *Twenty Years of Antonio Gramsci* (Lawrence and Wishart, 1977); bibliography of Gramsci and Gramsci studies in English.

Alastair B. Davidson: *Antonio Gramsci: towards an intellectual biography* (Merlin Press, 1977).

Giuseppe Fiori: *Antonio Gramsci: life of a revolutionary*, tr. Tom Nairn (New Left Books, 1970).

James Joll: *Gramsci* (Fontana, 1977).

Gwyn A. Williams: *Proletarian Order: Antonio Gramsci, factory councils and the origins of communism in Italy, 1911–21* (Pluto Press, 1975).

# KARL MANNHEIM*
## (1893–1947)

### Jean Floud

IN considering Mannheim's writings the comparison with Durkheim can hardly be avoided, although it cannot be pursued very far here. Both men were committed to the related ideas of a sociological theory of knowledge and a sociological science of society. Both sought to restate and resolve the old epistemological problems as sociological problems; and to convert politics into sociology by turning the old political problems of freedom, consent and obligation into new organizational problems of solidarity and consensus and the functional prerequisites of a stable social order. Their respective approaches to these problems were profoundly different, as were their intellectual styles; but they were fundamentally at one. Mannheim's subtleties, the Marxist strain in his intellectual pedigree and his strong feeling for social change did not prevent him from emerging as a utopian of the right, seeking the security of an integrated society, grounded in a common morality inculcated by education. As for Durkheim, so for Mannheim, education represented 'sociology in action' and it is interesting that both men were professors of Education as well as of Sociology.

Mannheim was a radical, but his radicalism was born of a deep conservatism. He yearned for stability. He wanted freedom, both in the narrower political sense and in the wider sense of freedom from irrational social and psychological pressures. But freedom

* This article is based on two lectures by Jean Floud which were reprinted – one in 1959 in a symposium published by Faber and edited by A. V. Judges, *The Function of Teaching*; the other in a Dutch journal *Sociologische Gids* published in 1963 'Karl Mannheim and the Sociology of Education': and on an essay in the *Times Literary Supplement* (30 January 1976, p. 116) reviewing Gunter W. Remmling's *The Sociology of Karl Mannheim*, Routledge and Kegan Paul, 1975.

is impossible in a disordered society; change, social reconstruction is therefore unavoidable.

One never feels that Mannheim welcomed change, in the manner of the true revolutionary, for its own sake. He was obsessed with the desire to synthesize past and present; he sought to take charge of change, to forestall it and to guide it. The spirit of exaltation that infuses so much of his writing about reconstruction derives not from any historicist sense of marching as the standard bearer of the future with history on his side, but from the joyful conviction that sociology, the science of social action, can banish or at least mitigate the horrors of social change. Change threatens stability because it is uneven in its impact, producing disharmonies, revealing inconsistencies and contradictions in society; and society should function as an integrated structure. Since, however, one cannot do away with change, it must be controlled, even encouraged when necessary, to maintain a dynamic social equilibrium.

It is in keeping with this mixed attitude towards change, of great aversion compounded with a compensating overmasterfulness, that, despite his preoccupation with it, Mannheim should have developed no theory of social change. In his early years he was a Marxist; but in abandoning economic determinism he did no more than assert the untenability of any monocausal theory, insisting on the interconnectedness of everything, but allowing for the special importance of economic factors in particular.

Despite the appearance of being concerned with dynamics, his real preoccupation was with the classical problems of social statics: the relations of the individual to society; social order and consensus; the reconciliation of freedom and organization; and then with the possibility of planned intervention into the social process. His heart was in stability, though for him stability took the sophisticated form of a planned, dynamic equilibrium.

The fullest and most stimulating exposition of Mannheim's distinctive contribution to the 'diagnosis of our time' is to be found, not in his books of that name, but in two of the *Essays on the Sociology of Culture* and the essay 'Rational and Irrational Elements in Modern Society', all from the early thirties.

His analysis of the social crisis is focused on the process of *democratization*, the process by which, with the advance of industrialism, increasing numbers of people participate in political, intellectual and cultural life. Democratization has two principal corollaries, and on these Mannheim concentrates his attention. First, the elements which he terms the 'governing élites' and, in particular, the intelligentsia, lose their homogeneity and social authority as their ranks are opened to recruits from all social strata. What was once a caste-like group with a virtual monopoly of public interpretation, a traditional prerogative of providing authoritative answers to the questions of the time, gives place to an open stratum, incapable, by its very nature, of formulating a unitary view of the world or a core of commonly acceptable values such as would lend spiritual consistency to a social system. The democratization of the intelligentsia is, perhaps, the major element in the disintegration of social consensus. What appears as an unhealthy scepticism, or a declining faith, or a fragmentation of the contemporary outlook has its social roots in this transformation of the intelligentsia. Secondly, 'as groups not yet familiar with political reality suddenly become charged with a political function', irrationality – always present in society, but under other social conditions either dormant or suitably canalized – forces its way into the arena of public life. Instead of a rationally informed conflict we get uninhibited emotional eruptions among the masses, a democracy of impulse (*Stimmungsdemokratie*) instead of a democracy of reason (*Vernunftsdemokratie*).

The democratization of the intelligentsia, the upsurge of the masses and the consequent threat to the delicately balanced distribution of rational and irrational forces, are the main points of Mannheim's diagnosis of the contemporary crisis. They surely reflect his early experiences as a young man in Hungary during and after the First World War. He was twenty-one in 1914 (he was born in 1893). Between October 1918 and August 1919, Hungary was convulsed in turn by radical and Bolshevist revolutions and a White counter-revolution.

The Hungarian masses were appallingly poor and illerate; on the other hand, the intelligentsia, predominantly Jewish and in almost extra-territorial relationship with the rest of Hungarian society, adopted what Oscar Jaszi, a distinguished participant in the events of the time, described as 'an altogether unique mixture of materialism and idealism. On the one side they fed from Marx, Lenin, Trotsky, Bukharin, on the other from Fichte and Hegel, the mild Rickert, Windelband, Kierkegaard, Husserl and even the medieval mystics!' 'The old order,' he wrote, 'had been caught between the millstones of the animal appetite of the mob and the transcendental enthusiasms of the young men.'

Mannheim was one of the young men. He was associated with the influential Sociological Society and its offshoot the Galileo Club, and he assisted Lukács in his freelance venture, the Free School of Social Science, where he taught philosophy. He served briefly under the revolutionary government in the ministry of education.

He left Hungary to settle in Germany with a problem to which he was to devote his life-work: how to reassert the role of reason in modern society and realize the nineteenth-century liberal ideal of applying organized intelligence to human affairs. He took with him, also, a solution to the problem, in principle, which he never abandoned: the ideal of a democratic society embodying 'the sovereignty of the industrious masses of peasants and town workers in the state, under the guidance of the genuinely creative intelligentsia'. In Germany, he applied himself to developing from the Marxist theory of ideology a 'sociology of knowledge' which he expounded in a number of essays and eventually in a systematic treatise, *Ideology and Utopia*, which appeared in 1929.

Mannheim had begun his career as sociologist in the context of the movement after World War I to recover the Hegelian roots of Marxism and develop further Hegel's remarkable legacy of insights into man and society which, by the late nineteenth century, had been overlaid by the undialectical materialism of the later Marx and Engels. The movement was effectively launched by Lukács in 1923 with the publication of his essays *History and Class Consciousness* and Mannheim was fully in sympathy with Lukács's rehegelianized Marxism – indeed he was imbued with it. However, he was reluctant to jettison the best of the legacy of the scientific positivism of the second half of the nineteenth century. His originality consisted in wanting to move beyond the theory of knowledge, grounded in philosophical Marxism, into a sociology of knowledge, grounded in 'scientific' (i.e. sociological) Marxism. He believed that relativism should be treated as a sociological rather than a philosophical problem.

Ideologies were not to be regarded as distortions of the truth, but as complementary aspects of it. Every social position affords its own perspective and the sociologist seeks to identify and elucidate these, and to locate the social origins of ideas, demonstrating typical relationships between ideologies and social situations. Thus, for example, in the study of German conservative thought which formed his doctoral dissertation, Mannheim seeks to show how a tendency to perceive the social process in organismic and morphological terms is inherent in the social position of the declining class of landowners.

The intelligentsia, he thought, was in a particularly favourable position to understand and collate the partial truths yielded by the various socially available perspectives. Its marginality and social diversity deprive it of an individual perspective; it is socially unattached (*freischwebend*) and, therefore, uncommitted; it is the natural carrier of 'objectivity' conceived as the correlate of a 'total perspective' arrived at by relating all the partial perspectives of particular social positions.

Mannheim has been heavily criticized on epistemological grounds for his attempts to evade the relativism implicit in a sociology of knowledge by substituting for it what he called 'relationism' (that is, the relating of 'partial perspectives' to form the 'total perspectives' which represents objectivity). He has also been much derided for his conception of the social role of the intelligentsia. Many of these criticisms have been shown to be beside the point; with the revival in recent years of interest in hermeneutics and interpretative sociologies his work is receiving more careful and appreciative treatment. Nevertheless, his theory of the existential determination of knowledge is unclear and its foundations shaky. Mathematics and the natural sciences could hardly be accommodated in his schema; and the term *seinsverbunden* is ambiguous in respect of both its elements:

'determined' and 'existence'. His theory of the intelligentsia as a group capable of a 'total perspective', as John Plamenatz has shown, derives from an uncritical acceptance of the Marxian notion of 'total ideology' and a fallacious analogy with optics.

Mannheim was not happy with Marxism – he simply found himself unable to dispense with the central tenets of Marxist sociology. He forever sought to evade his difficulties with the aid of disclaimers, *ad hoc* qualifications and diluted formulations of unacceptable Marxist propositions. He accepted the view that meaningful phenomena ask to be *interpreted* and that the method of the *Geisteswissenschaften*, which take such phenomena as their subject matter, is necessarily interpretative and not reductive. He went further and developed the view that meaningful phenomena are essentially social phenomena and can only be satisfactorily interpreted if they are socially 'placed' or 'located' in the collective experiences, beliefs, values and attitudes of particular social groups. As he put it, hermeneutics must be made 'adequate' by sociology and he tried to show how this should be done. But he was no exception to the rule that sociologists cannot live by hermeneutics alone, however 'adequate'. As a source of explanation for differences of *weltanschauung* or ideology, he always returned to the Marxist theory of class and class conflict in one weakened form or another. He was hampered to the end by the constraints of a theoretical position from which he was always seeking to escape but which he never forthrightly confronted and transcended.

By 1933, when Mannheim was again forced to flee and left Germany for England, he had begun to look beyond the notion of ideas as a function of the perspective afforded by a particular social position. He had begun to analyse the part played in the creation and flow of ideas and modes of thought by social processes such as competition, social relations such as 'social distance', and social units other than the classes with which he had hitherto been exclusively concerned, such as the generations. He finally conceived the plan of what he termed interchangeably a sociology of culture, or of the mind. This was to marry Hegel's insights into the creative character of mind, the structured context of men's actions and the social formation of their motives, about which Mannheim wrote perceptively and convincingly, with the empirical approach and procedures, developed by American sociology, which he greatly admired.

The essay with the unpromising title 'Towards the Sociology of the Mind: an Introduction', represents the high-point of the natural development of his ideas before this was arrested by the shock of his emigration and his total preoccupation thereafter with the problem of controlling the descent into disaster. This essay contains the best exposition of Mannheim's approach to sociology, his notion of its nature and scope and his idea of social structure and change. The introductory course which was given at the London School of Economics in 1934 and reproduced in *Systematic Sociology* is elementary to the point of triviality.

Mannheim's experience of life in this country made a profound impression on him. He found here a liberal social order with a cohesion and durability which his experiences in central Europe had led him to believe was virtually impossible. He found, too, an intelligentsia full of guilt-laden revulsion from totalitarianism yet disillusioned with liberalism, and convinced that there was no way back to an unplanned society. He felt new hope that a solution might be found, and he turned to developing his idea of 'social planning' and to expounding his views on education.

His idea of planning was first expounded in *Man and Society* which appeared in 1936. He starts from the fact that there is no unlimited power of free disposition and aims to devise a strategy of working with or against existing social currents from the most favourable points of control that can be discovered. Planning is 'predictive strategy' – an intervention in the social process by manipulation from key points. It is therefore, in principle, a restrained or limited activity; but it turns out that this ascetic policy signifies economy of means rather than modest aims. The planning, though not totalitarian, will be total, though 'a finer mastery of the social keyboard, a more accurate knowledge of social techniques, will make excessive interference unnecessary'. Freedom in a planned society is not to be achieved by limiting the powers of the planner, but by guaranteeing the existence of essential forms of freedom through the plan itself. It is not so much that there will be areas into which the long arm of the new law will not reach, as that cases of relief from its dispensation will be planned as a measure of social hygiene.

Mannheim's faith in the possibilities of applied sociology and psychology as the basis of planning was prodigious. As A. D. Lindsay, who got to know him very well, once remarked: 'Mannheim always resisted very strongly the suggestion that there was any limit to sociological knowledge, any suggestion that legislation, like moral action, was partly a leap in the dark. One always felt that he had a sociological faith that all these blanks of ignorance about society could be overcome.'

This *furor sociologicus* (as Albert Salomon once called it) shows itself on the most general level when he envisages the possibility of an age of 'administration', to follow an age of planning during which 'all or most of the historical forces which have arisen in the struggle have been brought under control through strategy' and 'all that we now call history, the unforeseeable, fateful dominance of uncontrolled social forces will (have) come to an end'. On a more particular level, the same *furor* assails us when we are told that a planned society will 'adapt the level of expectation' in the different social classes 'to wishes which it is possible to fulfil'; or when we find him advocating 'the planned guidance of people's lives on a sociological basis with the aid of psychology' and adding, with a touch of that staggering naiveté which was at once his most infuriating and endearing characteristic, 'in this way we are keeping in the foreground both the highest good of society and the peace of mind of the individual'.

Education as a social technique (*social education*: the planned educative impact of a variety of social arrangements) is central to Mannheim's prescription for 'democratic planning'. He was characteristically ingenious in uncovering the many ways in which the social environment makes its impress on the individual psyche and offered many suggestions for what he somewhat horrifyingly termed a 'planned attack on the self', that is, social education designed to produce a personality apt for participating in and sustaining a democratic society.

We must begin by attending to the masses. 'As soon as industrial society reaches the highest stage of individualism and slashes the bonds of custom and tradition through over-competition, urbanization and other processes, it leaves the individual without shelter . . . without any motive in primary groups, without a feeling of belonging . . .' Another name for uprootedness is emancipation. The difficulty is to capitalize the emancipation and to resist the tendency to massification (*Vermassung*), the flight from the responsibilities of spiritual freedom and personal autonomy. In the last resort, large-scale industrial societies cannot function successfully on the basis of mass conformism; successful division of labour needs the individualization it makes possible. On the other hand, the ravages of liberalism must be healed. We must begin by educating for a degree of conformity. We must 'rediscover the educational effects of primary groups' and 'create such groups where they are lacking' and 'stress their continuity and purposefulness'. And we must make up our minds about ultimate issues, producing a sound statement of belief which will take the place of the old dogma, and inform our whole educational effort. Everything possible must be done to destroy the psychological anarchy of liberal capitalism. We must, for instance, diminish the exaggerated appetite for competition, modify the emphasis on monetary rewards, re-evaluate work and leisure, and recapture the spirit of allegiance to responsible leadership.

As will be already obvious, Mannheim was no egalitarian, despite his profound faith in the perfectibility of man. He was deeply concerned with the selection of leaders, especially intellectual leaders, and voiced no scruples about segregating them during the period of their schooling. He was mainly concerned that the competition should be formally equal. He was concerned with the open road rather than with the equal start. Aside from this primary consideration, he was anxious that the whole body of the educated élite should not be drained off into exclusively vocational channels. He wanted a free-lance intelligentsia preserved: as an indispensable antidote to the bureaucratization of society, it would guarantee 'scope for free experimentation with the essential objectives of life'.

One of the elementary prerequisites of social creativeness is that the masses should not be able to criticize a social idea before it has been elaborated into workable form. 'It is very probable that a planned society will provide certain forms of closed social groups similar to our clubs, advisory councils or even sects, in which absolutely free discussion may take place without fear of premature broadcasting of views expressed.' Admission to these secret societies or orders must be on a democratic basis; members must maintain close and living contact with the masses; and channels must be provided through which the fruit of this sheltered liberal experimentation can, in the interests of keeping the plan flexible, reach the planners.

Intellectually speaking, Mannheim succumbed to terrible first-hand experiences of wars and of revolution. He stopped trying to understand specific situations better, and concentrated instead on preaching at large the gospel of salvation through sociology. So long as he did not plan, he applied his remarkably agile and fertile mind to understanding, and although the process is involute, the results are frequently very suggestive and sometimes highly illuminating. A good example is his discussion of humanism in the early essay on 'The Democratization of Culture'. Here he is directly in his own field, and his touch is sure. He talks – in fact, he 'sociologizes' in a most perceptive way – about humanism as a cultural and educational ideal, and broaches a critical exposition of an alternative democratic ideal which he sees emerging.

Had Mannheim continued to try to understand and diagnose, rather than to plan and legislate, he might have done a number of things. He might, for instance, have applied his talent for the sociology of knowledge to the modern man of science. There can be little doubt that, had he done so, he would have had to make considerable modifications in his notion of the intelligentsia, in his analysis of their characteristic qualities, and in particular, of their present and future social role. It is also certain that his democratic cultural or educational ideal (*Bildungsideal*) would have been the richer for an added dimension.

It is possible, moreover, that he might have arrived at a more critical view of the whole question of the relation between the so-called primary groups and the Great Society, and of the part to be played in it by a set of common values as the basis of social consensus. The suggestion that the remedy for the *anomie* of modern society lies in the cultivation and propagation of primary groups, which supposedly act as the nurseries, so to speak, of the higher norms of abstract morality which must govern conduct in the larger society, has gone virtually unchallenged since its prototype was first formulated in Germany in the 1880s. Durkheim, admittedly, did not subscribe to it. He accepted the social demise, under the effect of modern conditions, of the primary groups and did not seek, as did the German school, to resuscitate them. He argued that since occupational differentiation is the dominant characteristic of modern society, it is logical to take the occupational group as the basic social unit and endow it, on the analogy of the guilds, with an ethical or moral authority over its members. This suggestion is usually dismissed as mere syndicalism. His position was more logical, however, and his thought more rigorous than Mannheim's.

It is a matter of common observation that large-scale social organization can maintain a high degree of integration without widespread or intense attachment to an overriding value system. In applying ethical norms to the problems of political organization, the formulation of common ultimate ends is possibly less important – it is certainly less difficult – than the discovery of principles with the aid of which they can be linked with the detail of life. In other words, it is not usually general moral principles that become the subjects of doubt and controversy; it is the application of these principles to specific cases. Our understanding of the bonds which hold large-scale societies together is still rudimentary. Mannheim took a great deal of the theorizing of his predecessors and colleagues on faith. It is, perhaps, not surprising that he should in the end have turned to religion as the source of the common values which should integrate the democratic society. There are even hints that just before his untimely death in 1947, he was considering, in a manner reminiscent of Comte, the possibility that sociology might provide the theology of a new social religion of democracy. He never realized the vital difference between democratic planning and planning for democracy.

FURTHER READING

WORKS

*From Karl Mannheim*, ed. and introduced by Kurt H. Wolff (Oxford University Press, 1971).

CRITICAL STUDIES

John Plamenatz: *Ideology* (Pall Mall, 1970).

Gunter W. Remmling: *The Sociology of Karl Mannheim* (Routledge and Kegan Paul, 1975).

A. P. Simonds: *Karl Mannheim's Sociology of Knowledge* (Oxford University Press, 1978).

Sheldon S. Wolin: *Politics and Vision* (Allen and Unwin, 1961).

# TALCOTT PARSONS
## (*1902–* )

### Roland Robertson

UNLIKE so much sociological writing, it is seldom that one can scan Parsons' writing in order to get 'the general idea'. Indeed, diffusely compelling ideas are alien to Parsons' work. Parsons does not cajole, berate, or write in the charismatic mode. His writing style is by common consent often atrocious. In the superficial sense Parsons' work *is* – as many have maintained – dull. There is a puritanism of style which does often seem to be singularly at odds with the richness of the terrain, the human complexity, of that to which he is referring. What has to be understood, however, if Parsons is to be seriously encountered, is that the style of expression is closely bound to (which is not to say that it can be justified in terms of) the epistemological position which he developed early in his career in the 1930s. *Analytical realism* was the term which he adopted in his first major statement (*The Structure of Social Action*, 1937) to pinpoint a stance which involved shunning the idea that facticity was unproblematic – rejecting, that is, the notion that a sociological scientist can merely inspect and/or discuss the social world without a clear-cut sense of the *relationship between* analysis and 'reality'. Analytical realism is a commitment to *abstracting* from the flux of life as intellectually experienced, in terms of a systematically elaborated, analytical scheme. Thus Parsons calculatedly insulated his sociology from both intimate involvement with what others might call the facts of life and from the philosophy-with-a-message approach. Central to this self-insulation were the claims that what we call facts are actually *statements* about the world and that we cannot in the name of science either accept the factual surface of social life or impose our patterns of thought on the world without due regard for what it is we hope to accomplish, and for what purpose.

Talcott Parsons was born in 1902, attending Amherst College

as an undergraduate. His early ambition had been to enter medicine (an interest which has continuously informed his work), but he actually leaned more toward social science in his undergraduate years and from that basis he went to England upon graduation to spend a year at the London School of Economics. There he made the intellectual acquaintance of Hobhouse, Ginsberg, and Malinowski – only the last of these, according to Parsons, having made any constructive impression upon him. Parsons has written that many of the turns which his work has taken have been adventitious and entirely uncontrived. The offer of a period at a German university at that time is a very good example of such turns. The years which he spent at Heidelberg involved him deeply in German sociology, economic history and philosophy, and it was there that he began to systematize his interest in the relationship between sociology and economics, an interest which was at that time specifically centred upon the nature and development of capitalism. The work of Max Weber, who had died only a few years earlier, was to have the most lasting impression, both in respect of the analysis of the main features of industrial societies and in more theoretical-sociological terms. But the acquaintance with the work of the philosophy of Kant – whose impact on Parsons has been insufficiently discussed – was also very significant. Generally, in his short Heidelberg period Parsons became acutely aware of the great German debate about the relationship between the natural and the social sciences – a theme which was to be pivotal in his later work.

Upon returning to America, Parsons spent a short period teaching economics at Amherst, but moved quickly to a similar, junior position at Harvard in 1931 – remaining at Harvard until his retirement in 1973. Beginning in 1928, Parsons' early publications concentrated on economic matters – specifically the characteristics of capitalism and the relationships between economic and sociocultural factors. During this period he published a translation of Weber's *The Protestant Ethic and the Spirit of Capitalism* (1931), which, of course, has been the most influential essay on those themes. The early and mid-1930s at Harvard were very significant years in the crystallization of a general-theoretical, sociological scheme. Throughout his academic life Parsons has been extremely open to new ideas – sifting and reordering them for his own purposes. In that crucial period Parsons was particularly inspired by the ideas of the physiologist, Henderson, who convinced him of the pivotal scientific significance of the concept of *system* in scientific analysis *via* the work of Pareto. The latter's writings on economics and sociology and specific concern with the theme of *rationality* and its boundaries in social life were clearly – thought Parsons – of great relevance to his intellectual concerns. Also, during the same period, Parsons became acquainted for the first time with the work of Durkheim – much of that being centred upon the nature and foundations of modern industrial societies in long-term perspective (as well as with the claims of sociology to the status of an autonomous discipline). By no means exhausting the important influences of that period, particular mention should be made of the philosophy of Whitehead, part of whose work was very important in shaping Parsons' conception of analytical realism. That was the major source for the emphases upon abstraction and the necessity to avoid 'the fallacy of misplaced concreteness'.

By 1935 Parsons had completed the draft of a very long treatise on the analysis of social action, this with revision being published as *The Structure of Social Action* in 1937. This subsequently was to become recognized, but not rapidly so, as one of the major books in the history of sociology – some would say in the history of post-Enlightenment thought. In that book Parsons attacked various forms of positivism and empiricism, but at the same time attempted to steer firmly clear of the excesses of idealism. A variety of types of behaviourism, utilitarianism, and materialism were criticized in the former respect, while idealism was criticized for its metaphysical commitment to ideas such as 'the spirit of the age', its tendency toward relativism, and so on. Those parts of the book which were to attract the most enthusiastic attention were devoted to studies of four major social scientists: the English economist, Marshall; the German historian and sociologist, Weber; the French sociologist, Durkheim; and the Italian economist and sociologist, Pareto.

Parsons claimed that these four men could be regarded as having converged on the central problems of modern social science, in spite of their having worked independently of each other. Specifically, *via* analysis of these four men's works (plus subsidiary discussion of many other sociologists, economists, philosophers, and psychologists) Parsons tried to demonstrate a number of main points.

The first major point was that what is distinctive about the subject matter of the social scientist is that it consists of *social action*; that is to say, meaningful action on the part of human actors, the larger part of which is action *between* human agents. The second crucial argument was that insofar as social life consists most elementally in action there must arise a problem of how *order* is possible, for if one has started with the notion of action on the part of individuals, how are the actions related in such a way as to avoid chaos? It is crucial to recognize in this connection that the orderliness of *systems* of action was taken as a *fact*, not a possibility. The question was: given the fact of order, how is it *possible*? Thirdly, the treatment of the theme of action and the problem of order – argued Parsons – required an analytical approach (that of analytical realism) which would of necessity involve the notion of *system* in two major senses. On the one hand, treatment of orderliness in the sphere of action required that we see action as having structure: on the other hand, the actual analysis of such could proceed only in terms of a theoretical *system*, a system of interrelated concepts which would facilitate the abstraction from empirical reality of the basic ingredients of orderliness.

These arguments were developed primarily by taking 'Hobbes' problem' as the starting point – the problem of war-of-all-against-all under conditions of each agent pursuing his or her own goals – and sifting previous theories in order to establish a position which would take due account of the *variety* of types and aspects of action. In fact, even though, as we have said, Parsons severely criticized utilitarian and behaviouristic interpretations of action, in a rather different sense what he attempted to accomplish in *The Structure of Social Action*, and has continued to do ever since, was to put different conceptions of action in their 'proper place'. Thus he does not, for example, deny that there is a utilitarian dimension of action, nor that there is an *aspect* of action which conforms to the behaviouristic image. This *allocation* of different aspects of action is a frequent source of misunderstanding of Parsons' work, while at the same time it is one of its greatest assets. His theory of action involves a systematic attempt to integrate selectively, and thereby to transcend, many other theories. Different extant theories have been seen as only partial – as one-sided emphases on only particular dimensions of the human condition. In his view this was the great significance of Marshall, Pareto, Durkheim, and Weber. Each of them had been, for example, interested in the relationship between the calculatively rational forms of action and the aspects of social life which lie, so to speak, at the back of these forms of action or which are exempted from them. Marshall had been interested in the institutional setting of economic action; Pareto in the relationship between logical and non-logical action; Weber in the varieties of action with particular reference to the *historical* undergirding of modern instrumental rationality by value rationality (particularly as the latter was manifested in religious format); while Durkheim started his work by a critique of utilitarianism and materialism, by considering the 'non-contractual' basis of contract – in the course of this work increasingly emphasizing the moral properties of society and the societal origins of rationality.

In *The Structure of Social Action* Parsons emphasized the *voluntary* nature of social action, and it is around the allegation that he subsequently betrayed that principle – particularly in and after his 1951 books, *The Social System* and the co-authored *Toward a General Theory of Action* – that some controversy has raged. What has to be emphasized in this connection is that the principle of voluntariness was initially introduced as a way of characterizing action in its most basic form. Thus the latter involved the elemental circumstance of an *actor*, oriented towards the attainment of a *goal* (or goals) with certain *means* (later broadened by Parsonians to facilities) in a *situation*. It should be noted that the first two of these (actor and goal) comprise the essentially voluntary aspect of the action framework, while the latter two (means and situation) are to be regarded as *conditions*, with 'the situation' itself being the *least manipulable* condition – that which nowadays is sometimes labelled the *experiental*, in contrast to the *purely actional* aspect of systems of action. This elemental conception of action involved Parsons in *linking* prior one-sided emphases on objective, conditional factors with similarly one-sided subjective, orientational factors. Thus while great weight was given to the latter, its being emphasized as voluntaristic was *never* intended as meaning that there was total freedom (in the *everyday* sense of the word) of action on the part of any actor, *not even* in the artificially constructed situation of one actor.

In rejecting Hobbes' strong emphases upon coercive controls (although that perspective was later, in the 1960s, to be allocated a *space* in Parsons' paradigm), Parsons raised the notion of the possibility of there being a way to *combine* freedom of action with what he saw as a necessary controlling element. Taking Hobbes' problem as seriously as he did, Parsons had to cope with the problem of the integration of action, such that it would be possible to examine action *systems*. Clues to a solution, which drew selectively upon the work of Durkheim, Pareto, and Weber, were seen to lie in the controlling significance of *society itself* as a moral entity and the significance of 'ultimate values'. Thus beginning with *The Structure of Social Action* period and extending into the 1960s, Parsons gradually developed a conception of systems of action operating in terms of what came to be called a *cybernetic hierarchy* of controls and conditions. Controls are regarded in terms of the 'downward impact' of basic beliefs, values, and expressive symbols, while conditions are regarded in terms of the 'upward impact' of the physiological structure of human beings relative to external nature. More precisely: a general action system has four major analytic components (or sub-systems) – the cultural, the social, the psychological, and the biological. These stand in a hierarchy, there being a controlling flow from the first to the last of the sub-systems and a conditioning flow from the last to the first. In principle controlling and conditioning processes are *equally significant* – a notion which critics have often failed to notice,

Parsons himself having on occasions encouraged such mis-understanding by *ad hoc* over-emphasis upon the cultural factor.

This long-term transition in Parsons' thinking – from the elemental features of an action to the functioning of a system of action – was effected, however, in a very complex series of steps. Noting emphatically in *The Structure of Social Action* the need to spell-out in detail the relationship between action in its hypo-thetically very simple form and complex systems of action, Parsons began to attend in the late 1930s to the nature of *inter-*action. Work on that theme was slowly to result in the crystal-lization of the much talked-of *pattern-variables* scheme – the conceptual outlines of which had been wrought on the basis of attempting to grasp (with particular reference to professional organizations) the characteristics which distinguished traditional from modern societies. Basically, the pattern-variables scheme involves the abstract depiction of the variety of ways in which actors may interact. The theoretically stabilized version of this scheme emerged quite a long time after its most popularly known version in *The Social System* (1951). Indeed it was not until 1960 that Parsons gave a comprehensive exposition of the pattern-variables scheme of actors defining an interactional situation *in relation to* his model of a social *system* of action. In *The Structure of Social Action* Parsons had been particularly interested in the issue of *emergent properties* – the production of system characteristics which are not simply aggregations of elementary action. In *The Social System* (the focus of a great deal of the 1950s and 1960s hostility to Parsons' work), he maintained that it was impossible to derive directly the structure of social systems from the actor-situation frame of reference. The emphasis by the 1950s was thus increasingly placed on *functional* analysis.

Let us return, however, to the pattern-variables scheme. Remembering that the scheme has to do pivotally (but not only) with the bases of inter-action – elementally between two agents – we can now reproduce its outline as it unfolded in the 1950s. There are two general categories of pattern-variables of inter-action. On the one hand, there are problems of an *orientational* (or attitudinal) kind; on the other hand, there are 'choices' of what may be called a *locational* nature. In the first category, we speak of actors facing dilemmas of: first, *affectivity v. affective neutrality* – whether to seek immediate gratification or whether to renounce such in favour of instrumental or moral interests; and, second, *specificity v. diffuseness* – whether the scope of interest in alter should be based on specific matters at hand, or whether such interest should be broadly based on the diffuse significance of alter. In the second category, we may speak of actors facing dilemmas of: first, *universalism v. particularism* – whether to focus on alter, the other person, on the basis of a trans-situational, 'universal' precept, or on one particular to the situation; and, second, *achievement* (or performance) *v. ascription* (or quality) – whether to focus on a person's achieved attributes or upon those, such as sex or age, which are intrinsically ascriptive.

This scheme has been among the most influential aspects of Parsons' work, it having been used (often misused) for a variety of purposes, ranging from characterizations of the value systems of whole societies to role relationships in particular institutional settings. For Parsons himself, however, his primary interest in the pattern-variables scheme from about 1950 seems to have been in the problem of its relationship to the analysis of systems of action, with particular attention to relating it to his developing concern with the structure of social systems. Saving elaboration for later, it has to be emphasized at this juncture that by the late 1940s Parsons had begun to concentrate his intellectual energy on the elaboration of a beginning theory of *social* systems (or as he put it *the* social system). The social system in Parsons' work is *one* of the system levels in the overall action system. The action system, as we have seen, includes all of the aspects of action – *culture* (grounds of meaning, values, beliefs, and expressive symbols); structured *social* relationships; *personalities*; and *behavioural organisms* (anatomical structure, hereditary aspects, and patterns of physiological process). Thus only the second of these warrants the designation *social system* (of which *a society* is the most self-sufficient version). This systematic delineation of the overall action system was, however, only its very early stages during the late 1940s and early 1950s. A major problem in those latter years was to deal with the relationship between social action and a *social* system of patterned action and interaction. More specifically, how was the patterning of action and inter-action sustained? Paying much attention to problems of deviance from expected and 'normal' patterns of interaction, Parsons tackled this problem from three major perspectives. The first of these had to do with the nature of interaction as such, with particular reference to a very complex social system of the self-sufficient *societal* kind. The second had to do with the ways in which cultural ideas became embedded in – part and parcel of – the functioning of the system of social relations. The third had to do with the *contingencies* of interaction itself. We will deal with the third of these first.

Central to the phenomenon of interaction is its *double-contingency*. The notion of contingency has been of crucial, 'deep-structural' significance in Parsons' work. In its simplest form contingency appears in Parsons' theory of action with reference to two actors. Actor *a* in interaction with actor *b* knows that what he (*a*) chooses to do in a situation is contingent upon what actor *b* elects to do, and *vice versa*. Thus there is a problem of infinite regress, with no built-in solution. But, argued Parsons, there *must* be a 'solution'. There could be no predictability, no stability – indeed, no social system at all – without processes which prevent the problem of double-contingency from being all-pervasive, which would be an empirically impossible state of affairs for any length of time or on any but a very small scale of interaction.

Thus Parsons turned to the problem of the ways in which normative expectations are established and conformity to those expectations built up and sustained. The concept of role (some-times in conjunction with status) was introduced as a way of pinpointing the manner in which the 'anarchy' of the double-contingency circumstance is avoided. Double-contingency is thus, in terms of role analysis, structured in ways such that there are strong elements of predictability – actors interact within the confines of role expectations and definitions. The pattern-variables scheme, which we have already summarized, may thus be seen as providing the barest bones of the patterning of action, with role-*content* articulation comprising some of the most important flesh on the bones. For reasons of space we have had here to exclude summary of the ways in which Parsons built up the pattern-variables scheme *via* a delineation of action into cognitive, evaluative, and affective components, but it is important to note that in his characterization of *culture* the same three components appear. In tackling the problem of patterning from the perspective of the manner in which cultural ideas become operative in social relationships Parsons utilized two concepts – those of institutionalization and internalization. The first of these, *institutionalization*, refers to the processes of implementation of culture but particularly the *values* aspect of culture. Institutionalized values are values which have been drawn from the stock of ideas to which the society (or other social system) adheres and put to use in the social system. Values, being *preferred states of affairs*, cannot themselves, however, be adequate guides to action – they have to be made operative in the form of norms. Norms are prescriptions which may range from laws to highly informal guidelines to action. It is norms which specify the mode of collectivity *and role* organization within a system. Thus even though the pattern-variables scheme is claimed to be of universal applicability to any interaction, regardless of time or place, the actual contents of particular emphases within the pattern-variables alternatives derive from the institutionalization of culture within the social system. On the other hand, *internalization* refers to the processes whereby *personality* internalizes – takes into itself – the prevalent values and norms of a society. It was largely through the influence of Freud – with whom Parsons became increasingly acquainted in the 1940s and early 1950s – that Parsons aired this concept and related it intimately to Durkheim's views on the ways in which individuals were moulded by society (the key Freudian terms being introjection and identification). Thus internalization is the central aspect of the ways in which individuals became positively adjusted to the operation of the social system – in which they participate as individuals *in role* and not as individuals *in toto*. The aspects of culture which are most crucial in this respect are those having to do with expressive symbolism, relating to the cathectic aspect of personality.

Parsons' perspective on the patterning of action with reference to a very complex form of social system of the societal type is largely what his work has been about since the early 1950s. And it is in this connexion that the concept of *function* has been particularly evident – and to so many particularly problematic. It must quickly be added, however, that the beginning of functional analysis in Parsons' published work in the very early 1950s emerged in large, but not exclusive part, from the work of the social psychologist, Bales' work on interaction in small groups; and tying this into the pattern-variables scheme assisted in the attempt to characterize the contingencies of operation of a social system. Bales' work had shown that in small task groups there occurred a differentiation of function in the sense that over time there emerged within the group a discernible pattern of different kinds of problem – or of contingency – some people, for example, specializing in the function of the instrumentalities of the task, others performing functions of an expressive nature. These kinds of ideas, with the assistance of the pattern-variables scheme, were modified and extended to the operation of complex social systems, such that by the late 1950s Parsons had crystallized a *functional sub-system model* of the social system.

Whereas in *The Social System* phase the concept of function had been presented as an element of dynamism, emphasizing the functioning of the system – as a way of giving 'movement' to the structure of a system – it became rapidly the most general and significant of the concepts in Parsons' overall scheme. In the earlier stage function was, as it were, the oil which greased the machinery in what was often criticized as a *static* image of the social system. Later function was to be elevated to a much more important position in the Parsonian scheme. This has removed the sting from some criticisms that Parsons attempted to explain structures in terms of the idea that they were simply related to each other functionally or that they had to be there to meet certain functions, certain systemic requirements. As we shall see 'the oil which greases the machinery' was in the 1960s to become something else – namely the *media of interchange*.

Probably the central publication in terms of the transaction to a fully fledged functional sub-system model was the book which Parsons wrote with Smelser (*Economy and Society*, 1956), a book which marked a return to Parsons' interests in the relationship between economic and sociological theory. Parsons and Smelser developed a detailed functional delineation of the social system with special reference to *the economy*. Three facets of the general Parsonian scheme which were brought to fruition in *Economy and Society* need to be noted.

*First*, there was an emphasis upon the economy as a functional sub-system of the social system – meaning that the economy was identified not by concrete economic institutions but in reference to the functional significance of the economy for the social system as a whole. Thus the economy as a sub-system is identified in terms of all aspects of the social system which centre upon production – the maximization of utility. *Second*, the general functional significance of the economy in the social system is that of adaptation – it has to do with the adaptation of the social system to the latter's (primarily material) environment. Adaptation is one of four major functional foci of a social system, the others being goal-attainment (setting, and organizing for the pursuit of, collective goals); integration; and pattern-maintenance. Within a society as a social system these four functional sub-systems have respectively come to be labelled as: the economy; the polity; the societal community (centred on solidarity); and the fiduciary system (centred on basic moral patterns of the system). *Third*, even though *any* society will have these functional problems, the degree to which they are differentiated, in the sense of there being concrete structures specializing in them and individuals aware of them, is an empirical matter. Thus from 1956 onward there arose an increasing concern with *differentiation* in Parsons' work. That became the focal point of his grappling with the issue of *change*. Having emphasized so strongly in *The Social System* that his scheme remained highly problematic in respect of many of the most profound aspects of change (a 'confession' upon which his critics mercilessly seized), Parsons was at least from the period of *Economy and Society* much better equipped to deal with change – indeed to make change in the sense of differentiation absolutely central to his work. It was that focus which in large part apparently drew him to the study of long-term patterns of *evolution*.

In addition to these fruitional aspects of *Economy and Society*, we must note also two relatively new strands of analysis which were developed in that study. On the one hand, delineation of the four functional sub-systems of a social system (in terms of criteria which space precludes our discussing here, noting only that the pattern-variables scheme was bound-up with that delineation) required Parsons and Smelser to come to terms with the relationship between the sub-systems. Clearly a model could not be presented which simply allowed each sub-system, particularly in highly differentiated societies, to subsist on its own. That would have been a ridiculous idea in a scheme which emphasized functionality. Thus, drawing heavily upon ideas drawn from economic theory, Parsons and Smelser spelled-out a model of *interchanges* between the sub-systems. Central to the idea of interchange was the notion of its *doubleness* – two outputs and two inputs connecting each sub-system with each of the other sub-systems. (As has recently been argued, this contingent relationship between sub-systems has an interesting relationship to the idea of the double-contingency of interaction between two individuals.) Second, from *Economy and Society* onwards we find in Parsons' work an increasing interest in generalized *media* of interchange. In that book *money*, in particular, and *power* were talked about as the main bases in terms of which sub-systems are interrelated. That is, they *mediate* between the major aspects of a social system. Working primarily from the rather clear-cut case of money as a medium of exchange and a measure of value, Parsons extended that notion, with modifications, to an analysis of *four* media, each of which relates to a particular functional sub-system (*money* to the economy; *power* to the polity; *influence* to the societal community or integrative sub-system; *value-commitments* to the fiduciary – or pattern-maintenance – sub-system). Many difficulties have arisen about this scheme with reference to Parsons having used the economy (with money as the medium) as the paradigmatic starting point, for that has led to his work becoming more than tinged with a form of utilitarianism of which he had been so critical in the 1930s.

Media are seen in terms of *code* aspects (e.g. money as a measure of value) and *message* aspects (money as a medium of exchange). They are, as Parsons has argued, types of 'language' of which language in the everyday sense is prototypical. They enable 'things to get done' in particular ways. For certain types of social activity money is more effective as a 'language' than is the use of influence (attempting to persuade), or power (attempting to coerce) is more effective than value commitments (invoking issues concerning the sanctity of the basic values of the system). On the other hand, Parsons has extended the notions of inflation and deflation from the monetary case to the other media. Thus all four media of the social system are subject to processes of inflation and deflation, circumstances which are contingent upon a mixture of the supply of the relevant medium, its relationship to that which it can 'purchase' and its relationship to the three other media.

For a number of reasons the media of interchange remain analytically very problematic, but clearly essential, within the context of Parsonian action theory. Their essentiality – as the 'oils' which 'grease' the system – resides precisely in the fact that once having elaborated the twin ideas of functional subsystems and functional differentiation Parsons simply had to develop an additional set of ideas concerning the ways in which relatively independent spheres of action were related to each other in a dynamic sense. In his earlier work of the late 1940s and early 1950s Parsons tended simply to stress the cohesiveness of the social system with particular reference to the controlling significance of institutionalized and internalized culture. As he began, however, to explore in long-term historical and evolutionary perspective the manner in which systems become internally differentiated *in relation to* their environments he had to relinquish his rather cavalier (and much criticized) invocation of in-built equilibriating tendencies in social systems. The latter notion hardly appears at all in Parsons' work of the last fifteen years, it having been replaced by the concern with the *problematics* of mediation within systems and between environments and systems. Moreover, the concern with both very long-term and short-term processes of differentiation has, as part of this re-structuring of Parsons' theory, contributed to the diminution of concern with purely synchronic aspects of social systems and a greater concern with diachronic (that is, over-time) problems.

Thus Parsons' work since the mid-1960s has been marked by two major foci – namely, on the one hand, the generalized media of interchange, and, on the other hand, long-term processes of differentiation discussed primarily under the heading of *evolution*. The most crucial point to note about the latter (see Parsons, *The Evolution of Societies*, 1977) is that Parsons has been preoccupied with the evolution *of action* – of which the concern with *societies* or social systems – is but a part. For although Parsons has frequently maintained that the *sociologist* is most interested in the social realm his own work is addressed much more inclusively to human action in its cultural-symbolic, its psychological, its biological as well as its social dimensions. This has meant that since the mid-1960s he has insisted that his functional delineation of the *social* system can be applied by similar methodological precedures to action in its totality. Thus the delineation of the social system into adaptive, goal-attainment, integrative and pattern-maintenance realms has been extended, so that within the *overall context* of action the social system itself takes on an integrative-functional significance, with the behavioural organism having adaptative significance, the personality system having goal-attainment significance and the realm of culture having pattern-maintenance significance. That has meant as well that attempts have been made to address the idea of there being *media* of interchange at the total-action level; that is, media which facilitate interchange between culture, social system, personality systems and behavioural organisms.

In general terms the development of Parsons' social science during the past twenty years – the period since much of the hostility to his work crystalized in the mid-1950s – has been marked by a tightening of the scheme and a loosening of the 'world' to which the scheme applies. In the latter respect the emphasis upon differentiation has reduced a very great deal of the flavour of automaticity and utopianism in Parsons' work. In that respect the emphases upon shared, binding values, upon social-system equilibrium and the close fit between social system and personality, between culture and social system and between culture and personality have given way to a much more flexible but, of necessity, more complicated image of the human condition. The use of the term 'human condition' is, surely, a very appropriate one in connection with Talcott Parsons. It has become increasingly obvious that Parsons' work is centrally concerned with human *life*, a concern to which the study of society takes (an integrated) second place. His vision of life derives essentially from those great philosophers and social scientists who have, above all, been convinced of the contingencies of giving form to life. For the latter would be impossible without the giving of form to it. Beginning in the 1930s with an attempt to reconcile idealism and positivism Parsons has branched out – under the veil of very abstract talk – to produce a systematic image of the 'costs and benefits' of increasing differentiation. Differentiation of action basically invloves an increasing separation of spheres and domains of human life. That separation carries with it all kinds of advantages in terms of freeing certain aspects of life from the encumbrance of others. At the same time there arise attendant problems of mediating the relationships between these different aspects of life. Thus separation in the sense of differentiation amounts to growth both in autonomy *and* interdependence. Autonomy and interdependence – let us say, between the lives of individuals and the operation of social systems – are, as we learn from Parsons, concomitant processes. (The very idea of interdependence is predicated upon separation.) In that respect we can now more readily see that Parsons' conception of the problem of order is not so much about how *societies* are held together, but rather with the more general problem (which has much to do with alienation) of how life itself is co-ordinated. In that respect there are within Parsonian theory the seeds of a genuinely critical sociology. The activity of doing social science, emphasizes Parsons, has the long-term consequence of 'placing ego where id once was'. In other words, the *point* of social science in philosophical terms is to enhance collective, self-knowledge; knowledge which is freedom- inducing, even though it is a *knowledge of contingency.*

FURTHER READING

WORKS

*The Structure of Social Action* (Free Press, two paperbacks, 1968).
*Essays in Sociological Theory* (Free Press, 1954).
*The Social System* (Free Press, paperback, 1964).
*Towards a General Theory of Action* (Harper Torchbooks, paperback, 1962).*
*Working Papers in the Theory of Action* (Free Press, 1953).*
*Family, Socialization and Interaction Process* (Free Press, 1955).*
*Economy and Society* (Free Press, paperback, 1965).*
*Structure and Process in Modern Societies* (Free Press, 1960).
*Theories of Society* (Free Press, 1961).*
*Social Structure and Personality* (Free Press, paperback, 1964).
*Sociological Theory and Modern Society* (Free Press, 1967).
*Politics and Social Structure* (Free Press, 1969).
*The American University* (Harvard University Press, 1973).*
*The Evolution of Societies* (Prentice-Hall, paperback, 1977).
*Social Systems and the Evolution of Action Theory* (Free Press, 1977).
*Action Theory and the Human Condition* (Free Press, 1978).
* denotes Parsons was joint author.

CRITICAL STUDIES

Max Black (ed.): *The Social Theories of Talcott Parsons* (Prentice-Hall, 1961).
Harold J. Bershady, *Ideology and Social Knowledge* (Blackwell, 1973; Wiley, 1973).
Alvin W. Gouldner, *The Coming Crisis of Western Sociology* (Basic Books, 1970; Heinemann, 1971).
Benton Johnson, *Functionalism in Modern Sociology* (General Learning Press, 1975).
Jan J. Loubser, *et al.* (eds.): *Explorations in General Theory in Social Science* (Free Press, 1976).
Ken Menzies, *Talcott Parsons and the Social Image of Man* (Routledge, 1977).
Guy Rocher, *Talcott Parsons and American Sociology* (Paris, 1972; Nelson, 1974).

# THEODOR ADORNO
## (1903–1969)

### David Held

THE INSTITUTE FOR SOCIAL RESEARCH, founded in Germany in 1923, is the home of the so-called 'Frankfurt School'. It has been surrounded by controversy since its inception – controversy which still continues today. Theodor Adorno, officially a member of the Institute from 1938 onwards, was one of its most prominent representatives. The Institute's members included an extraordinary variety of individuals who were to become well-known in numerous fields: amongst others Max Horkheimer (philosopher, sociologist and social psychologist), Friedrick Pollock (economist and specialist on problems of national planning), Erich Fromm (psychoanalyst, social psychologist), Franz Neumann (political scientist with particular expertise in law) and Herbert Marcuse (philosopher and social theorist). But the work of the Institute's members has all too often been misunderstood. Adorno's writings have, in particular, been subject to this fate. The great complexity and difficulty of his whole style and approach has made matters worse. His thinking is often highly abstract and his writings deliberately obscure. Furthermore, he often does not intend his reader to take him at face value.

At first glance, some of Adorno's views on contemporary society seem bizarre. He suggested that we live in a world *completely* caught in a web spun by bureaucracy, administration and technocracy. The individual is, in his view, a thing of the past: the age of concentrated capital, planning and mass culture has destroyed the possibility of personal freedom. The capacity for critical thinking is dead and gone. Society and consciousness are 'totally reified'; they appear to have the qualities of natural objects – to possess the status of given and unchanging forms.

But the meaning of Adorno's thought cannot be fully comprehended if one concentrates simply on content at the expense of form. Adorno strived for a consistency between the style of his writing and its themes. The structure of many of his works *enacts* his concern with the development of repressive systems of thought and organization. Through 'provocative formulation' and 'dramatic emphasis', Adorno hoped to undermine ideologies and to create conditions through which the social world could become visible anew. The battery of techniques he employed to stir the reader include irony and hyperbole.

Above everything else, Adorno sought to sustain and create capacities for new and genuine critical thinking. In order to break the grip of all closed systems of thought (Hegelian idealism, for example, or the orthodox marxism of the Second or Third Internationals), and in order to prevent an unreflected affirmation of society (typical of 'bourgeois ideologies'), Adorno conceived of his writings as a series of analyses and interventions. His use of the forms of essay and aphorism (best seen in his *Minima Moralia*) reflects this concern to undermine all systems of thought that claim completeness.

He presented his themes in ways which demand from the reader not mere contemplation but a critical effort of original reconstruction. Through the criticism of ideologies, Adorno hoped to preserve independent thinking and receptivity to the possibility of radical social change. His aim was to develop a non-dogmatic critical theory of society.

Born in Frankfurt in 1903, Adorno was the son of a prosperous Jewish wine merchant. From secondary school onwards, he developed interests in both philosophy and music – his mother had been a professional singer, and it was her Italian maiden name which Adorno eventually adopted. After receiving his doctorate in 1924 for a work on the philosopher, Husserl, Adorno studied composition and piano with Alban Berg and Edward Steuermann in Vienna. He returned to Frankfurt in 1928, and three years later began teaching philosophy at the university. In 1934, with the advent of nazism, Adorno left Germany for England, working first in London and then in Oxford. Four years later, he moved to America, where he joined the Institute for Social Research (which had also fled from

Germany), and worked part-time with Paul Lazarsfeld at the Office of Radio Research.

Adorno and Horkheimer had been close friends since 1922. From the early thirties, when Adorno became a frequent contributor to the Institute's journal, the *Zeitschrift für Sozialforshung*, his work and Horkheimer's became increasingly complementary. Along with other members of the Institute, they moved to California in 1941 (where Marcuse, of course, was to settle). It was not until 1953, by which time the Institute was re-established in Germany, that Adorno resettled in Frankfurt. There he received a professorship and became a director of the Institute. He died in 1969.

The scope of Adorno's work is astonishing. His collected works (now being published in a standard edition in Germany) amount to 22 large volumes. They include writings within, and across the boundaries of, philosophy, sociology, psychology, musicology and cultural criticism. Adorno completed lengthy studies on Hegel, Husserl, Heidegger and Kierkegaard. In *Negative Dialectics* he developed a unique materialist and dialectical philosophy. *Dialetic of Enlightenment* (written with Horkheimer) stands as a major analysis of the origin and nature of instrumental reason.

The two volumes in the collected works which contain what its editors call Adorno's 'sociological writings', include theoretical studies on Weber, Durkheim, class and empirical methods, as well as a number of content analyses (of astrology, for example) and his contributions to the well-known book, *The Authoritarian Personality*. But Adorno's contribution to sociology is also apparent in highly original studies of culture, which include analyses of such diverse figures as Mahler, Schönberg, Brecht and Kafka, as well as discussions of the entertainment industry. In his last major work, *Aesthetische Theorie*, Adorno presented a novel philosophy of aesthetics. Given the range of Adorno's concerns, it is only possible to outline some of his major positions and the influences which helped to shape them.

The influences were complex and various. To begin with, although Adorno was steeped in the thought of Kant and Hegel, he only employed selected aspects of their ideas. He rejected

Kant's transcendental method, and Hegel's concept of absolute spirit. But Marx's work was even more important to his overall approach. Marx's critique of Hegel's notion of history, and the method he employed in his analysis of exchange value and commodity fetishism, provide models for Adorno's own method.

On Adorno's account, Marx showed how an examination of specific historical conditions, under which ideas and social structures develop, can be used to critically undermine the effects of bourgeois ideology. Adorno regarded Marx's method as the most adequate to grasp history's *current* dynamic; it is not a method that has universal validity. Following Nietzsche, he rejected all philosophical first principles: there are no ultimate foundations for knowledge and values. From Nietzsche and Walter Benjamin, Adorno inherited a concern with style and expression as integral elements of method.

Adorno's criticisms of philosophy, sociology and culture often turn on a critique of reification and fetishism in social life. These concerns derive, in part, from Lukács as well as from Marx's *Capital*. Reification and fetishism are terms for the processes whereby social phenomena take on the appearance of characteristics of things. Thus, social relations appear in the form of relations set by nature. But these and other phenomena, Adorno maintained, could not be examined wholly in economic and political terms. Like many other members of the Frankfurt school, Adorno held that explanations of social phenomena must include their sociological and psychological ramifications. Just as Marx had revealed crucial aspects of the present epoch's structure, so Freud (Adorno felt) had uncovered a great deal about the socio-psychological formation of the individual in the present epoch. Consequently, Adorno sought to integrate many of the substantive contributions of Marx and Freud. But he did not accept their positions uncritically. He shared Horkheimer's emphasis on the necessity of interdisciplinary research.

The upheavals of the nineteen-twenties, thirties and forties had a major impact on Adorno's thinking. Throughout his early life, Adorno had been somewhat optimistic about the chances for revolutionary change. Fascism, nazism and stalinism crushed this hope. Adorno was constantly concerned to rework his 'critical theory' in the light of these developments. His attitude to the possibility of political change was always ambivalent. But he did believe that an examination of the reasons for the failure of European radical movements, and the emergence of authoritariarism, might help to compel changes in consciousness and action.

Adorno referred to his own approach as 'negative dialectics' or 'immanent criticism'. For Adorno, dialectics does not describe the form of the objective workings of history. Rather, negative dialectics operates within the 'force-field' between the claims that are made about reality and reality itself. On Adorno's view, there is no theory which would hold good for every time and place and no eternally valid criterion on which to base a critique of society. Therefore, we can only measure and evaluate a given social phenomenon by investigating whether it falls short of its 'ideal image of itself'. (In Adorno's abstract language, this is the difference between an 'object's concept' and its actual state of affairs.) Negative dialectics is the critical assessment of these gaps.

For example, bourgeois society claims to be a society characterized by equality, with a free and just process of economic exchange. Yet, by virtue of its internal dynamics, it inevitably gives rise to structured inequality. By pointing to the discrepancy between what is claimed (in this case, a state of genuine equality) and what actually exists (structured inequality), a critical image is presented of what the object is and is not. Thus a critique is provided – a critique which points to unfulfilled possibilities. According to the position elaborated at length in *Negative Dialectics*, analysis and criticism are inseparable.

The imposition of categories, Adorno contended, is typical of all orthodox approaches to social science. Immanent criticism, on the other hand, identifies and assesses social phenomena through categories which are internal to the phenomena themselves, rather than imposed from the outside. This position does not prevent Adorno from using concepts from a number of theoretical frameworks. But, of course, they must be employed within the context of immanent criticism – i.e. they must be used to critically expose the gaps between 'ideal image' and 'actual reality'. Nor can they be employed without simultaneously being subjected to both rigorous philosophical analysis (of the ideas of society, of culture, of the individual, for instance) and to strict empirical inquiry.

While the world is always a product of interpretation, it is never, for Adorno, exhausted by interpretation. Only a number of representations of reality can provide an adequate approximation of it. Adorno employed language – through the construction of 'constellations of concepts – as a connotative or indicative device. His aim was to capture at least some aspects of reality. Thus, specific qualities of the social world, which are inaccessible to other types of thinking (particularly those types that subsume objects under classificatory schema), can be illuminated. Adorno is relentlessly critical of all belief systems that claim to have fully identified their objects. The false claims of 'bourgeois ideologies' are especially subject to this attack.

Many of Adorno's substantive intersts focus on the nature of capitalist society. His conception of capitalism begins from traditional marxian axioms. But unlike many marxists, who argue that class antagonisms and crises lead to breakdown and revolutionary transformation, Adorno maintained (especially in his later works) that crises can potentially be contained and class conflict stifled. While the notion of classes still demarcates relations of domination, constraint and inequity, it reflects, less and less, active, self-conscious relations of struggle.

Adorno did not produce detailed studies of the capitalist economy, or of the relation between the polity and economy. But throughout his *Sociological Writings* (Collected Works, vol. 8) the following constellation of elements appear central to his account of contemporary developments.

First, he identified a trend toward increasing integration of the economic and political. Monopolies emerge and intervene in the state, while the state intervenes to safeguard and maintain economic processes.

Second, the increasing interlocking of economy and polity ensures the subordination of local initiative to bureaucratic deliberation, and of the market allocation of resources to centralized planning. Society is coordinated, Adorno believed, by powerful (private and public) administrations increasingly self-sufficient but oriented single-mindedly towards production.

Third, with the spread of bureaucracy and organization, there is an extension of the rationalization of social life, through the spread of instrumental reason – a concern with the efficiency of means to pre-given goals.

Fourth, a continual extension of the division of labour fragments tasks. As tasks become increasingly mechanized, there are fewer chances for the worker to reflect upon and organize his own labour. Knowledge of the total work process becomes less accessible. The majority of occupations become atomized, isolated units.

Fifth, with the fragmentation of tasks and knowledge, the experience of class diminishes. Domination becomes ever more impersonal. People become means to the fulfilment of purposes which appear to have an existence of their own. The particular pattern of social relations which condition these processes – the capitalist relations of production – are reified. As more and more areas of social life take on the characteristics of mere commodities, reification is reinforced, and social relations become ever less comprehensible. Conflict centres increasingly on marginal issues which don't test the foundation of society.

Adorno's analysis of all these processes sought to expose the particular social basis of seemingly anonymous domination and to reveal, thereby, what hinders people 'coming to consciousness of themselves as subjects' capable of spontaneity and positive action.

Adorno's writings on major social developments often synthesize and rely upon the work of Marx, Weber, and Pollock. But he did produce highly original studies on the effect of these developments on culture, and on the effect of changes in culture on social structures. Nearly half of his works are on art and music. Adorno's approach to these cultural artefacts is strictly sociological, focusing on the way in which society expresses itself through its cultural life. Adorno believed that the products of the great artists of the bourgeois era, as well as those of the

Christian Middle Ages and the Renaissance, preserved a certain autonomy from the world of purely pragmatic interests. Through their *form* or *style*, these artists' works represented individual experiences in such a way as to illuminate their meaning. 'Autonomous' art, as Adorno called it, produces images of beauty and order or contradiction and dissonance – an aesthetic realm, which at once leaves and highlights reality. Its object world is derived from the established order, but it portrays this order in a non-conventional manner. As such, art has a cognitive and subversive character. Its 'truth-content' resides in its ability to restructure conventional patterns of meaning.

Today, Adorno maintained, most cultural entities have become commodities, while culture itself has become an 'industry'. The term, 'industry', here refers to the 'standardisation', and the 'pseudo-individualisation' or marginal differentiation, of cultural artefacts (for example, television Westerns or film music) and to the rationalization of promotion and distribution techniques.

Without regard for the integrity of artistic form, the culture industry concerns itself with the 'predominance of the effect'. It aims primarily at the creation of diversions and distractions, providing a temporary escape from the responsibilities and drudgery of everyday life. However, Adorno argued, the culture industry offers no genuine escape. For the relaxation it provides – free of demands and efforts – only serves to distract people from the basic pressures on their lives and to reproduce their will to work.

In analyses of television, art, popular music and astrology, Adorno tried to show how the products of the 'industry' simply duplicate and reinforce the structure of the world people seek to avoid. They strengthen the belief that negative factors in life are due to natural causes or chance, thus promoting a sense of fatalism, dependence and obligation. The culture industry produces a 'social cement' for the existing order. (Adorno did not hold that this was the fate of all art and music. He never tired of emphasizing, for example, that Schönberg's atonal music preserves a critical, negative function.)

Through immanent criticism of modern art and music,

Adorno sought to assess the nature of various cultural phenomena. In this inquiry he also tried to show how most leisure
activities are managed and controlled. The spheres of both
production and consumption, he further maintained, have
crucial influences on the socialization of the individual. Impersonal forces hold sway not only over individuals' beliefs but
over their impulses as well. Adorno's work in psychology investigated these effects.

Using many psychoanalytic concepts, Adorno examined the
way society constitutes the individual, producing social character types. He found that in the socialisation process, the importance of parents is dwindling. As families provide ever less
protection against the overpowering pressures of the outside
world, the legitimacy of the father's authority is undermined.

The result is, for example, that the male child does not aspire
to become like his father, but more and more like images projected by the culture industry in general (or by fascism in Nazi
Germany). The father retains a certain power. But his demands
and prohibitions are, at best, poorly internalised. The father's
power, therefore, appears arbitrary. In this situation the child
retains an abstract idea of force and strength, and searches for a
more powerful 'father' adequate to this image. A general state
of susceptibility is created to outside forces – to fascist dema-
gogues, for instance.

The classic study, *The Authoritarian Personality*, aimed at
analysing this susceptibility in terms of a personality syndrome
which crystallizes under pressures such as these. The study
endeavoured to establish interconnections between certain
character traits and political opinions which might be regarded
as potentially fascist, such as aggressive nationalism and racial
prejudice. It revealed a 'standardized' individual whose thinking
is rigid, prone to the use of stereotypes, blindly submissive to
conventional values and authority, and superstitious. The study
showed how deeply ideology was ingrained, and why it was that
people might accept belief systems 'contrary to their rational
interests'. The authoritarian character type was juxtaposed to an
autonomous individual capable of critical judgment.

Adorno believed that, despite developments in science,

technology and production which have increased the possibilities available to human beings, only a 'real hell' has been the result. Adorno was not, however, as is often thought, an unqualified pessimist. His work would make little sense in this light. His writings are contributions to the development of a non-authoritarian and non-bureaucratic politics. As a critic of society and culture, his work is of considerable significance.

Of course, many of Adorno's views are debatable. In my view, he does not possess an adequate theory of economics, politics, or of their relation to one another. His conception of capitalist (and socialist) development seems excessively influenced by his experience of fascism and nazism. He maintains an uneasy balance between theory and empirical studies. Attention is paid to both; yet, there is insufficient regard for historical detail. Nonetheless, the questions he raised and the problems he tackled remain of lasting importance.

#### FURTHER READING
WORKS IN ENGLISH TRANSLATION

*The Authoritarian Personality*, with E. Frenkel-Brunswik, J. Levinson, R. Nevitt Sanford (Norton, 1950).

'Culture Industry Reconsidered' in *New German Critique*, no. 6, 1975.

*Dialectic of Enlightenment*, with Max Horkheimer, tr. J. Cumming (Herder and Herder, 1972).

*Minima Moralia: reflections from damaged life*, tr. E. Jephcott (New Left Books, 1974).

*Negative Dialectics*, tr. E. B. Aston (Routledge and Kegan Paul, 1973).

*Philosophy of Modern Music*, tr. A. G. Mitchell and W. V. Blomster (Seabury, 1973).

*Prisms*, tr. S. and S. Weber (Neville Spearman, 1967).

'Sociology and psychology' in *New Left Review*, no. 46, 1967, and no. 47, 1968.

CRITICAL STUDIES

Jürgen Habermas: *Philosophisch – politische Profile* (Suhrkamp, Frankfurt, 1971).

Frederick Jameson: *Marxism and Form* (Princeton University Press, 1971).

Martin Jay: *The Dialectical Imagination* (Heinemann, 1973).

Gillian Rose: *The Melancholy Science: an introduction to the thought of Theodor W. Adorno* (Macmillan, 1978).

# NOTES ON CONTRIBUTORS

## J. A. Banks

Born 1920. Educated Enfield Grammar School (1931–37) and the London School of Economics (1947–52). Assistant Lecturer in Sociology at the University of Leicester (1952–54). Went to Liverpool to take up a research post; became Research Lecturer in Industrial Sociology in 1959, Senior Research Lecturer in 1960, and Professor of Sociology at University of Leicester in 1970. Author of *Prosperity and Parenthood* (1954), *Industrial Participation* (1963), *Marxist Sociology in Action* (1970), *Sociology of Social Movements* (1972), and *Trade Unionism* (1974). Joint author of *Technical Change and Industrial Relations* (1956) and *Feminism and Family Planning* (1964).

## John Beattie

Fellow of Linacre College, Oxford. Taught social anthropology at Oxford from 1953 to 1971, and at the university of Leiden from 1971 to 1976. Has also taught at the University of California (Berkeley) and at Cape Town University. Fellow, Center for Advanced Study in the Behavioral Sciences, Stanford, California, 1959–60 and 1966–67. Carried out field research in western Uganda 1951–53 and 1955. Books include *Bunyoro: an African Kingdom* (1960), *Other Cultures* (1964), and *The Nyoro State* (1971).

## F. Richard Cowell

Former civil servant, was secretary of the United Kingdom National Committee for UNESCO 1946–58. Awarded CMG, 1952. A graduate of King's College, London, and the London School of Economics, he held a Rockefeller Research Fellowship in the Social Sciences in the U.S.A. and Europe, 1929–31. In *Values in Human Society* (1970) he described Sorokin's theory of social development. He studied the cultural interpretation of Sociology in *Culture in Private and Public Life* (1959). Among his other works are *Cicero and the Roman Republic* (6th edition, 1972), *Everyday Life in Ancient Rome* (7th edition, 1972), and *The Garden as a Fine Art* (1978). He died in 1978.

## Ronald Fletcher

Born Yorkshire 1921. Studied Philosophy and Economics at the University of Bristol, and Sociology at the London School of Economics. 1953–63 Lecturer in Sociology at Bedford College and Birkbeck College, University of London. In 1964 Professor of Sociology and head of department at the new University of York. In 1968, profoundly dissatisfied with certain aspects of university life and administration, resigned from full-time employment, and now lives on the Suffolk coast and devotes himself to writing, though he has recently done some teaching at Reading University. Has lectured widely in adult education, for the British Council at home and overseas, and during recent years has undertaken several series of programmes on sociological themes, on radio and television. Author of *Instinct in Man* (1957), *Issues in Education* (1960), *The Family and Marriage in Britain* (1962), *A Humanist's Decalogue* (1964), *Human Needs and Social Order* (1965), *The Making of Sociology*, 2 vols. (1970–71), *John Stuart Mill: A logical critique of Sociology* (1972), *The Crisis of Industrial Civilisation* (1974); *The Framework of Society* (1976); editor of *The Science of Society and the Unity of Mankind*. He has also written books of a more general kind: *The Parkers at Saltram* (1971), *The Akenham Burial Case* (1974), *The Biography of a Victorian Village* (1977), *In a Country Churchyard* (1978).

## Jean Floud

Principal of Newnham College, Cambridge. Sociologist and former pupil of Karl Mannheim.

## Anthony Giddens

University Lecturer in Sociology, and Fellow of King's College, Cambridge.

## Salvador Giner

Born Barcelona, 1934; educated at Universities of Barcelona, Cologne and Chicago. Lecturer in Sociology at Reading University, 1965–72; Senior Lecturer at Lancaster, 1972–77. Since 1978 Reader at Brunel University. Visiting professorships at Puerto Rico and Carleton, Ottawa. Author of *Historia del pensamiento social* (1974, 1976), *Sociology* (1971, 1974), *Mass Society* (1976) and numerous studies of European social structures and the history of social theory.

## Morris Ginsberg

1889–1970. Educated University College, London. Lecturer in Philosophy at University College, London, 1914–23; Martin White Professor of Sociology in the University of London, London School of Economics 1929–54; Emeritus Professor, 1954; editor of *British Journal of Sociology* and *The Sociological Review*. Publications: *The Psychology of Society* (1921, 9th edition, 1964); *Studies in Sociology* (1932); *Sociology* (1934); *Essays on Sociology and Social Philosophy* (1961); *Nationalism; a reappraisal* (1961); (editor) *Law and Opinion in England in the Twentieth Century* (1959); *The Material Culture and Social Institutions of the Simpler Peoples* (1915, joint author); *L. T. Hobhouse: His Life and Work* (joint author, 1931); *On Justice in Society* (1965).

## John H. Goldthorpe

Born 1935, Great Houghton, South Yorkshire. Educated at Wath-upon-Dearne Grammar School, University College, London, and the London School of Economics. Taught sociology at the University of Leicester, 1957–60, then at Cambridge as University Lecturer and Fellow of King's College; since 1969 Official Fellow, Nuffield College, Oxford. Author (with David Lockwood and others) of *The Affluent Worker* studies, (with Keith Hope) of *The Social Grading of Occupations*, and of numerous papers in the fields of industrial sociology, social stratification and sociological theory. Married (wife teaches French literature at Oxford) with two children. *Class Structure and Social Mobility in Modern Britain* is forthcoming.

## Julius Gould

Born 1924. Read classics and PPE at Balliol College, Oxford. From 1957–64, Reader in Social Institutions at London School of Economics. 1958, Visiting Professor at the University of California, Berkeley. 1960–61, Rockefeller Fellow at Harvard. Since 1964, Professor of Sociology at University of Nottingham, and currently Dean of the Faculty of Law and Social Sciences; Visiting Professor, Cornell University, 1971. Member of the UK National Commission for UNESCO and Chairman of its Social Sciences Advisory Committee. Member of Economic Planning Council for the East Midlands Region. Publications include *The Rational Society* (1971) and *The Attack on Higher Education* (1977); editor, *Penguin Social*

*Science Surveys*; joint editor, *Dictionary of the Social Sciences* and *Jewish Life in Modern Britain*. Contributor to many journals here and abroad.

## David Held

Born 1951. Graduated 1973 from University of Manchester Institute of Science and Technology. Completed Ph.D. in Political Science at Massachusetts Institute of Technology in 1976. Currently a University of Wales Fellow at University College, Cardiff, and a Junior Research Fellow at Wolfson College, Oxford.

## Everett Cherrington Hughes

1927–38 taught at McGill University, Montreal, studying the effect of industrialization and urbanization upon the relations of French with English Canadians. 1938–61, at the University of Chicago, working on multi-ethnic societies and on professional occupations. From 1961 to 1968 on the staff of Brandeis University. From 1968 to 1977 on the staff of Boston College. He has written: *French Canada in Transition* (1943, 1963); *Boys in White: Student Culture in Medical School* (1961, 1977, in collaboration); *Making the Grade: the Academic Side of College Life* (1969, in collaboration); *The Sociological Eye* (1971).

## Godfrey Lienhardt

Born 1921. Lecturer in African Sociology, Institute of Social Anthropology, University of Oxford, since 1949. Sometime Visiting Professor, College of Arts and Sciences, Baghdad, and the University of Ghana. Editor (with E. E. Evans-Pritchard and W. H. Whiteley) of *The Oxford Library of African Literature*. Chief publications: *Divinity and Experience: the Religion of the Dinka* (1961) and *Social Anthropology* (1964).

## Steven Lukes

Born 1941, is a Fellow in Politics at Balliol College, Oxford. Was formerly a Research Fellow at Nuffield College, Oxford, and taught for a time at Keele University. He has published articles on political theory, moral philosophy, the history of sociology, and social theory, and is the author of *Emile Durkheim, His Life and Work* (1973), *Individualism* (1973), *Power: A Radical View* (1974), and *Essays in Social Theory* (1977).

## Neil McInnes

An Australian writer who lives in Paris, is the author of *Eurocommunism* (1976), *The Communist Parties of Western Europe* (1975), *The Western Marxists* (1972), and other essays on socialism and philosophy.

## Donald G. MacRae

Born 1921. Professor of Sociology, London School of Economics, since 1961. Martin White Professor of Sociology, University of London, 1978. Formerly lecturer in Sociology, University of Oxford; Visiting Professor at Universities of Ghana, California (Berkeley); Fellow, Center for Advanced Studies in the Behavioral Sciences, Stanford; etc. Author of *Ideology and Society* (1960), *Ages and Stages* (1973), *Max Weber* (1974). Past editor of *British Journal of Sociology*. Editor of Heinemann books on sociology.

## John Rex

Born Port Elizabeth, South Africa, 1925; educated Grey High School and Rhodes University. Lecturer, Leeds University, 1949–62, Birmingham University, 1962–64. Professor of Social Theory and Institutions, Durham University, 1964–70. Professor of Sociology, University of Warwick, since 1970. Author of *Key Problems of Sociological Theory* (1961); (with R. Moore) *Race, Community and Conflict* (1967); *Race Relations in Sociological Theory* (1970); *Discovering Sociology* (1973); *Race, Colonialism and the City* (1973); *Sociology and the Demystification of the Modern World* (1974).

## Audrey I. Richards

Took her B.A. (Natural Sciences) at Cambridge (1922) and Ph.D. (Anthropology) at the London School of Economics (1931). Lectured at the London School of Economics (1931–50) and at the University of Witwatersrand (1938–41) between spells of anthropological fieldwork in Zambia and the Northern Transvaal. War years spent in the Colonial Office acting as Secretary of a Social Welfare Committee and the Colonial Social Science Research Council. Director of the East African Institute of Social Research, Makerere University College (1950–56) and did fieldwork in Buganda. Smuts Reader, Cambridge University, 1960–65. Director, Centre of African Studies, Cambridge 1961–6. President, Royal

Anthropological Institute, 1959–61. President, African Studies Association, 1964–66. Author of works on the Bemba of North Zambia, the Ganda of Uganda, and an Essex village.

## Roland Robertson

Born in Norwich, England, 1938. Currently Professor of Sociology, University of Pittsburgh. Has held teaching positions at the Universities of Leeds, Essex and York (where he was Professor and Head of Department of Sociology, 1970–74). Author of *The Sociological Interpretation of Religion* (1970) and *Meaning and Change* (1977). Co-author of *International Systems and the Modernization of Societies* (1968) and *Deviance, Crime and Socio-Legal Control* (1973). Editor of *Sociology of Religion* (1969).

## Alan Ryan

Reader in Politics in the University of Oxford since 1978, and Fellow and tutor in politics at New College, Oxford, since 1969; educated Christ's Hospital and Balliol College, Oxford; has taught at the Universities of Keele, Essex, Texas and California; author of two books on J. S. Mill, and of *The Philosophy of the Social Sciences* (1970), and editor of *Social Explanation* (1973). Regular contributor to *New Society*, and other journals. Currently working on the political theory of property.

## T. S. Simey (*Lord Simey of Toxteth*)

Was Professor of Social Sciences at the University of Liverpool. He graduated in the Modern Greats school at Oxford, and was Lecturer in Public Administration at Liverpool from 1931. His employment by the Colonial Office from 1941 to 1945 as Social Welfare Adviser to West Indies Development and Welfare was a formative period in his thinking. Member of Crowther Committee, and Fulton Committee on Civil Service. Created Life Peer in 1965. His publications include: *Principles of Social Administration* (1937), (with Mrs Margaret Simey) *Charles Booth, Social Scientist* (1960), *Social Science and Social Purpose* (1968). He died in 1969, age 63.

## Laurie Taylor

Professor of Sociology at University of York, graduated in psychology from Birkbeck College, London, and then completed postgraduate studies in sociology at University of Leicester. His books include *Psychological Survival* (with Stanley Cohen, 1972);

*Deviance and Society* (1973); *Crime, Deviance and Socio-Legal Control* (with Roland Robertson, 1974); *Escape Attempts: The Theory and Practice of Resistance to Everyday Life* (with Stanley Cohen, 1976) and *Prison Secrets* (with Stanley Cohen, 1978). He has also edited *Politics and Deviance* (with Ian Taylor, 1973) and *Young People and Civil Conflict in Northern Ireland* (with Sarah Nelson, 1977).

## Malcolm Warner

Born 1937 in Manchester. History Scholar, Trinity College, Cambridge. Read Economics, followed by Politics Ph.D. (on the Webbs as Intellectuals in Politics). Taught and researched in several British and American universities. Currently Professor and Research Coordinator of the Joint Graduate Programme of the Administrative Staff College (Henley) and Brunel University. He has recently published (with J. D. Edelstein) *Comparative Union Democracy: Organisation and Opposition in British and American Unions* (1975).

## Gwyn A. Williams

Born 1925, is Professor of History at University College Cardiff and was formerly at York and lecturer at Aberystwyth. Publications include several articles on Welsh history, *The Merthyr Rising* (1978), *Artisans and Sans-culottes* (1968), *Goya and the Impossible Revolution* (1976), *Proletarian Order: Antonio Gramsci, factory councils and the origins of communism in Italy 1911–21* (1975) and (translator and editor) Paolo Spriano, *The Occupation of the Factories: Italy 1920* (1975).

## Michael Wood

Born 1936. Professor of English and Comparative Literature at Columbia University, New York. Formerly Fellow of St John's College, Cambridge. Author of *Stendhal* (1971) and *America in the Movies* (1975).